Exploring
Research-driven Building Design

Edited by
Marilyne Andersen
Emmanuel Rey

Foreword by
Martin Vetterli
Jean-Nicolas Aebischer
Astrid Epiney

Contributions by
Hamed Alavi
Marilyne Andersen
Arianna Brambilla
Derek Christie
Anne-Claude Cosandey
Philippe Couty
Stefano Cozza
Hugo Gasnier
Nicolas Henchoz
Endrit Hoxha
Thomas Jusselme
Vincent Kaufmann
Denis Lalanne
Jean-Marie Le Tiec
Cédric Liardet
Thierry Maeder
Marc Antoine Messer
Arnaud Misse
Julien Nembrini
Cécile Nyffeler
Luca Pattaroni
Florinel Radu
Emmanuel Rey
Thibaut Schafer
Raphaël Tuor
Himanshu Verma
Dominic Villeneuve
Didier Vuarnoz
Renato Zülli

15	**Foreword**
17	**Introduction**

Project foundations

27	①	The *smart living lab* and its flagship building
39	②	Research at the service of building design
55	③	An occupant-driven perspective

Experimental research

77	④	Intensification of use: an exploratory study
107	⑤	Low-carbon thermal inertia
141	⑥	Low carbon building energy system: design and operation

Process design

177	⑦	Architecture in making
207	⑧	A data-driven approach for lifecycle performance
239	⑨	Lessons learned from a living lab research process

257	**Conclusion**

261	List of acronyms
262	Illustration credits
264	Authors
268	Stakeholders
272	Acknowledgements & Imprint

Foreword

Martin Vetterli
President,
École polytechnique fédérale de Lausanne

Jean-Nicolas Aebischer
Director,
School of Engineering and Architecture of Fribourg

Astrid Epiney
Rector,
University of Fribourg

Resulting from a cooperative project between three Swiss universities— the School of Architecture, Civil and Environmental Engineering (ENAC) at the École polytechnique fédérale de Lausanne (EPFL), the School of Engineering and Architecture of Fribourg (HEIA-FR) and the University of Fribourg (UNIFR)—the *smart living lab* is a research and development centre designed to explore the future of the built environment. The project will be located within an innovative structure at the strategic blueFACTORY site in Fribourg, a brownfield being sustainably redeveloped as part of the Swiss Innovation Park (called "Switzerland Innovation"), and will serve as an emblem of the project's aim to translate academic research into actual buildings.

Edited under the direction of Professors Marilyne Andersen and Emmanuel Rey, who helped define the *smart living lab*'s vision from its very inception, a series of books entitled "Towards 2050" will showcase this ambitious undertaking in its various stages. The series notably aims to capitalize on the scientific findings generated during the interdisciplinary development of the building, which will be home to the *smart living lab*. Another project goal is to disseminate this knowledge to scientists, decision-makers and practitioners involved in architectural production and spatial development more generally.

What makes the *smart living lab* approach unique is its attempt to create a cutting-edge working/living space (i.e. a container). The lab will also be the home of an interdisciplinary centre that strives for excellence in the field of innovative technologies and building-related concepts (i.e. a content). This book, entitled "Exploring," the second in the series, presents a detailed overview of the critical research phase. Led by the "Building2050" group, researchers focused on how to best meet the future *smart living lab* building's sustainability goals. The construction sector being one of the world's largest energy consumers and CO_2 emitters, the "Building2050" group is seeking strategies to improve the *smart living lab* building's energy and carbon performance in anticipation of stringent requirements for 2050. This collection brings together the original, interdisciplinary works of 30 researchers active within our three institutions. It highlights the approach that led to the scientific definition of the expected performances for the future *smart living lab* building with regard to architectural quality, climate issues, potential bioclimatic strategies, energy performance, the integration of renewable energies, life cycle analysis and functional flexibility.

We would like to thank Professors Marilyne Andersen and Emmanuel Rey for their unfailing commitment to supervising this vast, interdisciplinary research project, as well as all the contributors and Scientific Committee members involved in the creation of this book. We look forward to networking the many skills boasted by our respective institutions, and hope this approach foreshadows future synergies and fosters new and innovative approaches to interdisciplinarity.

Introduction

Marilyne Andersen
Emmanuel Rey

Entitled "Thinking. Visions for Architectural Design," the first volume of the "Towards 2050" book series has provided an ensemble of complementary, sometimes contradictory, sometimes overlapping expert voices as to what a sustainable built future may—or should—entail. The next volumes aim to showcase a quite unique endeavour, namely to uncover the path starting with a conceptual ambition and leading to a built and occupied edifice. This challenge will be completed though an iterative research process in three main stages: help delimit the solution space from the state of knowledge in research rather than in practice, accompany the design and construction processes by proposing novel methods to inform them, and ultimately confront the result to the initial expectations through a post-occupancy evaluation. The present book, entitled "Exploring. Research-driven Building Design," focuses on the first of these three stages, i.e. the research that provided, through the project's foundations, the experimental research that was conducted and the process that was designed, the boundary conditions on which to base a more tangible ambition for an actual place of living and for (academic) work.

This work offers a multi-disciplinary perspective of what this kind of effort might entail, with the objective to share results with a broad spectrum of disciplines, whether directly or indirectly connected to the built environment. While the research it showcases was developed within a specific framework—supporting the design of the future building of the *smart living lab* in Fribourg, Switzerland—it aims to serve a broader community of academics and professionals in the fields of architecture, engineering and construction, as many of its findings and chosen approaches can be applicable, or at least relevant, to a very large spectrum of contexts and projects. The development of this book allowed us to bring new knowledge and tools that may help anyone better understand what ingredients need to be successfully integrated into the design and construction of a building emblematic of the "future"—and, maybe most importantly, how they influence and interact with one another.

What do we actually mean by "future"? The envisioned building aims to be experimental, user-centered, demonstrative and respectful of its environment in terms of its construction and operation footprint. The focus is therefore not so much on its level of automation or on how intensively the most recent technology has been embedded into it. Rather, it aims at minimizing the risk of its own obsolescence by emphasising sobriety, adaptability and a smart use of resources over overly-deterministic programmatic or functional choices. The only needs a building can be said with certainty to still aim to serve in a somewhat distant future—say by 2050—are the fundamental and cultural needs of its human inhabitants, which bring us back to the reason of their existence: providing shelter with a maximum level of comfort and, more largely, well-being. In the perspective of real sustainability transitions, these needs should be met while limiting the use of non-renewable resources and hence increasing efficiency, whether regarding material, energy or space.

Towards these goals, a lot of attention was—and should be—placed on the architectural quality, the whole lifecycle of the building, the choice of materials, their assembly into systems and the interactions happening between the latter. The overarching principle is to favour passive means over active means to ensure comfort for the building users, but not to favour predicted energy performance over human comfort or usability.

With these ambitions in mind, the most challenging aspect inevitably remains their reconciled integration. The present book aims to offers new insights as to how research can effectively contribute to this endeavour, and ultimately translate into foundations for a different, more holistic design approach.

Project foundations

Like many endeavours, big or small, the *smart living lab* started as an idea on the corner of a table. But it quickly acquired its overarching concept: to be exemplary both as a container—a building—and in terms of its contents—an academic, inter-institutional and inter-disciplinary center on the future of the built environment. The next step was to articulate specific objectives and a framework able to achieve this. In other words, to establish the project foundations.

This first part presents how the adventure started and what we wanted to achieve. It introduces the strategy that was implemented and the objectives that were set to support the design of a building thirty years ahead of its time through research outcomes, with an underlying aim: placing human and environmental needs in an appropriate and valuable equilibrium.

① The *smart living lab* and its flagship building

Anne-Claude Cosandey
Marilyne Andersen
Emmanuel Rey

The present chapter will introduce the context from which the *smart living lab* emerged, the objectives, principles and goals for its development, and the resulting "Smart Living Building Research Program."

The *smart living lab* is a research and development centre designed to explore the future of the built environment. It was born of an academic partnership between three higher education institutions, each representative of Switzerland's different education systems (CRUS et al. 2009): the Ecole polytechnique fédérale de Lausanne (EPFL), the School of Engineering and Architecture of Fribourg (a member of the University of Applied Science of Western Switzerland (HEIA-FR) and the University of Fribourg (UNIFR). These institutions propose complementary approaches: the EPFL and UNIFR conduct research at a more global level, whereas the HEIA-FR focuses more on its application to practice and industry. All put strong emphasis on engineering and architectural sciences, which complement humanities and social science studies (law, management and human behavioural research).

Through the *smart living lab*, the three institutions will pursue a common goal: to provide a unique platform for research and innovation on the most topical, exciting questions relative to the future of the built environment. The institutions used a bold strategy to make this a tangible reality: to design and construct a building that will embody this future and serve as a test tube for exploring ways to get one step further. This building will be the future home of the *smart living lab*.

A specific research programme was designed to meet the ambitious goals the lab has set for itself. However, the first step was defining the principles for such a building: it should be emblematic of the future, designed in the present and based on learnings from the past, and should serve as a living laboratory for its users. The programme, quite simply called the "Smart Living Building Research Program" produced a diverse set of outcomes that will be explored in greater detail in the following chapters.

1.1 Strategic project for regional development

Following the relocation of Fribourg's Cardinal Brewery in 2011, after more than a hundred years of industrial activities on the site, the latter was acquired by the City and State of Fribourg. The plan was to turn the site into an innovation district called blueFACTORY. This site is at the core of the canton's regional development strategy (Etat de Fribourg 2017) and is part of the Switzerland Innovation initiative (Switzerland Innovation 2018).

The blueFACTORY site has inherent qualities due to its proximity to the Fribourg train station ^{Figure 1.1}, which itself is well connected to both the Lake Geneva region and the Zürich area. Currently under renovation, the site will be used for a variety of purposes, including housing, offices, commercial areas, etc. It is also unique in its strong commitment to a zero carbon economy, as tenants are requested to sign a charter (Bluefactory Fribourg Freiburg SA 2014) which specifies a *zero carbon policy*. In 2014, the ownership and development

Fig. 1.1 The blueFACTORY site's surroundings

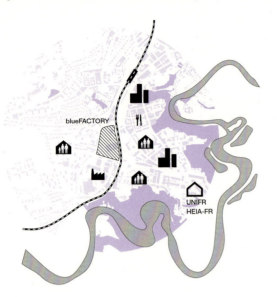

Fig. 1.2 Fribourg's strategic position in Switzerland

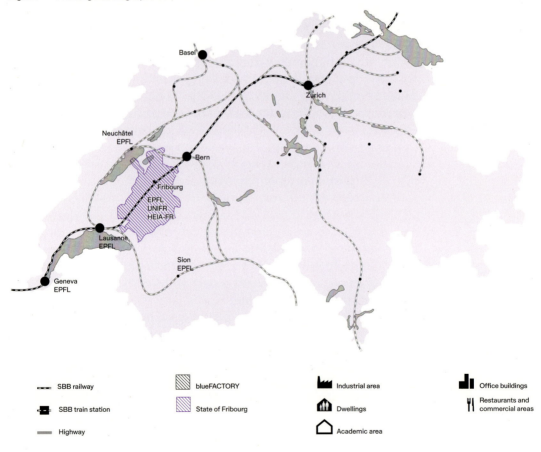

30   Exploring

of the site were delegated to a public limited company called Bluefactory Fribourg Freiburg SA (BFF SA).

To stimulate its development, the State of Fribourg has decided to initiate and support a variety of technological platforms (Etat de Fribourg 2017). The *smart living lab* is one such platform. It was for this reason that the State of Fribourg approached the EPFL in January 2012, to gauge its interest in developing a satellite campus on the blueFACTORY site dedicated to a theme relevant to both parties. The EPFL accepted the proposal, which was in line with its larger strategy to develop satellite campuses in different areas of western Switzerland ^{Figure 1.2}, having already founded specialized "antennae" in Neuchâtel (micro-engineering) (Catsaros et al. 2014) (Rey 2014), Sion (green chemistry, energy and environment), and Geneva (biotechnology).

An iterative process ultimately led to the emergence of the appropriate potential development theme. In addition to the built environment—which was ultimately accepted—other possible topics, including nanomaterials and nutrition, were also proposed. In November 2012, the State Council determined that the EPFL Fribourg antenna's focus would be the built environment, one of the State's main economic activities. The *smart living lab* proposal, which thus far had been jointly developed by the EPFL and HEIA-FR, was to become the flagship project for establishing the EPFL's presence in Fribourg, in partnership with both HEIA-FR and UNIFR (Andersen and Rey 2013). Thus was the EPFL's new satellite campus (or antenna) born in Fribourg, 80 km from Lausanne.

The goal of the project is to create a working and living space (a container) that is ahead of its time and a centre for interinstitutional and interdisciplinary excellence in the areas of innovative technologies and construction techniques. Both a place of knowledge and a motor for technological transfer, the building will be a centre for post-occupancy research projects by involving its own users—the researchers—in the trials.

With this aim in mind, a formal agreement detailing the antenna's financial, academic and organizational structure was signed on March 11, 2014 between EPFL and the State of Fribourg. This included, among other things, a commitment from the State of Fribourg together with EPFL to finance a group called Building2050, whose activities would be specifically dedicated to the development of the "Smart Living Building Research Program." This programme aims to establish the state of the art and to determine the theoretical, empirical and experimental findings on which to base operational and performance criteria. Determining these criteria, which ranged from environmental to social, was necessary in order to best serve the *smart living lab* building's primary mission: to become a signature building for sustainability that showcases the advantages of a research-driven design process by embodying these principles as a "building for the future." Its mission was also to offer its users and researchers a unique platform to experiment with new ideas,

① The *smart living lab* and its flagship building

be it testing new technologies, developing alternative energy systems, studying and influencing human well-being, behaviour and interactions, or innovating in terms of decision processes.

All in all, from its inception, the development of the *smart living lab* and its building ^{Table 1.3} has involved an original network of stakeholders and, to our knowledge, unprecedented governance.

Key dates

The definition and construction of the *smart living lab* building project will be based on a predetermined framework and involve a specific set of actors. While the building's users will be *smart living lab* researchers, the project will be financed by the State of Fribourg and developed by BFF SA, the site's owner. Though highly innovative and original, the design and construction processes will be subject to public procurement law.

To ensure the project satisfies the *smart living lab*'s goals as per the considerations presented in this book, a "collaborative competition" has been launched. The competition will allow for interaction between several interdisciplinary design teams and researchers, and thus will provide greater understanding of the issues during the building's predesign process.

1.2 The research and innovation embodied in the *smart living lab* building

The research activities within the *smart living lab* building will be driven by the goal of enhancing its users' well-being while limiting resource consumption through digital improvement. In other words, the *lab*'s interdisciplinary research will contribute to economic development (which will involve both its users and private sector actors) by experimenting and evaluating performances broadly and at different levels, based on actual use by individuals.

Nine research groups ^{Table 1.4} will form the nucleus for collaboration between the three universities, while additional research groups (from the universities and beyond) will serve as affiliates through specific research projects. These research groups will contribute to four areas of research, which are:

Well-being & behaviours: Improving human health and comfort by optimizing indoor environmental quality and behaviours.

Interactions & design processes: Understanding and building a dialogue among stakeholders in the building's lifecycle in order to develop tools for designing, modelling and operating the buildings.

Construction technologies: Monitoring resource efficiency and accelerating implementation of new construction processes.

Energy systems: Developing smart, energy-efficient systems and technologies, improving their management, and foreseeing legal and economic consequences.

Tab. 1.3 Key milestones and agreements for the design and construction of the *smart living lab* building

Year	Month	Milestone
2011	June	Re-purchase of the land by the City and the State of Fribourg
2012	Jan.	Contact initiated between the State of Fribourg and EPFL
	March	First concept note defining the fundamental principles of the *smart living lab* (Andersen and Rey 2012)
	Summer	Development of a detailed vision by a working group comprised of representatives of EPFL and HEIA-FR (Andersen et al. 2012)
2013	April	*Antenne EPFL sur le site blueFACTORY* tentative agreement between the State of Fribourg and EPFL, April 23, 2013
2014	March	*Implantation de l'EPFL à Fribourg* agreement between the State of Fribourg and EPFL, March 11, 2014
	May	*Octroi d'une aide financière en faveur du projet smart living lab et de la création d'une antenne permanente de l'Ecole polytechnique fédérale de Lausanne dans le quartier d'innovation blueFACTORY* cantonal council decree, May 15, 2014
2015	Dec.	Temporary move of the first researchers into a blueFACTORY neighbourhood facility called Halle Bleue, December 1, 2015
2016	June	*Construction du bâtiment dédié au smart living lab sur le site blueFACTORY entre l'Etat de Fribourg et Bluefactory Fribourg-Freiburg SA (BFFSA)* agreement, June 21, 2016
2017	Nov.	*Plan d'Affectation Cantonal (PAC) de blueFACTORY* public enquiry by the State of Fribourg, November 23, 2017
2018	May	*Octroi d'une aide financière en faveur de la construction du "Smart Living Building" (SLB)* cantonal council decree
	July	Ratification by the Fribourg State Council of the PAC
	Sept.	Launch of the collaborative architectural competition in the form of a *Mandat d'Etude Parallèle (MEP)*
2018–2019	(forthcoming)	Preliminary project competition
2019	(forthcoming)	Project definition
2020–2022	(forthcoming)	Project realization

Tab. 1.4 The *smart living lab* core groups

Institution	Group	Full name
EPFL	FAR	Construction and Architecture
	HOBEL	Human-Oriented Built Environment Lab
	SXL	Structural eXploration Lab
	TEBEL	Thermal Engineering for the Built Environment Laboratory
HEIA-FR	Energy institute	
	Transform institute	
UNIFR	Human-IST	Human Centered Interaction Science and Technology
	IImt	International institute of management in technology
	Institute for Swiss and international construction law	

The *smart living lab*'s future building will provide 130 work spaces for *smart living lab* researchers on an approximate surface area of 5000 square meters. The building will embody the seven values defined by the heads of the research groups, which are to:

1) Catalyse and imbue progress;
2) Foster investigative rigour and lateral thinking;
3) Enhance individual experience and guarantee fair conditions for everyone;
4) Support collaboration and the transmission of knowledge;
5) Honour its surrounding environment and its cultural context;
6) Embody sustainability in all its forms, embrace industrial ecology and circular economy; and
7) Evolve and be capable of self-redefinition.

The following chapters in this book will mainly address values 1, 3 and 6. This includes setting environmental goals based on the information gleaned from state of the art research (Chapter ②) and determining the types and intensity of usage (Chapters ③ and ④), which will lead to the development of tools and methods that could further enhance environmental performance (Chapter ⑤ to ⑧).

These outcomes have been included in an overview of the "collaborative competition" to be launched. Other recommendations relative to values 2, 4, 5 and 7 were defined by the *smart living lab* researchers through collaborative workshops.

1.3 A living, "live-in" lab

Beyond these values and based on these processes lies the overarching principle of a building that serves as both a "living lab" and a "live-in lab," as its name suggests.

The living lab concept makes end users the focus of an R&D process, also known as user-centric design. As presented by Westerlund and Leminen (Westerlund and Leminen 2011), living labs can thus be defined as "physical regions or virtual realities where stakeholders form public–private–people partnerships (4 Ps) of firms, public agencies, universities, institutes, and users that collaborate to create, prototype, validate, and test new technologies, services, products, and systems in real-life contexts." Their users not only act as sources of information, but as drivers of innovation, as well as testers, developers, and designers on par with other living lab contributors.

Though not necessarily specific to the built environment as a field, the living lab concept is seen here as a form of open innovation that provides multiple benefits, including cost savings, improved user value, and better innovation performance. The *smart living lab* will apply this same innovation process to the various projects it develops, including its own building.

As a live-in laboratory, the research carried out will be more specific to the built environment. Such live-in laboratories are real-life buildings that serve as housing or actual work environments. They emerged from the need for comprehensive data on real, complex, naturalistic environments to develop user-friendly devices for the home (Nyström et al. 2014).

As one-to-one scale prototypes, they can be used for testing and evaluating new solutions for energy efficiency, sustainability, smart buildings, etc., set up like real homes, where test subjects are asked to try out new products and systems for a variable period of time. Such labs help researchers in bridging the gap between laboratory testing and larger studies in real homes. Unlike the living lab concept, however, test subjects are not necessarily involved in the design of these "live-in laboratories" (Fishkin and International Conference on Pervasive Computing 2006).

The *smart living lab* hopes to satisfy both definitions simultaneously. The living lab concept provides an open innovation framework for involving *smart living lab* researchers as testers, developers, and designers in innovation for their primary research tool: their building as a live-in laboratory. Chapter ⑨ makes several recommendations in service to this goal.

1.4 Summary

An interdisciplinary approach will therefore be at the core of the *smart living lab*'s research activities. As the project is not based on a single discipline or scientific approach, it is through complementarity and hybridization that the *smart living lab*'s value as a research centre will be enhanced. Theory combines with practice, empirical evidence and general hypotheses.

This multi-faceted approach finds particularly fertile ground in the field of the built environment, both in terms of research and practice. Simultaneously integrating multiple criteria in the development and transformation of buildings is inherent to any sustainability-based approach. To successfully carry out research in this field and in order to construct innovative buildings, it is necessary to enrich the design process using approaches that are multi-dimensional, evaluative, interdisciplinary, and participative (Rey 2014).

How to address the *smart living lab*'s goals for its own building led to the creation of a dedicated research programme. The following chapters will describe the main phases of development of this multi-dimensional programme and their outcomes.

Acknowledgements

The authors would like to thank the Canton of Fribourg for its financial support and, more broadly, the multiple stakeholders from the École polytechnique fédérale de Lausanne (EPFL), the School of Engineering and Architecture of Fribourg (HEIA-FR) and the University of Fribourg, who have contributed to the development of the *smart living lab* vision since its genesis.

References

Andersen, Marilyne, and Emmanuel Rey. 2012. "SMART LIVING LAB. Note succincte esquissant la vision d'une antenne EPFL au sein du PST Fribourg." EPFL, Lausanne.

Andersen, Marilyne, and Emmanuel Rey. 2013. "Le projet SLL à Fribourg: un bâtiment du futur en site réel." *La vie économique*, 26–27.

Andersen, Marilyne, Emmanuel Rey, Jacques Bersier, and Jean-Philippe Bacher. 2012. "SMART LIVING LAB. Note succincte du groupe de travail." Bluefactory Fribourg Freiburg SA. 2014. "Charte d'utilisation du site blueFACTORY."

Catsaros, Christophe, Pauline Rapaz, Cedric van der Poel, Emmanuel Rey, Willi Frei, and Cyril Baumann. 2014. "Microcity". *Espazium, Tracés edition, sec. cahier spécial*. https://documents.epfl.ch/groups/l/la/last-unit/www/PRESSE/140502_Cahier%20Microcity_DEF.pdf.

CRUS, KFH, and COHEP. 2009. "Les trois types de hautes écoles au sein du système d'enseignement supérieur suisse." https://www.swissuniversities.ch/fileadmin/swissuniversities/Dokumente/Kammern/Kammer_PH/Dok/2009_Beschreibung_HS-Typen_f.pdf.

Etat de Fribourg. 2017. "Programme gouvernemental et plan financier 2017–2021." PS Fribourg. November 7, 2017. https://www.ps-fr.ch/fr/programme-gouvernemental-et-plan-financier-2017-2021.

Fishkin, Kenneth P. 2006. "International Conference on Pervasive Computing." *Pervasive computing: 4th international conference: proceedings.* Berlin: Springer.

Nyström, Anna-Greta, Seppo Leminen, Westerlund Mika, and Kortelainen Mika. 2014. "Actor Roles and Role Patterns Influencing Innovation in Living Labs." *Industrial Marketing Management* 43 (January). https://doi.org/10.1016/j.indmarman.2013.12.016.

Rey, Emmanuel. 2014. "Synegies territoriales pour les lieux de savoir. Stratégies expérimentées dans le cadre du projet Microcity à Neuchâtel. (Suisse)." https://infoscience.epfl.ch/record/201009.

"Switzerland Innovation." 2018. *Switzerland Innovation*. 2018. https://www.switzerland-innovation.com/.

Westerlund, Mika, and Seppo Leminen. 2011. "Managing the Challenges of Becoming an Open Innovation Company: Experiences from Living Labs." *Technology Innovation Management Review*; Ottawa. https://search.proquest.com/docview/1614474666?accountid=27198.

② Research at the service of building design

Thomas Jusselme

The "Smart Living Building Research Program" was developed to fuel the design and construction processes of the future building, which will serve as a base for more than hundred *smart living lab* researchers. This second chapter will provide details of the strategy used to develop this programme and the questions it aimed to answer.

The key criteria of the *smart living lab* strategy are:
1) a building of exceptional architectural quality
2) excellent life cycle performance
3) usability over time

Hence, a preliminary research phase called the "Smart Living Building Research Program" ("SLB Research Program") was developed to help in formulating a scientific design brief that will serve as a basis for the building's design. This phase, which embodies the principles of design-based research, will also steer the future design process through relevant research findings.

This chapter will provide an overview of the SLB Research Program methodology and clarify the relationship between the following chapters and the SLB objectives.

The last IPCC Special Report (IPCC et al. 2018) on the impact of global warming of 1.5° C calls for a carbon neutrality around 2050, i.e. the amount of CO_2 in the atmosphere must no longer increase at that time. To that end, the goals of the Swiss 2000-Watt Society in 2050 provided a framework for the project's main environmental objectives. The Kaya identity then allowed us to define the major research areas so as to determine the steps necessary to meet the building's objectives. Finally, we used complementary top-down and bottom-up approaches to explore these research areas from both a global and a more focused perspective.

2.1 The 2000-watt vision

The Swiss Federal Institute of Technology in Zürich introduced the 2000-Watt Society concept in 1998. The concept highlights the need to reduce primary energy demands and carbon footprints Figure 2.1 to 2000 watts and 1 tCO_{2-eq}[1] per capita respectively before 2150 (Kesselring and Winter 1995, Jochem et al. 2004). These objectives were calculated based on the impact of an entire society divided by its population. The 1 tCO_{2-eq} per capita target addresses climate change as described by the Intergovernmental Panel on Climate Change (Pachauri et al. 2014), whereas the 2000-Watt per capita target is based on human needs. According to the United Nations Development Programme, these targets are necessary for developed countries to reach a Human Development Index of 0.8 (Goldemberg et al. 2004).

Inspired by the 2000 Watt vision, we chose to target a more intermediate objective at a closer horizon — that of 2050 — with a cumulative energy demand (CED) of 3500 watts and Global Warming Potential (GWP) impact of 2 tCO_{2-eq} per capita. Considering that the current average footprint of Swiss residents is 6.5 tCO_{2-eq} and 4900 watts per capita (Société à 2000 Watts 2016), this indeed raises a challenge, particularly as regard carbon emissions, which must be reduced nearly threefold. Previous research (Notter et al. 2013) shows

[1] CO_{2-eq}: equivalent carbon dioxide

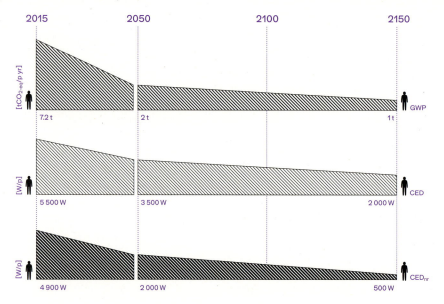

Fig. 2.1   The 2000-Watt objectives

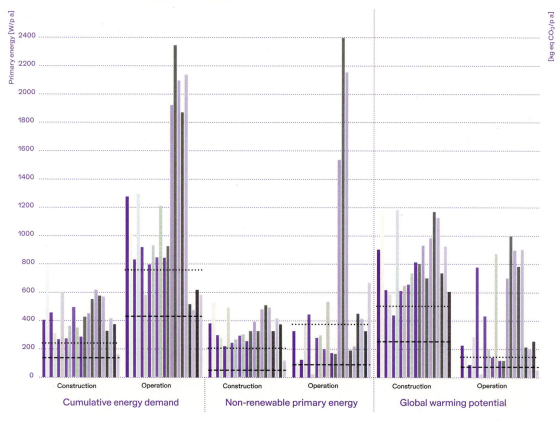

Fig. 2.2   Compared impacts of 20 buildings with the 2050- and 2150-target values of the 2000-Watt Society (Jusselme et al. 2015)

⋯⋯ Targets for 2050   – – – Targets for 2150

42   Exploring

that a portion of the Swiss population already has a footprint of less than 2000 Watts, but that no portion falls below 1 $tCO_{2\text{-eq}}$.

The same observations were true for the built environment. We conducted a comparative study of the environmental performance of twenty best-practice buildings (Jusselme et al. 2015) and the 2000-Watt Society in 2050 targets, as illustrated by the Swiss SIA 2040 norm (SIA 2011). Only one or two buildings actually reached the individual targets, and none were compliant with all of the targets simultaneously (i.e. CED, CED_{nr} and GWP) Figure 2.2. Notably, the construction phase and GWP impacts were the most challenging.

This first section allowed us to better understand the 2000-Watt Society, the 2050 objectives and their challenges relative to current building best practices. We will now look at how we identified the main building performance targets in the hopes of meeting these objectives.

2.2 From the Kaya identity...

A Japanese energy economist named Yoichi Kaya illustrated in a simple, pragmatic way the mechanisms that result in the human production of greenhouse gases in what is called the Kaya identity (Kaya and Yokobori 1997). This identity Figure 2.3 states that greenhouse gases are the product of the world population, the per capita Growth Domestic Product (GDP), world GDP's energy intensity and the carbon intensity of the energy. By 2050, the GDP may have doubled (if it continues to rise at a rate of 2% – 3% a year) (Ward 2011), and the world population is expected to have reached 9.7 billion inhabitants, a 33% increase (United Nations 2015). The current carbon emissions average is three tons per year per capita (Metz 2001). Reducing these emissions to two tons by 2050 while the GDP and world population continue to grow will put great strain on the GDP's energy intensity and the carbon intensity of the energy factors.

Using the same approach, the Kaya identity was applied to the Swiss building context Figure 2.4 by replacing the GDP with built surface (Jusselme et al. 2015). Building greenhouse gas emissions are expressed as the product of the Swiss population, the per-capita built surfaces, the built surfaces' energy intensity and the carbon intensity of the energy. Again, a prospective overview for 2050 shows that the Swiss population will have risen to nine million inhabitants, a 14% increase (Kohli et al. 2010), and built and heated surfaces will probably have reached 940 million m^2, a 50% increase.

Understanding the mechanism that causes Swiss buildings to produce greenhouse gases helped us to define the main areas of investigation in the framework of the SLB Research Program.

Fig. 2.3   The Kaya identity shows the main drivers of greenhouse gas production, namely population, per capita GDP, energy intensity and carbon intensity

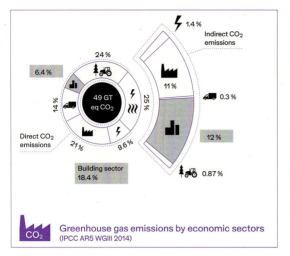

Greenhouse gas emissions by economic sectors (IPCC AR5 WGIII 2014)

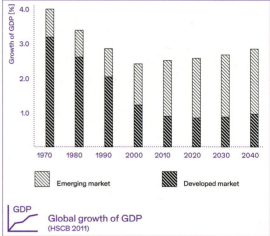

Global growth of GDP (HSCB 2011)

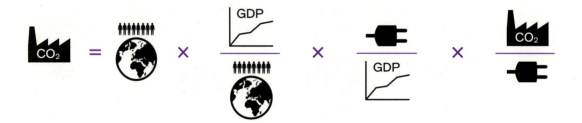

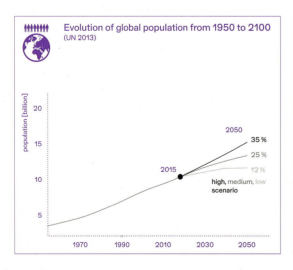

Evolution of global population from 1950 to 2100 (UN 2013)

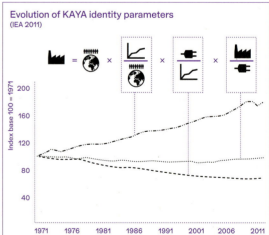

Evolution of KAYA identity parameters (IEA 2011)

Fig. 2.4   The Kaya identity applied to the Swiss building context

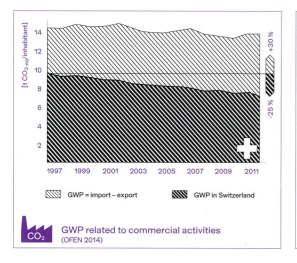

GWP related to commercial activities
(OFEN 2014)

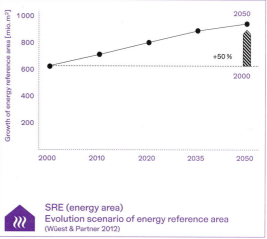

SRE (energy area)
Evolution scenario of energy reference area
(Wüest & Partner 2012)

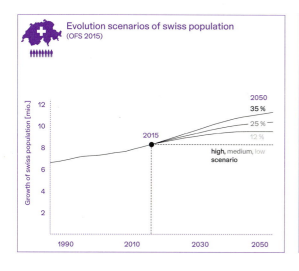

Evolution scenarios of swiss population
(OFS 2015)

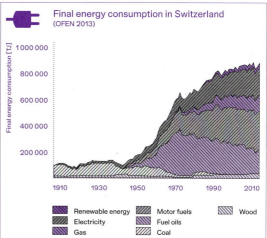

Final energy consumption in Switzerland
(OFEN 2013)

2.3 …to the targeted research fields

Applying the Kaya identity to the Swiss building context allowed us to formulate the following questions, which served as fundamental drivers for the SLB Research Program.

Some of these questions related to users:
- By how much can the building area per capita be reduced?
- By how much can building usability be increased?
- What are the real environmental benefits of such a strategy?
- What are the acceptable limits in terms of comfort and discomfort?

These questions were investigated in an exploratory framework in our own offices (more details in Chapter ④).

Other questions were related to carbon footprint:
- What were the main strategies used to reduce the energy footprint of built surfaces?
- What does the embodied energy of the building components represent, and which materials would help improve a building's life cycle?
- How do human-building interactions affect energy performance?

Chapter ⑤ provides an overview of the research conducted as part of an experimental building module specifically designed to answer these questions.

Further questions focused on energy demand:
- How can we lower the carbon content of the energy buildings consume?
- Is it possible to assess and monitor the time-dependent carbon content of the supplied energy?
- How can we correlate a building's energy demand to the production of renewable energy?

We investigated these issues at the scale of the "Smart Living Building," as reported in Chapter ⑥.

We designed the three aforementioned experiments in order to make useful recommendations regarding the design of the future building, its life cycle performance and its usability. The application of these recommendations, however, does not automatically result in high architectural quality; on the contrary, it could potentially increase the complexity of the design process by adding new constraints and demanding additional skills on the part of designers. For this reason, two additional methodological questions were formulated:
- What impact should the SLB objectives have on the design process?

- Which design methodology would best support innovation and architectural quality?

Chapter ⑦ provides an overview of the research, starting with the theoretical framework and going all the way up to the collaborative, iterative design proposal for the building.

We also questioned its applicability in an actual design process:
- How can life cycle performance criteria be integrated earlier in the design process?
- Which decision-making tools can assist the design process to that end?
- Is it possible to illustrate the technical and architectural consequences of the 2000-Watt targets to enhance designers' understanding?

Chapter ⑧ addresses these issues and describes a new exploratory approach for sustainable architecture. These issues had two consequences on the SLB Research Program. The first was raising awareness of the importance of the building as an entity with hundreds of components and user interactions, for which we used a holistic, interdisciplinary approach. However, one of the main goals was to identify specific targets and key pragmatic strategies to help designers meet the SLB objectives. The second was the need to divide the building into subcomponents using what is called a target cascading approach. We used these two complementary methodological guidelines throughout our work, switching from a holistic, top-down approach to a targeted, bottom-up approach, both of which will be described in the following sections.

2.4 Holism and interdisciplinarity

An environmental assessment looks at multivariable, interdisciplinary, intercorrelated issues (Marszal et al. 2011). Improving a building system or component can improve one performance indicator while negatively impacting a building's overall performance. Thus, for example:
- Double-flow heat recovery mechanical ventilation decreases a building's demand for heating, but increases the electricity consumption of the ventilation.
- Increasing insulation of the facades lowers the demand for heating but increases the building's embodied impacts.

Therefore, the SLB performance indicators were assessed using a cradle-to-cradle approach that included the entire building life cycle.

The construction of the future *smart living lab* building will also have an impact at the urban scale, mainly in terms of mobility and food. In addition to the building itself, the environmental impact of users will be compounded by the building's location, which will determine commuting and eating habits during working hours. As the Notter, Meyer and Althaus study based on a sample of Swiss households (Notter et al. 2013) shows, the cumulative impacts linked to the building's infrastructure, food and mobility represent 33 %, 14 % and 47 % of the GWP impact per inhabitant respectively. Therefore, we included the building infrastructure and all mobility-related impacts in the scope of the analysis. Food was excluded, as the designers' ability to address this issue was too limited.

The direct consequence of this holistic approach was a wide range of areas to be investigated. For this reason, the SLB Research Program team was highly interdisciplinary, and included building physicists, energy scientists, sociologists, architects, computer scientists, various designers and others (specified in the Acknowledgements).

2.5   Reductionism and target cascading

In the previous section we highlighted the importance of a research programme that uses a holistic approach to maintain the building's overall coherence. However, this approach also increases the complexity of the design process, as each building component must be considered within the larger scope of the entire building and thus be re-assessed in this evolving context. This is particularly critical for designers during the initial stages, where multiple and rapid changes and back-and-forth between the creative and analytical phases take place. Moreover, though the initial design phase is the least detailed, it is also that in which designers have the greatest influence on the design.

That is why we developed a methodology to complement the holistic approach called target cascading. We applied this reductionist method, which originated in the mechanical sciences (Kim 2001), to illustrate how top-down objectives from the 2000-Watt Society can be divided into sub-objectives at the building system and component levels. In so doing, it is possible to steer the designers from component targets towards the overall building objectives in a pragmatic way (Hoxha et al. 2016). Using a Sankey diagram, we can illustrate Figure 2.5 how the 2 $tCO_{2\text{-eq}}$ per capita target can be applied to office, residential and school buildings based on their respective systems and components. The target cascading method, which was used for most of the programme's research projects, is further described in Chapter ⑧, as it is also part of a new exploratory method for early design phases.

Fig. 2.5 Target cascading from the 2000-Watt Society objectives for building systems and component targets

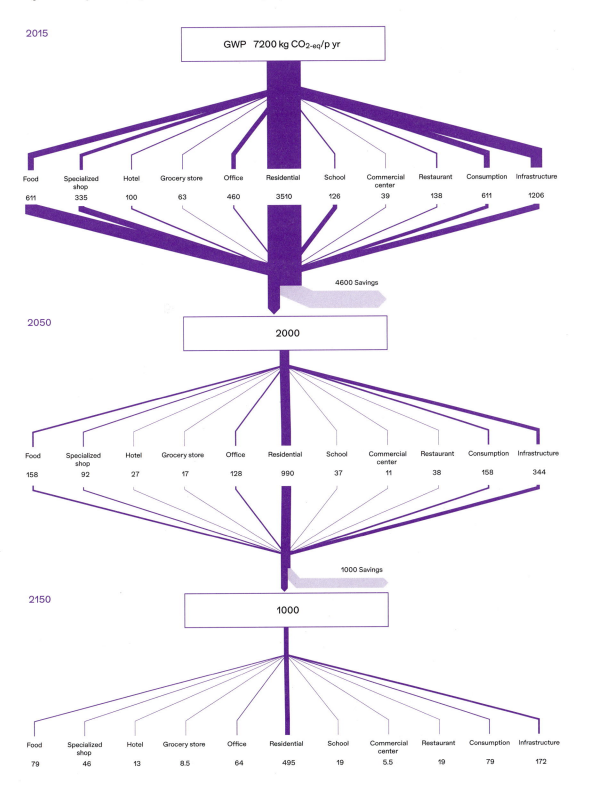

Fig. 2.6 From strategy to design brief

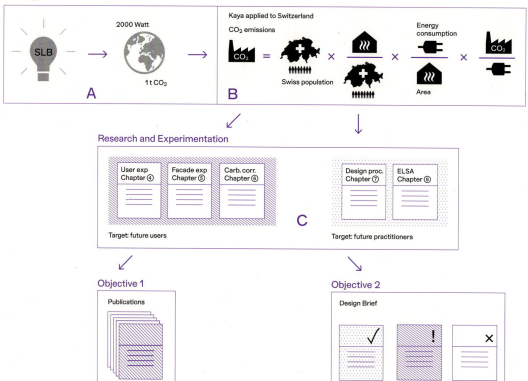

Exploring

2.6 In a few words…

The SLB Research Program was a unique opportunity to unite an interdisciplinary community of scientists around a common research subject: the future *smart living lab* building. The 2000-Watt Society concept provided the SLB Research Program with a foundation ^{Figure 2.6} on which to define its objectives (A). Building upon this idea, researchers identified the Cumulative Energy Demand (CED), the non-renewable Cumulative Energy Demand (CED_{nr}) and the Global Warming Potential (GWP) as the main impact factors to monitor. The Kaya identity was adapted so as to understand the impact of greenhouse gases and define the main areas of research investigation (B), namely the usability of the built surface, the building energy intensity and the carbon intensity of energy. These areas were explored (C) in the three research experiments (Chapters ④, ⑤ and ⑥) and in two methodological issues (Chapters ⑦ and ⑧).

Roughly thirty scientific articles and reports were published based on this research material. Additionally—and of key importance for the *smart living lab* building—a scientific design brief with operational recommendations was created to support the SLB design process.

Acknowledgements

The author would like to thank all of the researchers involved in the implementation of the "Smart Living Building Research Program," and especially the Building2050 team for its invaluable support.

Related publications
Jusselme, Thomas. 2015. "Building 2050 – Research Programme" EPFL, Fribourg. Available at http://building2050.epfl.ch/

References
Goldemberg, José, Thomas B. Johansson, Dennis Anderson. 2004. "United Nations Development Programme, United Nations, Department of Economic and Social Affairs, and World Energy Council. *World Energy Assessment: Overview: 2004 Update*". New York: United Nations Development Programme, Bureau for Development Policy.
Hoxha, Endrit, Thomas Jusselme, Arianna Brambilla, Stefano Cozza, Marilyne Andersen, and Emmanuel Rey. 2016. "Impact Targets as Guidelines towards Low Carbon Buildings: Preliminary Concept." In *PLEA*. Los Angeles, USA.
IPCC, Valérie Masson-Delmotte, Panmao Zhai, Hans Pörtner, Debra Roberts, Jim Skea, Priyadarshi Shukla, Anna Pirani, Wilfran Moufouma-Okia, Clotilde Péan, Roz Pidcock, Sarah Connors, J.B. Robin Matthews, Yan Chen, Xuhui Zhou, Melissa Gomis, and Elisabeth Lonnoy, Tom Maycock, Melinda Tignor, Tim Waterfield (eds.). 2018. "Summary for Policymakers of IPCC Special Report on Global Warming of 1.5°C Approved by Governments." World Meteorological Organization, Geneva, Switzerland. http://www.ipcc.ch/news_and_events/pr_181008_P48_spm.shtml.
Jochem, Eberhard, Göran Andersson, Daniel Favrat, Heinz Gutscher, Konrad Hungerbühler, Phillipp Rudolf von Roh, Daniel Spreng, Alexander Wokaun, and Mark Zimmermann. 2004. "A White Book for R&D of Energy-Efficient Technologies." Switzerland: Novantlantis. https://goo.gl/UGBiAM.
Jusselme, Thomas, Arianna Brambilla, Endrit Hoxha, Yingying Jiang, Didier Vuarnoz, and Stefano Cozza. 2015. "Building 2050 – State-of-the-Arts and Preliminary Guidelines." EPFL, Fribourg.
Kaya, Yōichi, and Keiichi Yokobori, eds. 1997. "*Environment, Energy, and Economy: Strategies for Sustainability.*" Tokyo; New York: United Nations University Press.
Kesselring, Paul, and Carl-

Jochen Winter. 1995. "World Energy Scenarios: A Two-Kilowatt Society-Plausible Future or Illusion." In *Energy Days 94. Proceedings*.

Kim, Hyung Min. 2001. "Target Cascading in Optimal System Design." Michigan, USA: Department of Mechanical Engineering, University of Michigan.

Kohli, Raymond, and Bundesamt für Statistik. 2010. "*Les scénarios de l'évolution démographique de la Suisse 2010–2060.*" Neuchâtel: Office fédéral de la statistique.

Marszal, Anna Joanna, Per Heiselberg, Julien Bourrelle, Eike Musall, Karsten Voss, Igor Sartori, and Assunta Napolitano. 2011. "Zero Energy Building – A Review of Definitions and Calculation Methodologies." *Energy and Buildings* 43 (4): 971–79. https://doi.org/10.1016/j.enbuild.2010.12.022.

Metz, Bert. 2001. "Climate Change 2001: Mitigation: Contribution of Working Group III to the Third Assessment Report of the Intergovernmental Panel on Climate Change." Vol. 3. Cambridge University Press.

Notter, Dominic A., Reto Meyer, and Hans-Jörg Althaus. 2013. "The Western Lifestyle and Its Long Way to Sustainability." *Environmental Science and Technology* 47 (9): 4014–21. https://doi.org/10.1021/es3037548.

Pachauri, Rajendra K., Myles R. Allen, Vicente R. Barros, John Broome, Wolfgang Cramer, Renate Christ, John A. Church, Leon Clarke, Qin Dahe, and Purnamita Dasgupta. 2014. "*Climate Change 2014: Synthesis Report. Contribution of Working Groups I, II and III to the Fifth Assessment Report of the Intergovernmental Panel on Climate Change.*" IPCC.

SIA. 2011. "SIA 2040 / 2011 La voie SIA vers l'efficacité énergétique." SIA Société suisse des ingénieurs et des architectes.

Société à 2000 watts. 2016. "La Suisse, sur la voie de la société à 2000 Watts." 2016. http://www.2000watt.ch/fr/societe-a-2000-watts/facts-figures/.

United Nations. 2015. "World Population Prospects: The 2015 Revision – Key Findings and Advance Tabls." United Nations, Department of Economic and Social Affairs.

Ward, Karen. 2011. "The World in 2050 – Quantifying the Shift in the Global Economy." HSBC Bank plc. \\antfrgenas1.epfl.ch\antfr-ge\4Building-2050\03.Ressources\vision 2050\hsbc-bwob-theworldin2050-fr.pdf.

③ An occupant-driven perspective

Dominic Villeneuve
Thierry Maeder
Hamed Alavi
Vincent Kaufmann
Denis Lalanne

The social design approach presented in this chapter was developed to ensure that the new *smart living lab* building includes not only sustainable environmental and economic aspects, but also social aspects. By better understanding the preferences and attitudes of its future occupants and its three founding institutions, the team will be able to successfully incorporate the former in the design process.

This chapter presents the building's human dimensions as well as the twofold, socially-driven approach used to design the new *smart living lab* building. The approach was designed based on both the building's managers and its future occupants. For the former, the goal was to ensure that the project managers' programming principles were explicit in terms of social uses and well-being through a top-down study. The study aimed to establish the project's principles and steer projections by exploring the discourses and positions of the institutions involved in the project. For the occupants, the aim was to determine occupants' needs using a bottom-up approach. The two approaches, conducted in parallel, aimed to analyse the expectations of employees, in other words, those who will be most affected by the building in terms of layout and work environment, and to combine this with careful observation and analysis of their behaviours in the existing building via sensors.

Therefore, the main goal of the study was to provide both empirical and theoretical support for designing technical solutions for the future academic building. The particularity of this project, besides serving as the new premises for three institutions[2] with different needs and expectations, lies in the specific nature of academic research, which requires creativity and cooperation, as well as time and space for highly focused individual work. Moreover, the building is meant to be an example both in terms of sustainable design and efficiency, and in terms of the well-being of its occupants. This implies a multidimensional approach that takes into consideration institutional, individual and technical parameters, and their impact on one another.

This social design approach is at the interface of the project's key principles and future occupants' needs. It addresses users' relationships to their workspace, how the building's spatial layout will affect comfort, uses and appropriation, as well as the form and modalities of the collaboration between the three schools in the new building. The approach had two main objectives: the first was to define realistic objectives for social sustainability, while the second was to propose concrete programming recommendations to be incorporated into the building's future architectural programme design. This involves translating the objectives and values projected by the Scientific Committee and the future occupants, and finding spatial compromises for the building's designers so that the *smart living lab* can serve as an example and model in this respect, both technically and architecturally.

3.1 Social Design Methodology
3.1.1 Top-down approach

The top-down approach sought to define the priority principles that emerged from project managers, namely the three institutional partners responsible for the project, and to establish

[2] École polytechnique fédérale de Lausanne, Haute école d'ingénierie et d'architecture de Fribourg and University of Fribourg.

common principles that would serve as a roadmap for the subsequent phases of the building's development.

This consisted of an analysis of written sources—working documents for internal use, legal documents (convention and State Council's message) and memoranda (inventory, etc.)—supplemented with four additional twenty-minute interviews. The interviews addressed general topics (including the values conveyed by the *smart living lab*, key social issues and the lab's image and identity), as well as more specific issues relative to the spatial layout and functioning of the future building (notions of environmental awareness, mobility, flexible working schedules, ancillary services, etc.). The interviews provided an initial idea of how to prioritize the issues based on the importance the respondents themselves gave them. The final component of the empirical portion of the study consisted of discussions in a plenary session between the research team and the institutions.

Through a thorough analysis of the documentation, including a series of successive readings, we were able to identify and synthesize the cross-cutting themes of the different documents, and to summarize them into key consensus principles for the *smart living lab* project. The results of the first research phase were synthesized and presented to the project managers to elicit reactions. Comments and concerns were noted, and common ground for the second phase of the study (namely the bottom-up approach) was redefined.

3.1.2 Bottom-up approach

The aim of the bottom-up approach was to identify similarities and differences in the relationships between individuals and the built environment, and in the expectations of academics and university staff. This part of the research also helped highlight areas in which the adoption of behaviours in keeping with the *smart living lab* philosophy (building regulations, commuting, recycling, etc.) could be encouraged. The bottom-up approach drew upon two main sources: a qualitative survey in the form of semi-structured interviews with employees involved in different types of academic activities, and a quantitative survey via an online questionnaire of employees of the three institutions.

Semi-structured qualitative interviews with eleven staff members from the School of Engineering and Architecture of Fribourg[3] and the University of Fribourg were conducted from May 27 to July 3, 2015. The interviews included two administrative assistants, three scientific collaborators, five professors and one PhD student. The interview grid consisted of three themes:
- Employees' relationship to the built environment. Respondents were asked to describe their work environment at different scales (the city, the

3 Haute école d'ingénierie et d'architecture de Fribourg

neighbourhood, their office, etc.) and all of the elements found therein in extensive detail.
- Daily practices and appropriation of the premises. In this part of the interview, respondents described a typical day's activities.
- Expectations in terms of living/work environments, facilities and local amenities. In that last part of the interview, respondents were invited to discuss their expectations and their ideal working environment.

In parallel, a quantitative survey on behaviours and expectations regarding the work environment (ecology, values, commuting, working space, activities, colleague relations, and the office ideal) was conducted among the employees of the three institutions. The questionnaire, which was sent to all employees of the three institutions, was returned by 1598 people. 1167 were complete and usable for statistical analysis.

Three exploratory studies to capture and analyse occupants' movements inside and outside the building were conducted in the *smart living lab* (Blue Hall):

Outdoor behaviour: In order to understand the specific work context of participants relative to other working locations, volunteers were equipped with GPS tracking software on their smartphones for one week. This enabled us to track and analyse how often the participants worked from home or from secondary office locations, as well as the transport modes used to get to and from the experimentation site. An individual mobility map was created for each participant subsequent to the tracking period. Interviews were then done to discuss and interpret these results with the participants to understand why they chose to work at one location instead of another and the factors involved in these choices.

Macro indoor behaviour: In this study, bracelets with Bluetooth beacons were given to the twenty-two occupants. Twelve rooms were monitored for two weeks. Based on the data, it was possible to tell at any given time whether any of the twenty-two occupants were present in one of the twelve rooms, and if so, which one. After careful data mining and analysis, characteristic profiles of the occupants were created based on their daily space-use patterns in the building, their movement between rooms, and their habits. Some occupants were highly predictable, with sedentary and routine behaviours. Others, on the contrary, were quite unpredictable and changed behaviours. This experiment helped in defining occupants' profiles and needs. The details of the study, statistical analysis and results are available in a previous publication (Verma et al. 2017).

Micro indoor behaviour: In this second study (described in detail in Chapter ④), two refurbished rooms were monitored with infra-red sensors, making it possible to locate occupants at the centimetre granularity in those rooms. The qualities of the two rooms were rather different: one was designed for collaborative use and the other for quiet, individual work. There were no assigned seats, and occupants could choose their room and sit according to their preferences and/or needs in the moment. Over eight weeks, the space-use behaviour of the thirty-three participants was monitored in the two refurbished rooms, as well as ten other areas in the building (cafeteria, meeting rooms, and the atrium). In addition, we used environmental sensing (CO_2, temperature, noise, humidity, etc.), as well as qualitative observations and interviews. The superposition of space-use patterns on the spatial configuration of offices revealed statistically verified results, demonstrating how certain visual attributes of a workspace—namely visual exposure and visual openness—can determine its relative occupancy rate. The details of the study design, data collection process, analyses, and findings are available in a previous publication (Alavi et al. 2018). The collected data is available to other researchers involved in the *smart living lab* project and will be available to the public research community through a shared corpus.

3.2 Results

Guidelines for the future building's design could be drawn from these qualitative and quantitative investigations.

The top-down approach helped in establishing a conceptual base and in building a consensus regarding what were identified as the four key principles of the *smart living lab*: innovation, ecology, well-being, and cooperation ^{Figure 3.1}. Based on these four principles, we established courses of action for their implementation, as well as means for achieving them. Moreover, this approach was also useful in identifying possible conflicts between the means to achieve the goals and potential solutions to contradictory goals, the most emblematic case being the dichotomy between well-being and ecology relative to building automation. The complexity of the interference between the values ^{Figure 3.1 (white circles)} required an additional step in terms of the programmatic design of the *smart living lab*. The latter consisted in creating interdependent clusters that encapsulate the four principles in a systemic way. The four conceptual clusters of values ^{Figure 3.1 (coloured shapes)} were expressed in the programmatic recommendations as: Creativity, Emulation, Human ecology, and Outreach.

Finally, a literature review was used to evaluate certain solutions, particularly in terms of employee well-being and productivity and their relevance to the lab. Notably, it emerged that greater employee autonomy with regard to working schedules, location and workspace layout seemed beneficial in all respects. The literature review also indicated the advantage of moving away from the idea of an open-space layout by highlighting the importance of isolation (visual and sound) for intellectual work. This led us to consider desk

Fig. 3.1 Four clusters of values

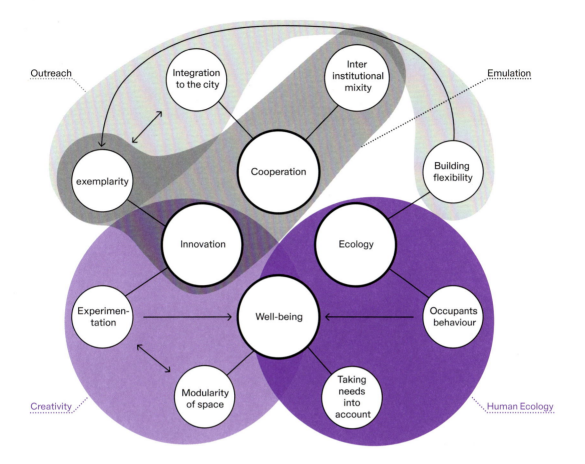

Fig. 3.2   Aspirations according to age

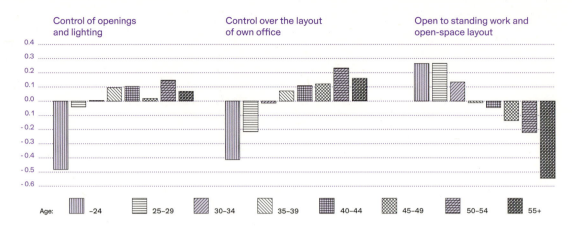

Fig. 3.3   Aspirations according to education level

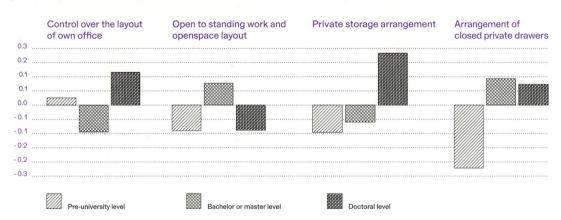

62   Exploring

sharing as an option, to meet the lab's environmental and collaborative objectives.

The bottom-up approach shed light on potential future occupants' expectations of the lab. For example, the survey revealed that alternative mobility access (public transit, walking and cycling) to the building was a key factor of employee well-being and productivity. Effectively, when potential users were asked "What are the most important characteristics of an ideal workplace?", the answers were distributed in the following way (the percentage rate in parenthesis corresponds to the percentage of respondents who felt that the given feature was of great importance):

1) Access by public transport (73%)
2) Brightness (70%)
3) Walking access (58%)
4) Quality of interior space (57%)
5) Outdoor view (52%)
6) Green areas nearby (41%)
7) Break areas (40%)
8) Meeting spaces (37%)
9) Parking options (35%)
10) On-site childcare (28%)
11) Car access (28%)
12) Design and decoration (19%)
13) Cloakrooms or showers (13%)

The quantitative survey revealed that neither respondents' gender nor their home institution were decisive factors in determining their responses. Their field of activity, age and education level, on the other hand, were powerful determinants of differentiation across a whole series of analyses that aimed to measure the degree of convergence between the project's principles and employees' experiences and aspirations. Regarding the field of activity, it is clear that workspace needs differ according to the field of research. This notably relates to the type of research (theoretical vs. experimental/laboratory work, individual vs. team work). It also appears that different practices and aspirations are associated with differences in age [Figure 3.2]. Though it is impossible to determine with complete certitude, as we lack longitudinal data, there seems to be a generation effect, especially among younger generations, who considered it less important to control their working environment (brightness and layout) and were more open to standing work stations and an open-space layout. Similarly, depending on whether respondents had a university degree or not, similar differentiation based on education level was also identified, with significant differences in terms of workplace aspirations [Figure 3.3].

3.2.1 Typology of work lifestyles

To identify lifestyle typologies, we built upon the Urban Sociology Laboratory's (LaSUR) work on residential lifestyles (Thomas et al. 2013). Conceptually, three relational dimensions to the workplace must be considered: social, sensitive and functional. Combining these dimensions, we did a classification analysis on the results of the quantitative survey using a dynamic cloud model (Ward's method). This methodology identified five groups of work lifestyles among the future occupants of the *smart living lab*.

Group 1 — Part-time, Rigid Solitary Work: This group is comprised of individuals who have their own offices. They rarely eat with their colleagues, in part because of their relatively strong propensity for part-time work. They rarely participate in meetings, have numerous face-to-face discussions, and take morning and afternoon breaks with their colleagues. They tend to arrive rather early, have fixed schedules and do not telecommute.

Group 2 — Work as a Second Home: In this group, we find people who eat together with colleagues, often share an office with several colleagues, frequently use headphones, have a personal desk, arrive at work rather late, work full-time (and more than all the other groups) as well as on weekends, and like to take breaks. We can therefore say that their social life at work is highly developed, and that the time they spend there suggests they almost "live at work."

Group 3 — Flexible Work Schedules, with Many Meetings: People in this group have their own offices and often spend time alone in them. They are also seriously affected by "meeting-itis" (most have more than two per day), have many face-to-face discussions, and usually leave their office doors open. They do not take many breaks, and rarely eat with colleagues. Telecommuting is habitual, and their schedules are flexible.

Group 4 — Annoyed About Rigid Work: This group applies to people who are largely dissatisfied with their work environment and working conditions. They do not eat with colleagues, but rather with friends or family members. They often work in areas that are shared by a number of people, and can often be seen wearing headphones. They rarely have a desk of their own.

Group 5 — Part-time, Rigid Team Work: This group is comprised of people who are not dissimilar from those in Group 1. They have rigid schedules, often arrive slightly late, and often work part time. They differ from Group 1 in that they take fewer breaks, have lunch with colleagues, have few face-to-face discussions, and often share their desks.

As suggested by the group titles, these working lifestyles are directly linked to individuals' professional positions. People in Group 1 were mostly administrative assistants, in general slightly older than the mean and with little training. Group 2 was mainly comprised of people with a bachelor's or master's degree and who were much younger than the mean. Group 3 had more Ph.D. holders and was older than the mean. Group 4 included people of all ages with a slightly lower educational level than the mean. Group 5 typically included people in management services.

Among the working lifestyles of the study participants we identified, only one—Group 4—distinguished itself by its high level of dissatisfaction. Upon further analysis of this group, we observed that no specific population was overrepresented; the only overrepresentation was people who would like to telecommute but cannot. More importantly, 55% of Group 4 participants would like to manage their office space but, again, cannot (versus 22% for the entire sample). Participants in Group 4 shared offices with other people at the time of the survey, but did not necessarily express a desire to work with fewer people. 11% currently had no door but would like one (versus 3% for the entire sample). We found Group 4 participants to be more demanding in terms of the quality of the interior space (69% versus 58% for the entire sample), and would like the opportunity to redesign their offices. We also noted that they were overrepresented among those who would like to have private storage spaces. Finally, it is interesting to note that, while there was a strong statistical association between professional status and working lifestyle among the other groups, we could not find any such statistical association for Group 4. In fact, while the group had a diverse range of profiles in terms of establishment, training, status, origin, age, gender, etc., the members of Group 4 stood out in their high standards relative to the quality of interior spaces. They also had in common the fact that many suffered due to the inability to appropriate their workspace, with 55% regretting not being able to organize their workspaces as they wished.

3.2.2 Programming recommendations

A set of recommendations based on a synthesis of both approaches was developed for use by the building's designers in subsequent stages of the project. This research process' uniqueness lies in its areas of investigation: while many studies on management and ergonomics that explore the links between workplace and productivity exist, such studies rarely apply to the academic world, where the notion of productivity is more difficult to define.

Unlike ergonomic studies, which tend to focus on notions of productivity, creativity, and general wellness, the *smart living lab*'s context and original goals require the incorporation of extremely varied dimensions (well-being, innovation, energy efficiency, economic impact, influence, etc.) while meeting the expectations of the three institutions. Using a one-dimensional evaluation system (is it good or bad for productivity/creativity?) was, in this case, impossible, which is why we used multidimensional approaches and attempted to identify discrepancies between the various alternatives (which alternative can meet expectations without negatively impacting the others?).

Moreover, as the *smart living lab* is the result of a collaboration between three academic institutions with distinct expectations, work organizations, and workplace cultures, a top-down analysis was needed to establish the common principles of the project's broad guidelines. This characteristic was not found in the various studies considered and added a layer of complexity. The future building is designed to house a specific type of activity: research. It is therefore essential to be attentive to the conditions that are conducive to research work and the complex relationship between the need for mingling with other scientists and the need for solitude and time to reflect. The sociological study thus emphasized the importance of job autonomy as an essential condition for research work. This means giving employees considerable freedom and flexibility in their working environment, for example by facilitating the reorganization of workspaces, offering different working environments, and/or allowing for flexible working schedules.

In order to foster these complex rhythms, we proposed unifying the building around a basic, two-level system of primary and secondary workstations, the idea being that employees will always have a classic seated workstation at their disposal. These so-called "primary" workstations can be assigned or not, depending on whether a desk sharing system has been implemented. In parallel, secondary workstations—which are unassigned—will allow for other working methods, small meeting rooms, standing workstations, etc. The secondary network should help bolster the primary system.

Thus, the building should be understood as a complex system that helps support and create a dialogue between the *smart living lab*'s four key conceptual clusters identified in the top-down approach: Creativity, Emulation, Human Ecology, and Outreach. For each key principle, we listed a series of recommendations born of a combination of the institutions' demands, employees' expectations, and the special requirements of the academic work anticipated in the *smart living lab*.

3.2.3 Four key principles

Creativity: Autonomy is at the heart of the creative process. The result was a series of recommendations, notably concerning the organization of primary workstations, but providing a relevant basis for all of the workspaces. To begin with, workspaces must accommodate solitude for demanding intellectual work, away from noise and crowds. Second, workspaces and the layout of the units should be easily reconfigurable (positioning of the workstation, customizing the space, adaptation to changes in working teams or at the end of experiments, etc.). Third, because of the different types of work (administrative work, personalized supervision of students, etc.), it is important that primary workstation units be reconfigurable into a modular system for one to five people. While the one-person unit (i.e. the individual office) remains an important feature in the structure of the academic system, the five-person limit reflects the need for isolation from noise and interruptions. The primary units are therefore a key challenge for the system — a kind of reinvention of working conditions at intermediate scales that is neither a system of closed offices nor a general open space.

Emulation: Innovation in the sciences lies not only in the creative capacity of individual researchers, but also in the quality of social interactions and opportunities for forging new partnerships. The building must, therefore, provide both the everyday social spaces necessary for quality relationships with colleagues, and opportunities for bringing together the different worlds present in the *smart living lab*. First, the building's structure should respect the unique identities of the three institutions. While there are no plans to mix researchers from the different schools within the primary workspaces, interinstitutional exchanges should be encouraged in secondary spaces. Rather than floors or strict compartmentalization, solutions that pool services and collaborative spaces shall be favoured. Second, exchanges between the three institutions should be encouraged by creating large common areas that are available for use as so-called secondary workstations (collaborative or not) with different working configurations (e.g. standing workstations, sofa spaces, silent boxes, small workrooms, etc.). The common areas must also include rest areas that are accessible to all employees (cafeterias, lounges, discussion areas, etc.). Third, each research unit needs its own meeting place. The survey found that there was a need for small-scale break areas where people can sit around a table with colleagues from the same research unit.

Human ecology: Designed as an exemplary system to illustrate and experiment with built environments of the future, the building must have exceptional environmental qualities, especially as pertains to users' experience and expectations. In this regard, the initial survey provided clear indications of employee preferences and practices for the three institutions.

1) The building must allow for maximum user control as regards managing light, temperature, ventilation, blinds, and opening windows, while incorporating the highest standards of energy efficiency. Solutions may include the automation of management systems, but should never override the user's choice. The building must propose and en-

courage low environmental impact behaviours rather than impose them.
2) The building should, so far as possible, give priority to natural lighting, and primary workstations should always have an outdoor view.
3) An open and inclusive discussion regarding materials, colours, and the presence of plants in the building should be launched by the designers, as these three elements emerged as important for many future users.

Outreach: Finally, the building should serve as a platform for exchange with society at large, both by facilitating the sharing of its innovation beyond the institution and by offering itself as a venue for extramural initiatives. First, although a sensitive issue for academic buildings, the question of opening the building to the public must be addressed. This relationship could, for example, take the form of services in the building that are open to the public (restaurant/cafeteria, exhibition rooms, etc.). In terms of programming, a discussion regarding making the premises available to start-ups could also be opened. Second, the spaces must be adaptable in order to withstand obsolescence. Since the building itself should reflect the research conducted by the institutions within it, the sustainability of the building design directly impacts its reputation. Thus, the attention paid to the building's iconic status and scalability should also apply to workspaces. The latter must be able to easily evolve to meet the institutions' future needs, be highly resilient to programming changes over the building's lifetime and serve as a model in the long term.

3.3 Summary

The socially-driven design study for the *smart living lab* project helped to clarify a number of directions in terms of the design of the future building. The top-down approach established a conceptual and consensual basis for what have been defined as the four main principles of the *smart living lab*, namely cooperation, innovation, well-being and ecology. Based on these four principles, means of implementation as well as reflection on the conditions for realising them were established. Finally, a literature review helped in evaluating certain potential solutions with regard to employee well-being and productivity, and their relevance for the *smart living lab*. In particular, it appeared that greater employee autonomy in terms of schedules and workspace locations/configurations was beneficial in all respects. The literature review also excluded open space as a spatial design solution, highlighted the importance of isolation (visual and sound) for intellectual work, and led us to consider desk sharing as an option to meet the *smart living lab*'s ecological and collaborative goals. Finally, the bottom-up approach shed light on the expectations of the building's potential future occupants, making it possible to clarify the applicability of certain design options. In addition to being a valuable decision-making support tool for the design of the *smart living lab*, this study offers insight on contemporary workspace design, especially as it applies to the academic sector.

Acknowledgements
The author would like to thank all of the researchers involved in the implementation of the "Smart Living Building Research Program," and especially the Building2050 team for its invaluable support.

Partners
Urban Sociology Lab: Vincent Kaufmann, Thierry Maeder, Dominic Villeneuve
Human-IST Institute: Hamed Alavi, Denis Lalanne

References
Alavi, Hamed S., Himanshu Verma, Jakub Mlynar, and Denis Lalanne. 2018. "The Hide and Seek of Workspace: Towards Human-Centric Sustainable Architecture." *ACM Press*: 1–12. https://doi.org/10.1145/3173574.3173649.

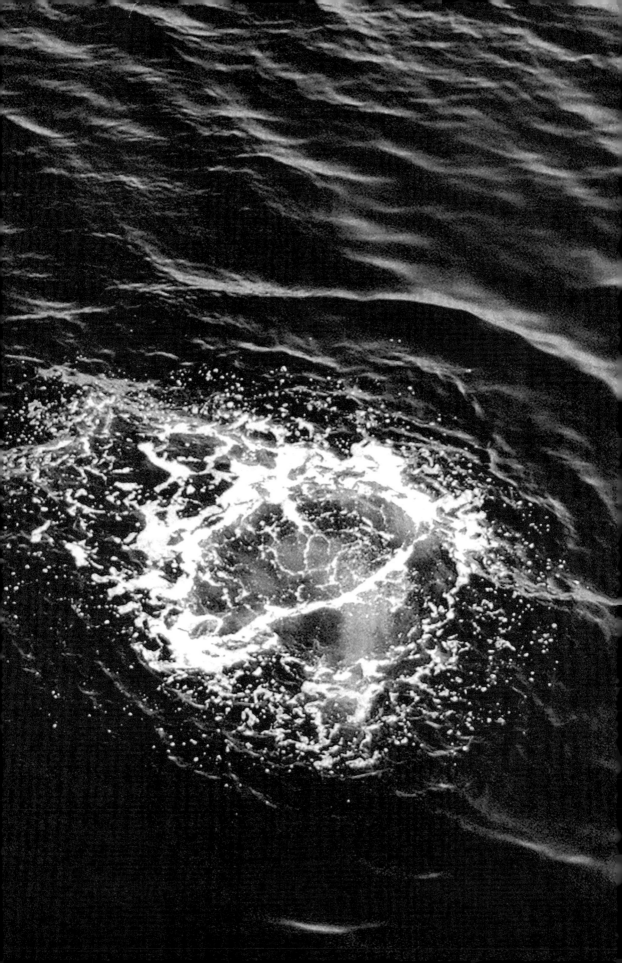

Experimental research

Building upon the now established foundational framework, the next step is to generate new knowledge able to answer open questions and define the boundaries of the possible, given both the ambitions of the project and the conditions in which it will be developed. Geographic location may be as impactful as available technology for instance, which led to the necessity to develop experimental research aiming to address what was identified as the potentially most highly impacting factors in driving the ultimate performance of the future building.

This second part presents the assumptions and outcomes of three different experiments that were conducted to address this need. They range from users' needs regarding space and comfort, to the requirements of the building's envelope and the energy strategy when aiming for a minimal carbon footprint and maximal occupant satisfaction.

④ Intensification of use: an exploratory study

Thomas Jusselme
Endrit Hoxha
Cédric Liardet
Himanshu Verma
Derek Christie
Marc-Antoine Messer
Luca Pattaroni

This chapter investigates the life cycle performance benefits of intensifying use of an office environment, taking into account the impact on user comfort. It highlights the need to revisit how building performance should be measured—not per square meter as a functional unit but in terms of actual occupation through a user-centred approach, notably at the post-occupancy stage.

The Kaya identity adapted to the Swiss building context (Chapter ②) demonstrates that one of the main drivers of GHG emissions is the relationship between built surfaces and the population that uses them ^{Figure 4.1 (purple box)}. According to standard projections, built surfaces in Switzerland are expected to increase by 50 % between 2010 and 2050 (OFEN, n.d.), versus 14 % population growth (Kohli et al. 2010). As the latter is notoriously difficult to manage, the remaining controllable factors are decreasing the built surface per capita or increasing the number of users per built surface, i.e. enhancing the usability of space. This issue is highly relevant for architects and engineers, the hope being that novel design strategies that lead to densification by improving buildings' usability.

In order to intensify use, users themselves must be the focus of the design process. Chapter ③ provides insight aimed at better understanding of user behaviour. However, more emphasis must be put on understanding how this knowledge can inform the design process to minimize buildings' environmental impact by intensifying use of their spaces. How can we increase the usability of these spaces? To what extent can we densify while maintaining an acceptable (and preferably high) level of comfort? Does densification really improve environmental performance, and if so, to what extent?

To answer these questions, we conducted an experiment in the existing (temporary) smart living lab premises in Fribourg, Switzerland, in 2016–2017 in accordance with the principles of a live-in lab (Chapter ①). This chapter describes how we conducted the experiment, the case study and methodology, and the results. The objective was twofold: first, to collect data on design strategies that would help in the construction of the future smart living lab building and, second, to obtain research findings that can be shared with practitioners and the research community.

4.1 Experimental framework
4.1.1 Building usability in the scientific literature

Usability is defined by ISO 9241-11 as the "extent to which a product can be used by specified users to achieve specified goals with effectiveness, efficiency and satisfaction in a specified context of use" (ISO 1998). The concept was developed in the 1970s with the emergence of computer-based technologies and is now widely used in the development of software and web applications. The research community most active on the question of usability is human-computer interactions.

However, since the early 2000s, usability has also become an emerging issue in the building sector. In 2000, Leaman pointed to the challenges of meeting building users' needs and the lack of user-centred design practices and building usability assessment methods (Leaman 2000). More recently, works focusing on the question of building usability (Alexander 2010, Fenker 2008, Hansen et al. 2011) stress that usability should be a process whereby decision-makers learn how users behave in a given situation and use this knowledge to inform the future building design.

However, two major points are seemingly missing from these research works. First, the environmental impact of built space is not considered relative to the satisfaction and efficiency experienced by its users. Second, to the best of our knowledge none of the usability assessments uses quantitative techniques, which can be particularly useful for gaining a deeper understanding of user behaviour, especially when combined with qualitative methods.

It was with the goal of filling this perceived research gap that we decided on a mixed-method design based on quantitative and qualitative approaches to evaluate multiple uses of space in different situations. In each of these situations, we measured space occupancy (quantitatively) and user satisfaction/behaviour (quantitatively and qualitatively), and assessed the overall environmental impacts.

4.1.2 Methodology

We designed the experiment by:
1) Monitoring the comfort, occupancy rates and environmental performance of two typical 65 m² offices belonging to the current (temporary) smart living lab environment.
2) Creating strategies and a new office layout designed to increase occupancy rates and thus densify use.
3) Implementing the new office environment in the two 65 m² rooms.
4) Using these rooms as workplaces for our own research teams and inviting colleagues to use them in order to intensify their use.
5) Monitoring the comfort, occupancy rates and environmental performance of these offices during and after the intensification phase.
6) Analysing the data collected to compare the situations qualitatively and quantitatively prior to and following the intensification phase.

Given the wide range of methods used in this experiment, we set up an interdisciplinary research team in which several research groups were represented. The EPFL's Building2050 group developed the general methodology and environmental impact assessments, and implemented the experiment. The Human-IST Institute of the University of Fribourg (UNIFR) handled the quantitative assessment regarding space occupancy. The EPFL's Urban Sociology Laboratory designed a user comfort qualitative assessment. Finally, Atelier-Oï, an interior design firm, was responsible for the case study design and implementation.

Fig. 4.1 The Kaya identity applied to the Swiss context, which highlights densifying use of the built environment (purple box) as a key factor for mitigating GHG emissions Figure 2.4

GWP related to commercial activities

SRE (energy area) Evolution scenario of energy reference area

Evolution scenarios of Swiss population

Final energy consumption in Switzerland

Fig. 4.2 Experiment timeline

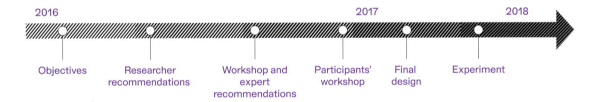

4.1.3 Timeline

In early 2016, the research teams established a comprehensive experiment methodology [Figure 4.2]. In summer 2016, design recommendations based on previous studies were used to develop a proposal for an initial workspace layout. The layout and methodology were discussed with internal and external experts during a workshop in October 2016. Based on their recommendations, a new layout was submitted to the future users of the experimental workspaces in November 2016. In early 2017, the final design was validated after several iterations between researchers, designers and future users. In March 2017, the first phase of the experiment started, with observations of the initial (baseline) workspaces. In May 2017, the second phase began with the new workplace layout and an increased number of users. The experiment ended in late May 2017, after three months of monitoring.

4.2 Case study
4.2.1 Context

This experiment should be understood as an exploratory field intervention, wherein an office environment was used to enrich the results from a real case study. It required the participation of a population that was willing to move before and after the experiment period and be monitored for several months. Due to the intrusive nature of the methodology, we decided to use the office environment of two of the groups involved in the study itself (Building2050 and Human-IST) as the experiment context, in the spirit of the live-in lab (Chapter ①). Working in a lab made it easier to find willing participants for the experiment, as they themselves are the ones who will benefit from the findings. The two main advantages were:

1) It enabled immediate feedback, which is useful for an exploratory study whose findings could inspire more extensive field studies of an independent population, so as to eliminate any bias in the results
2) The results will be extremely useful in designing the future smart living lab building programme, as the designers will have knowledge of some of its current users' working patterns and needs, given that it involves actual users of the future SLB.

The current smart living offices used for the experiment were located in a temporary building known as the "Blue Hall," which is located in Fribourg, Switzerland. The former industrial building belonged to a brewery (Chapter ①) and was converted into offices in 2015 using 126 prefabricated wooden boxes with an atrium covered by a glass roof [Figure 4.3]. New polycarbonate facades allow for natural light inside the building and, at the same time, harmonize

Fig. 4.3 Inside view of the Blue Hall and its atrium with its glass roof

Fig. 4.4 Typical office before experiment

Fig. 4.5 Comparison of 25 % and 100 % desk-sharing with the same number of people in the same spaces

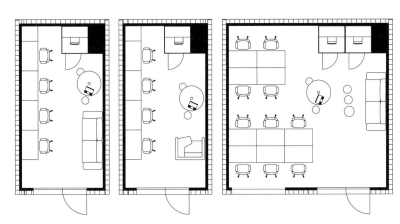

25 % desk-sharing for 23 people

2.5 m² per desk
18 personnal desk = 18 × 2.5 = 45 m²
10 alternative workplaces = 25 m²
Additional space = 7 m²
Necessary area = 84 m² (4 boxes)
Density = 84 m² / 23 = 3.6 m²

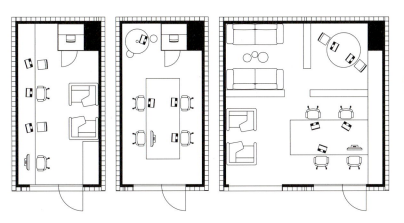

100 % desk-sharing for 23 people

12 normal desk = 12 × 2.5 = 30 m²
10 alternative workplaces = 25 m²
Additional space = 29 m²
Necessary area = 84 m² (4 boxes)
Density = 84 m² / 23 = 3.6 m²

④ Intensification of use: an exploratory study

Fig. 4.6   The layouts of the "Interactive room" (left) and the "Quiet room" (right)

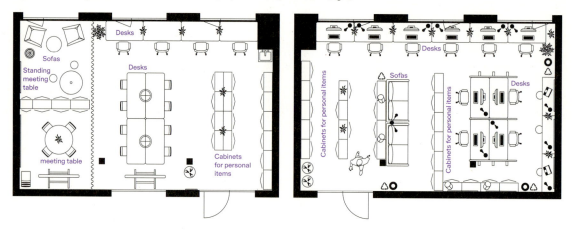

Fig. 4.7   Photos of the "Quiet room"

Fig. 4.8   Photos of the "Interactive room"

the exterior. In early 2017, windows were added to the facades to increase natural light and offer outdoor views.

The main materials used for the structure and envelope of the boxes were wood (for the walls), concrete (for the floors) and wood wool (for the insulation). The openings have triple-glazed windows and doors with wood-aluminium frames. With the exception of the floor slab (with a thermal transmittance of 0.15 $Wm^{-2}K^{-1}$), all other elements in the building envelope have a thermal transmittance of 0.1 $Wm^{-2}K^{-1}$).

Half of the offices in the building are occupied by companies working in innovation and eco-technology. The other half is used by the smart living lab, which includes several research groups, not all of which participated in the experiment. Initially, the study participants all worked at individual desks ^{Figure 4.4}.

4.2.2 A new layout for office densification

In order to analyse the intensity of use, we developed an iterative procedure for the design of workspace layouts based on three different criteria: the location of the workspace, the number of participants and the percentage of desk-sharing.

A workshop with the future experiment participants, aiming to better understand their preferences for privacy, collaboration, large spaces, diversity and separation of tasks/activities, was held in November 2016.

A comparison of layout solutions ^{Figure 4.5} showed that a small percentage of desk-sharing (25%) did not allow us to greatly intensify use, as it would compromise user comfort due to the small size of the desks. It would also conflict with the current ergonomic norms of the Swiss labour code[4] (*Commentaire des ordonnances 3 et 4 relatives à la loi sur le travail*, n.d.).

In order to maximize the intensification effect, we decided to create more workstations than the number required by Swiss norms and to test a 100% desk-sharing strategy.

The final design solution ^{Fig. 4.6–8} was inspired by Myerson's concept (Myerson and Bichard 2016) of spaces for concentration and spaces for collaboration. Hence, we proposed an activity-based working layout with what we called a "Quiet room" and an "Interactive room."

The Quiet room was 65 m² and targeted the following tasks:
- **Concentration:** a quiet environment without noisy activities or sources of distraction that is separate from other spaces.
- **Contemplation:** an area for breaks with natural elements that foster creative thinking.

[4] In naturally ventilated rooms, a minimum air volume of 12 m³ per person per room is required. When artificial ventilation alone is used, an air volume of at least 10 m³ per person must be available. Depending on the amount of equipment, a workstation must have an uninterrupted floor space of at least 6 to 10 m². In open-plan offices, an average of 10 to 25 m² of non-adjacent, cumulated floor space per workstation is necessary.

The Interactive room (also 65 m²) was designed for:
- **Collaboration:** an environment with spaces for sharing documents and the appropriate technological equipment to support remote collaboration, comprised of movable, flexible elements.
- **Communication:** availability of technologies allowing users to combine physical and virtual means of communication.

We implemented the changes by transforming both of the 65 m² offices already used by members of the living lab (one by the Building2050 group, the other by the Human-IST group) into the Quiet and Interactive rooms. The living lab members in these two groups participated in the experiment and were asked to give informed consent. In the first stage, the occupants of the two original offices were simply relocated to the newly-transformed "Quiet" and "Interactive" rooms (their working conditions had changed, but no significant densification took place). In the second stage, members of the smart living lab who worked in other offices were also invited to work in the Quiet and Interactive rooms in view of intensifying use.

4.3 Experiment protocol
4.3.1 Technical procedure for monitoring actual presence

Our monitoring of occupants' presence in different areas with varied functions followed the principles of pervasive sensing, as described in the literature (Ilic et al. 2009). This type of method depends on observing individuals and how they behave and interact. Ambient and/or wearable devices are typically used to collect data. For our experiment, the study of occupancy behaviour and the computation of occupancy rates was adapted from our own work (Verma et al. 2017). We used Bluetooth bracelets to model the space-use behaviour of occupants in an office building. We find a similar approach for studying individuals' activities in Atallah and Yang (Atallah and Yang 2009), where Bluetooth wristbands and ambient blob sensors were used to model the activities of patients in a hospital and predict abnormal behaviour. Unlike research based on self-completion questionnaires (Kelley 2003), the use of Bluetooth bracelets allows for scalability in terms of the study duration and sample size (Verma et al. 2017).

Thirty-three participants (ten women and twenty-three men) were provided with bracelets equipped with Bluetooth Beacons[5] programmed to broadcast a Bluetooth packet every second. We installed Bluetooth data loggers[6] in twelve different rooms in a section of the Blue Hall building. A data logger corresponding to the room the participant was in at any given moment received the packets transmitted by the bracelet. In this way, we were able to

[5] EMBC01 from EM Microelectronic, Switzerland

[6] Raspberry Pi 2 Model B

Fig. 4.9 Bluetooth Bracelet and Data-Logger

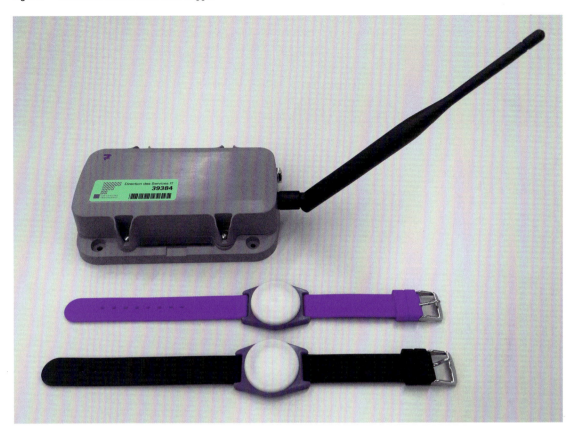

estimate the participant's position in the building. Besides the Interactive and Quiet rooms, five meeting rooms, a cafeteria, the atrium and three open-plan offices were monitored during the course of the study. Bracelets were distributed to participants and data-loggers used to collect data ^{Figure 4.9}. The participants were asked to wear the bracelets during their normal working day and to bring the bracelets home after work (though no tracking occurred outside the Blue Hall area). Signs reminding participants to wear their bracelets were placed near the entrances of various rooms within the Blue Hall.

Each bracelet transmitted a packet with a unique identifier, which enabled us to identify study participants and record their space-use behaviour during a normal working day (7 am – 6 pm). Upon receiving a Bluetooth packet, the data loggers recorded the timestamp corresponding to each packet and the received signal strength (RSSI). This information later allowed us to filter out false positives and correct the data collected. We recorded the participants' occupancy information for ten weeks.

4.3.2 Qualifying user satisfaction

We used sociological methods to understand how people experienced and evaluated the changes that occurred in the office environment during the experiment. The combined use of interviews and observation allowed us to investigate user experience in terms of well-being, social relations and workspace ergonomics. We paid particular attention to the creative nature of the work done by many of the study participants. The literature on cognitive psychology effectively suggests that creative activities are associated with forms of information management, including cluttered desks (Vohs et al. 2013) and/or the piling up of documents (Abrahamson 2002).

A total of twenty-five short, standardised, questionnaire-based interviews were conducted during the course of the experiment. The questions addressed not only people's direct experience in the workrooms, but also their relationship to the broader spatial and institutional context. As the literature on environmental psychology suggests, perceptions and meanings relative to a specific place should be analysed within a larger system of settings (Rapoport, 1964). Our hypothesis was that the perceived quality of the workspace is linked to broader dimensions, such as the availability of other work places, commuting distances, the reasons for and degree of freedom in working on or off premises, the type of contract (full-time, part-time or temporary), etc.

The interviews were complemented with photographs and a detailed observation of the premises. Particular attention was paid to desks and other work surfaces, as well as to the presence (or absence) of objects such as bags, documents or personal computers. We observed the extent to which users attempted to create a personal space (by leaving objects on desks or elsewhere, removing things from the shelves, etc.), as well as any elements related to the choice of workstation (hesitation, place changes during the day, etc.).

Social interactions were also observed, including occasional interactions with others and formal/informal discussions or meetings. We also made note of noise levels and possible adaptations to noise (use of headphones, etc.).

Three dimensions allowing for the deconstruction of the broad "user satisfaction" concept were analysed in section 4.5 using this data:
1) The impact of differentiated working premises on social relations and working attitudes
2) Users' qualitative perception of these changes
3) The spatial appropriation of workstations

4.3.3 Measuring environmental impacts

We defined the scope of the environmental impact assessment so as to encompass the embodied impact of the building itself. When evaluating the contribution of the space's many dimensions relative to the overall environmental impact, special attention was paid to indoor furniture (tables, chairs, etc.) and hardware (computers, screens, etc.). Indeed, building-scale life cycle assessments almost never consider furniture within their boundaries. In our case, as the latter will have a key role in intensifying the use of the spaces, we decided to consider it within the boundaries of our environmental impact assessment.

Thus, the life cycle assessment (LCA) method was used to evaluate building impacts, including all life cycle phases. In LCA, defining the functional unit is crucial. Several units are established in European norm EN-15978 (2012) but are limited by their inability to consider how buildings are actually used. Indeed, a building may have very low impacts per m^2, but very high impacts per actual user due to a low occupancy rate.

For this reason, it was necessary to create a novel functional unit that takes into account the efficient use of building space. To that end, the impact assessment of this experiment before and after densification will be expressed hereafter according to the following functional units, introduced within the frame of this study:

Per SIA employee per year: This is determined by the Swiss SIA 2024 norm (SIA 2024 2015), which gives a ratio of average employee per square meter.

Per employee per year: In this case, the actual number of employees working within the assessment boundaries is used.

Per fulltime equivalent employee per year: Here, the actual number of employees working within the assessment boundaries is corrected by their administrative presence (according to their employment contract).

Per fulltime equivalent employee per actual presence per year: In this case, the actual number of employees working within the assessment boundaries is corrected by their actual presence, which was monitored using the Bluetooth Bracelet described previously.

The embodied impact evaluation was based on the KBOB database for office buildings. The database presented by Hoxha and Jusselme (Hoxha and Jusselme 2017) was used for existing furniture while the Ecoinvent database was used (Kellenberger et al. 2007) for new furniture. The energy consumption for lighting and equipment was monitored using specific sensors. Heating, hot water and cooling were not monitored due to technical considerations. The latter would most likely not have affected the robustness of the results, as hot water consumption is notoriously low in office buildings and therefore not within the physical boundaries of this experiment. Also, the experiment was conducted in the spring, when heating and cooling loads in office buildings were nul or very low. The environmental performance was calculated according to the "2000-Watt Society" vision (Jochem et al. 2004). Thus, the indicators for primary energy, non-renewable energy and global warming were evaluated. The primary (renewable and non-renewable) indicators were calculated according to the impact assessment method described in Bösch et al. (Bösch et al. 2007). Global warming potential was calculated according to the impact assessment method described by IPCC (2007).

4.4 User occupancy results

This section aims to present and comment on the results obtained by monitoring office users with Bluetooth bracelets to analyse the intensification of use.

4.4.1 Occupancy Rates

To compute the occupancy rate for each room in the user study, we proceeded as follows:
A) we divided the work day into 1-minute time intervals
B) for each time window, we estimated the total number of occupants who, individually, spent more than half of the duration of the window in the room
C) assigned this number to the room's occupancy rate.

As the computations for occupancy rates were aggregated for small time intervals (one minute for each time window), we were able to capture the dynamics of participants' space-use behaviour during the study.

Using this method, we can see the densification effect of the two rooms used for the experiment ^{Figure 4.10}. The Building2050 room, which became the Interactive room, saw its density double

Fig. 4.10 Variation in actual occupancy rates during the course of the experiment. The rise in densification was a continuous process that occurred over several weeks

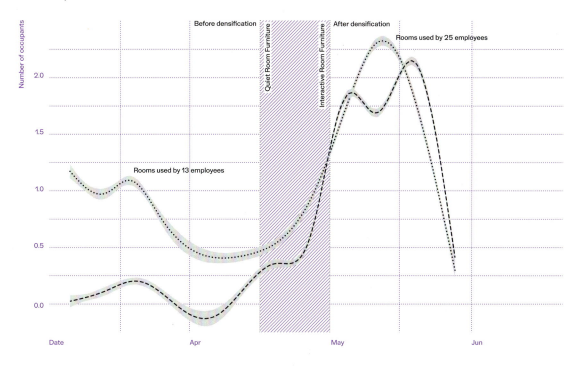

Fig. 4.11 Typical occupancy rates for the Interactive (Building2050) and Quiet (Human-IST) rooms

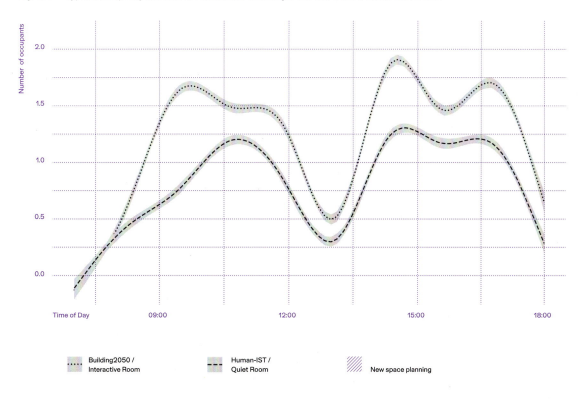

Fig. 4.12   Smoothed line graphs show how the densification of the Building2050 and H-IST rooms affected other office spaces during the experiment

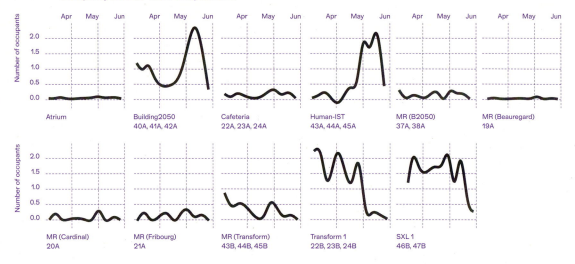

Fig. 4.13   Number of employees in pre-/post-densification and according to SIA 2024 (2015) (Hoxha et al., 2018)

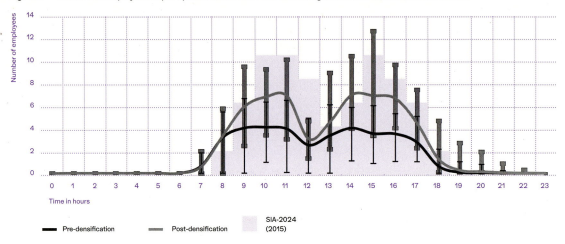

Tab. 4.14   Comparison of occupancy rates according to the SIA norm, nominal employees, fulltime-equivalent employees and actual fulltime-equivalent employees

Occupancy	Pre-densification	Post-densification	Densification rate
SIA occupancy	9.0	9.0	0 %
Employees	13.0	25.0	+92 %
Full-Time-Equivalent Employees	10.1	17.5	+73 %
Effective Full-Time-Equivalent Employees	3.8	6.2	+63 %

from one to two occupants on average during the course of the experiment. The density in the Human-IST room (which became the Quiet room) increased from almost nil to one close to that of the Interactive room. Although density increased, a gap between the actual average occupancy rate and the theoretical number of employees using the rooms was observed.

We gain deeper insight into the data from the next graph Figure 4.11, which plots the variation in occupancy rates for the Interactive and Quiet rooms for a typical workday following the implementation of the new layout. The two peaks (in the morning and in the afternoon) were separated by a sharp drop around noon, when most participants went for lunch outside of the building or at the cafeteria. The Interactive room had a higher occupancy rate, with +0.5 occupants on average versus the Quiet room.

Finally, all other rooms that could potentially be used by the study participants were monitored for any change in their use linked to the experiment.

The increase in occupancy rates in the Interactive (Label: Building2050) and Quiet (Label: Human-IST) rooms corresponds to the densification phase, during which several other research groups were asked to share these two rooms for their daily work Figure 4.12. This was shown by the decrease in occupancy rates in other offices, like Transform and SXL.

4.4.2 Comparison between norms and reality

We compared the actual occupancy rates pre-/post-densification and those of Swiss norm SIA 2024 (2015), which are usually considered reasonable for any energy assessment during a building design phase Figure 4.13. According to SIA 2024, the number of employees in an office is evaluated based on the assumption that each employee requires a net floor area of $14\,m^2$. In this experiment, with $130\,m^2$ of net floor area, the two offices should have been able to accommodate nine employees. In reality, the space housed thirteen employees prior to densification and twenty-five post-densification.

As a significant portion of employees worked part-time, they were represented using their associated work percentage (e.g. 60% for an employee who worked three days a week). The total number of equivalent fulltime employees at the pre-densification stage was 10.1, versus 17.5 post densification. Another factor to take into account was the actual employee presence in the office. In fact, employees often spent less than the 8.2 hours per day that is the typical working day in Switzerland in the office for different reasons (meetings, holidays, sick leave, duty travel, lunch and coffee breaks, etc.). Thus, when we divide the total number of hours of actual presence by a full working day, we obtain what we call "Actual Fulltime-Equivalent Employees," with an average occupancy of only 3.8 for the two rooms in the pre-densification phase. During post-densification, this value rose to 6.2 (the occupancy rates are summarized in Table 4.14). According to the figures, we observed 0 % densification if we consider the surface of the offices as the reference unit, 92 % if we consider nominal employees, 73 % using full-time-equivalent employees and 63 % for actual fulltime-equivalent employees.

To conclude, it is clear that the SIA 2024 norm based on the occupancy ratio per area cannot document a densification strategy. Looking at actual employee occupancy, major differences can be found between relative and absolute rates, as well as between official working hours and actual presence. In our case, the difference was particularly notable, as the offices are used for academic research purposes. These spaces do, in fact, have a low occupancy rate due to "nomad" employees, many of who have part-time contracts or work in several different buildings or even cities.

4.5 Assessing subjective comfort and attitudes towards change

This section aims to describe how office users reacted to the creation of the Quiet and Interactive rooms, and the subsequent densification. As mentioned in section 4.3 of this chapter, direct observation and questionnaire-based interviews were the methods used both at the baseline and over the course of the experiment. The questionnaire included items about the Quiet and Interactive rooms as well as questions about the broader context, such as the entire building (Blue Hall) and participants' home-work organization so as to identify possible interactions between the broader context and what took place in the converted offices.

4.5.1 The role of the broader context

The Blue Hall was perceived rather negatively due to its lack of natural light and unadjustable air conditioning. The common areas were described as cold, unattractive and poorly-insulated acoustically. However, the building had undergone improvements in the months prior the beginning of the experiment, with the installation of windows in the facade. For many participants, the latter—albeit unrelated to our experiment—was more momentous than any part of the experiment itself.

During the baseline period, i.e. prior to the creation of the Quiet and Interactive rooms, the workrooms were relatively basic, with workstations (usually assigned) accommodating six to nine people. As three institutions and an even greater number of laboratories used the various workrooms in Blue Hall, their occupancy rate and functions varied greatly. In general, those that served as a secondary site for institutions whose main offices were elsewhere were seldom used, while those that served as main offices were occupied more often. As it turned out, many participants had workplaces in other buildings, and sometimes even other towns or cities. For various reasons, these alternative workplaces were sometimes preferred (distance from home, proximity to colleagues, convenience of the facilities, etc.).

These observations suggest that changes in office spaces should always be considered relative to the entire building and the broader system of possible workplaces of each participant.

4.5.2 The impact of differentiated working premises

The interviews and observations show that the differentiation strategy—creating Quiet and Interactive, i.e. non-standard, rooms—worked well on a functional and social level, as users adopted differentiated behaviours and strategies according to the setting. As stated in the literature, a space's quality depends on the clarity of its "script" (Rapoport, 1964), meaning the ease with which the behaviour expected in that setting can be recognized. In this respect, the two rooms clearly correlated with different working and social behaviours. The atmosphere in the Interactive room was far noisier than that in the Quiet room. When asked which adjectives they would use to describe each room, "calm," "quiet," "isolated" and "enabling concentration" were used to describe the Quiet room, whereas the Interactive room was described as "lively," "motivating," "friendly" and "dynamic."

In the Interactive room, it was not uncommon to observe people speaking loudly to one another across the space, with questions such as "Would anyone like coffee?". We also observed several people speaking together while standing in a group, or one person standing speaking to someone sitting at a desk several metres away. We also observed meetings between four to five team members.

Nevertheless, one person in the Interactive room told us that it was sometimes necessary to go into the corridor or into a formal meeting room to hold discussions with other team members. Another participant mentioned that the two corners of the Interactive room (the areas with small round tables, to the left upon entering the room ^{Figure 4.8}) were too small and close together, and not sufficiently insulated acoustically for parallel meetings to take place. During one of our observation phases, one corner of the room was used for at least thirty minutes by a single person, who isolated herself by closing the curtain and could be seen using the drawing board in a concentrated, focused way. However, other participants told us that, in their opinion, the curtain was not sufficient for creating a sense of privacy. Overall, noise was an important issue in the Interactive room, as evidenced by the fact that some study participants informally referred to it as the "Noisy room."

This suggests that two key aspects must be considered in designing an interactive room that can sustain interactive lifestyles:

- The general acoustic quality of the room
- The ability to section off portions of the room to enable multiple parallel interactions

As seen in the photographs below, optimal use was made of the different types of furniture in the Interactive room, except for the workstations facing the window. This suggests that the interactive room functioned as an attractor, motivating the presence of people who had the choice to work alone elsewhere and in better conditions. As academic work requires both long periods of concentration and short meetings, it is important to reflect further on the location of such differentiated spaces, as their juxtaposition within the same building may not be the best solution.

The situation was quite different in the Quiet room. Upon entering in the morning, one immediately noticed that the room was not only quieter but also less used.

The need for a more complex spatial system: One key observation was the behaviour of Quiet room users when they received or made phone calls. In both cases, they immediately left the room, but rather than heading for the Interactive Room, they remained in the Atrium (lobby) for the duration of the call. Evidently, people do not go into the Interactive room just for a phone call. This was confirmed by interviews with several study participants.

On a broader level, this would suggest that the spatial system should include at least three or four different types of spaces.

Hierarchy of workspaces: In the Quiet room, the four main workstations (in square formation) were almost always occupied by jackets, books, computers, bags, etc. in the afternoon. However, only two or three people were usually present and working in silence. There was a clear gradient or hierarchy between the more desirable workstations—where personal belongings were left—and the less desirable ones, which were unoccupied most of the day. The observed hierarchy corresponded very closely to the self-declared hierarchy described in the next section ^{Figure 4.15}.

Learning process: Internal mobility between the Interactive and Quiet rooms was rather limited initially. During the first week of observation, we found almost no examples of people who moved from one to the other during the course of the day. However, another round of observations carried out towards the end of the experiment revealed more instances of people moving between the rooms. This suggests that adopting new routines and behaviours following changes in office spaces takes time (at least two to three weeks, based on our observations).

When commenting on the experience of the converted rooms, participants often reiterated their general concern about the poor quality of the building. For example, several people complained about the lack of natural sunlight. We take this as evidence that, in the context of this research project, the general quality of the building was considered more important than the quality of the offices. When asked about their experience of the working spaces, people often focused on external conditions such as temperature and light. There was recurring criticism of temperature regulation issues within the building. Additionally, many participants considered the office spaces too dark.

This implies that the whole experience must be evaluated with care, especially when drawing general conclusions about the actual experience of densification.

4.5.3 Perceptions of office/desk quality

The creation of the Quiet and Interactive Rooms complexified the environmental context, i.e. the layout of the desks changed in terms of their orientation, proximity to other desks, windows and doors and natural vs. artificial light. This plays an important role in terms of densification. Indeed, in the case of a clear hierarchy of good and bad places, an increase in the number of users leads to a "struggle for places" (Lussault 2009). As we will now show, this did not occur during this experiment, though a clear hierarchy of places that was agreed upon by almost all the users indeed existed (i.e. the users largely agreed about the desirability of the various workspaces). This is due to the fact that, although densification was observed, it was relatively low. Hence, the daily increase of use never surpassed the amount of available "good" seats.

A clear hierarchy of workplaces: The diagrams Figure 4.15 represent what users described as their favourite (white pellets) and least favourite places (purple pellets). In the Quiet room, the four central workstation positions received overwhelmingly positive ratings, whereas the window and lateral sections of both rooms mostly received negative ratings. This does not imply that these positions served no purpose or that they should be removed; rather, they may fulfil a function other than human occupation. Although this was not investigated and would therefore require further study, it is possible that simply seeing relatively unappealing empty seats lent to the feeling expressed by many participants that a) the offices were not overcrowded and b) that they (the participants) had managed to secure decent seats. More specifically, having one's back to the door or having to reveal one's screen to other users or passers-by were cited as key negative attributes in both rooms.

Densification without conflicts: The absence of conflict with regard to the choice or distribution of places could be due to the overall satisfaction with the design of the two rooms. However, it may also be linked to the relatively low density and limited duration of the experiment.

On a more general level, our findings suggest that densification strategies should take into account the quality of a maximum spatial occupancy relative to the possibility of creating equally-

Fig. 4.15   "Good" and "bad" places in the Interactive (left) and Quiet (right) rooms

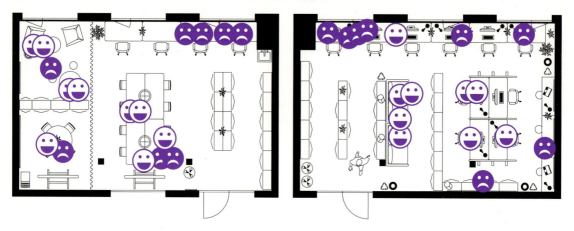

Fig. 4.16   Dynamic occupation of the Interactive room (left), except for the window area (right)

Fig. 4.17   Popular (left) and less popular (right) workstations in the Quiet room

valued workplaces. Nevertheless, they also suggest that adding extra, unoccupied workspaces—to give users the impression that they still have a choice of free seats—might be an effective strategy for increasing experienced user comfort.

4.5.4 Spatial appropriation of workspaces

In this research, the appropriation or personalisation of workspaces refers to the deliberate leaving of materials and/or personal items on or next to tables and chairs at lunchtime and, in some cases, overnight. The photos ^{Figure 4.16} show how various workspaces were appropriated (right) or not (left) during the experimentation phase.

Detailed observation showed that personalized spaces were used differently from non-personalized ones. The former were "busier" and seemed to be taken over by habitual users who used the space in a similar way each day, allowing them to "settle in."

Even over a limited period we observed very clear appropriation strategies clearly linked to the attractiveness of certain workspaces in the Quiet room ^{Figure 4.17}. Such observations confirm the idea that appropriation strategies are an important part of the conducting and quality of scientific work. Creative work requires an appropriation of space. Hence, the idea of making appropriation possible should be carefully discussed in densification strategies for academic offices, especially when they entail "clean desk" approaches. If more time is spent concentrating than interacting, it is important to create more "Quiet" rooms than "Interactive" ones at the scale of the entire building.

4.6 User-centred environmental assessment

A life cycle assessment of the two offices before (pre-) and after (post-) densification was done following the methodology described in section 4.3.3 ^{Table 4.18} shows the results obtained per unit of energy reference area and per year for the primary energy (CED), non-renewable energy (CED_{nr}) and global warming potential (GWP) indicators for both situations.

To begin, comparing the pre- and post-densification results, we observed that life cycle performances were almost the same for both situations, with a maximum variation of 5% for the GWP indicator when the results were expressed per square meter. There was a slight increase in the embodied impact of appliances and furniture, which was compensated for by a decrease in the impact of energy consumed by equipment and lighting. This is understandable, given that densification required the implementation of a new layout with more furniture and office equipment, while the separation of spaces into the Interactive and Quiet rooms helped reduce the impacts of lighting and equipment. Effectively, employees did not always use the computer monitors (screens) available in the Quiet room, which helped to minimize energy impacts. Moreover, participants preferred to use individual table lights rather than general overhead lighting in this room.

Another major finding was the relative environmental impact of the equipment and furniture. We chose to include all the building components physically present within the boundaries of the experiment, which is not often the case for building LCA. Ultimately, equipment and furniture represented 35 % of the GWP, with 32 % for embodied impacts only, which points to the importance of considering them within the scope of building LCA. What is more, they should be chosen specifically based on their embodied impacts.

Looking at the results ^{Table 4.18}, it is clear that the LCA results expressed per "energy reference area per year" do not highlight any benefits of densification. In fact, on the contrary, impacts even increased slightly. For this reason, the impacts of the offices pre- and post-densification are presented using the other functional units described in section 4.3.3, as well as the results of the Bluetooth bracelet monitoring campaign ^{Figure 4.19}. According to SIA 2024, for the number of employees, the conclusions were almost identical before and after densification, as this unit is correlated to the built surface, with 14 m^2 for each employee. The results show that the effect of densification on the building's impacts can only be measured using the other units. From the data ^{Figure 4.19}, we observe that densifying working spaces minimizes impacts for all the functional units that measure the per employee impact (difference between full and dashed lines) by approximately 40 %.

However, there are clear differences when comparing the results in absolute values. We can easily deduce that, when it comes to an accurate functional unit such as the fulltime equivalent employees per actual presence (representing the lowest employee presence), the impact per person is three times higher than when expressed by the other units ^{Figure 4.19}. Thus, the absolute benefits are much higher when we compare pre- and post-densification.

4.7 Limitations

There are several limitations associated with this experiment. Some are investigated here, though not exhaustively. First, with regard to appropriation and spatial conflicts—which emerge in time—the duration of the experiment was quite short.

Research activities tend to be cumulative. Hence, it would take questions regarding the storage of documents months to emerge.

Several participants found the experiment's target themes to be secondary to other, more important aspects regarding comfort at work, including having an outdoor view. The windows installed in early 2017 did improve the light quality. Nevertheless,

Tab. 4.18   Environmental impacts of offices pre- and post-densification (Hoxha et al., 2018)

Components	CED Cumulative energy demand (MWh/m² ERA yr)		CED$_{nr}$ Nonrenewable energy (MWh/m² ERA yr)		GWP Global Warming Potential (kg CO$_{2-eq}$/m² ERA yr)	
	Pre-densification	Post-densification	Pre-densification	Post-densification	Pre-densification	Post-densification
Lighting energy consumption	40	38	33	32	1.4	1.3
Appliances' energy consumption	24	23	20	19	0.8	0.8
Appliances & furniture	28	33	25	30	6.4	7.7
Equipment & installation	27	27	21	21	4.6	4.6
Building components	73	73	37	37	9.7	9.7
Total	192	193	137	139	22.9	24.1

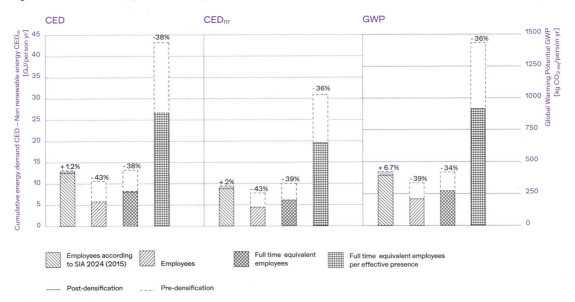

Fig. 4.19   Environmental impacts of building pre- and post-densification (Hoxha et al., 2018)

many respondents still regretted not having a direct view outdoors. The indoor temperature (which was considered poorly regulated) and ventilation (often deemed insufficient) were the second and third most common points mentioned. As such, the study participants already perceived the space as confined and somewhat oppressive, independent of the experiment. The fact that aspects unrelated to the experiment were predominant in people's minds—more so than the experiment itself—can be viewed as a major limitation. On the other hand, this means that participants were relatively unfazed by the experiment and thus able to analyse and express their feelings about it freely.

Also, the fact that almost all the study participants were scientists must be acknowledged: it is well known that such sub-populations are more open to innovation and experimentation than other social groups. Some of the positive appreciations relative to the experiment may therefore be attributable to this openness. Notably, several of the researchers involved in the project were part of the experiment itself or belonged to the same labs. The proximity between the researchers carrying out the study and the participants may well have produced a social desirability bias (a belief that we wish to be true) or a confirmation bias (a belief we already hold). Effectively, regarding the qualitative comfort assessment, participants may have reacted to the purpose of the experiment itself and not only to the changes in the space. However, the quantitative assessment of the effects of densification and its environmental impact might not have been significantly affected by this bias, as they were monitored by sensors rather than described by participants.

Finally, the scope of the experiment was limited to the two office boxes. The induced impacts of these two boxes at the building level (or beyond) were not investigated. In fact, the tracking campaign showed that the increase in density in the two rooms was compensated for by a decrease in density in the other offices. Thus, in our case, the environmental benefits were valid only at the office level, not at the building level. This demonstrates that the densification strategy must be applied to smaller built environments in order to have positive environmental impacts. Otherwise, the latter will simply shift from one place to another.

The majority of these limitations highlight the need to switch from an exploratory approach to an extensive survey that targets a wider, independent population in order to turn these promising first results into robust conclusions.

4.8   Towards more usability in building sustainability

According to the Kaya identity, occupation density is one of the key drivers for lowering energy use and carbon emissions. The purpose of this pilot study was to verify this hypothesis by measuring the energy consumption, carbon emissions and comfort levels of two offices before and after intensification of use. We found that a low-energy building may be highly performant per square meter, and yet be highly inefficient per user if it is almost empty. The intensification was the result of a new office layout that incorporated a desk-sharing strategy and separated the two offices functionally for different activities. One, the Quiet room, was used for tasks requiring concentration. The other, the Interactive room, was used for tasks requiring interaction.

The study participants largely appreciated the differences between the two rooms. At the conclusion of the investigation, it was clear that the possibility of moving from one room to another improved self-assessed comfort at work and, therefore, potentially increased productivity. However, given the limited duration of the experiment, it is difficult to assess whether there are specificities linked to academic work that might become obstacles to the longtime viability of such a desk-sharing model. Some of the participants, especially those working in architecture, said that they had left more sizeable/bulky work items at another office. This leads to a new hypothesis that study participants developed strategies to cope with the densification. We suggest investigating this hypothesis as part of the emerging research agenda in this field. Regardless, it would seem that the densification of the space did not affect experiment participants negatively, quite probably because the density ratio was still reasonable after densification: from 34 m² per actual fulltime employee (FTE) to 20 m² per actual FTE.

The environmental assessment for both situations was done using a life cycle analysis based on different functional units, from the built surface to the actual FTE. To that end, we used the principles of pervasive sensing to monitor the presence of occupants in these rooms. Our sensing approach required that the participants wear a Bluetooth bracelet during the normal workday. By monitoring the reception of the Bluetooth packets transmitted by the bracelets, we were able to accurately compute occupancy rates for very short time intervals. These occupancy rates were used to express the life cycle analysis results in different functional units. When compared to the built surface, the building impacts increased slightly. When compared to the actual number of employees, we observed a potential decrease in the environmental impact of 40%. Densification thus appeared to be very efficient, with the potential to significantly reduce the life cycle impact per employee without decreasing the overall comfort experienced by occupants (in the context of this experimentation).

We demonstrated that the current functional unit (energy reference area per year) was not appropriate for evaluating the actual densification benefits, which in turn revealed a major strategy for improving building performance. To obtain a proper evaluation, the functional unit "fulltime equivalent of actual presence" was introduced. We suggest this unit be used in future LCA studies involving buildings, at least for post-occupancy assessments. Thus, in addition to the mechanism that attributes building impacts to an actual population, this pilot study developed a methodology for implementing a user-centred approach for assessing the environmental impact of buildings that could be further developed and used by researchers and practitioners. These future developments should focus on the induced impacts on user comfort. Based on this pilot study, an extensive survey with a broader population and over a longer period would be of great interest.

Acknowledgements
We would like to thank all of our colleagues from the *smart living lab* who contributed to this experiment for their participation and valuable comments and suggestions.

Partners
Atelier Oï: Raphaël Dutoit, Patrick Reymond
Building2050 / EPFL: Thomas Jusselme, Endrit Hoxha, Cédric Liardet
Human-IST / Fribourg University: Himanshu Verma, Hamed Alavi, Denis Lalanne
LASUR / EPFL: Derek Christie, Dominic Villeneuve, Thierry Maeder, Luca Pattaroni, Emmanuel Ravalet, Sébastien Munafò, Virginie Baranger, Marc-Antoine Messer, Vincent Kaufmann

Related publications
Alavi, Hamed S., Himanshu Verma, Jakub Mlynar, and Denis Lalanne. 2018. "The Hide and Seek of Workspace: Towards Human-Centric Sustainable Architecture." *ACM Press*: 1–12. https://doi.org/10.1145/3173574.3173649.
Hoxha, Endrit, and Thomas Jusselme. 2017. "On the Necessity of Improving the Environmental Impacts of Furniture and Appliances in Net-zero Energy Buildings." *Science of the Total Environment*: 596–597, 405–416. https://doi.org/ 10.1016/j.scitotenv.2017.03.107
Hoxha, Endrit, and Thomas Jusselme. 2018. "Measuring the Effect of Office Densification on the Energy and Carbon Lifecycle Performance." (To be submitted)
Alavi, Hamed S., Himanshu Verma, and Denis Lalanne. 2017. "Studying Space Use: Bringing HCI Tools to Architectural Projects". *ACM Press*: 3856–3866. https://doi.org/10.1145/3025453.3026055

References
Abrahamson, Eric. 2002. "Disorganization Theory and Disorganizational Behavior: Towards an Etiology of Messes." *Research in Organizational Behavior* 24 (January): 139–80. https://doi.org/10.1016/S0191-3085(02)24005-8.
Alexander, Keith. 2008. "Usability of Workplaces – Phase 2." CIB. https://doi.org/10.13140/2.1.3993.9202.
Atallah, Louis, and Guang-Zhong Yang. 2009. "The Use of Pervasive Sensing for Behaviour Profiling – a Survey." *Pervasive and Mobile Computing* 5 (5): 447–64. https://doi.org/10.1016/j.pmcj.2009.06.009.
Bösch, Michael E., Stefanie Hellweg, Mark A. J. Huijbregts, and Rolf Frischknecht. 2007. "Applying Cumulative Exergy Demand (CExD) Indicators to the Ecoinvent Database." *The International Journal of Life Cycle Assessment* 12 (3): 181–90. https://doi.org/10.1065/lca2006.11.282.
"Commentaire des ordonnances 3 et 4 relatives à la loi sur le travail." n.d. Accessed March 27, 2018. https://www.seco.admin.ch/seco/fr/home/Publikationen_Dienstleistungen/Publikationen_und_Formulare/Arbeit/Arbeitsbedingungen/Wegleitungen_zum_Arbeitsgesetz/wegleitung-zu-den-verordnungen-3-und-4-zum-arbeitsgesetz.html.
Fenker, Michael. 2008. "Towards a Theoretical Framework for Usability of Buildings." Vol. CIB report 316. CIB. https://halshs.archives-ouvertes.fr/halshs-01290227/document.

Hansen, Geir K., Siri H. Blakstad, and Wibeke Knudsen. 2011. "USEtool. Evaluating Usability. Methods Handbook." *Ntnu*.

Hoxha, Endrit, and Thomas Jusselme. 2017. "On the Necessity of Improving the Environmental Impacts of Furniture and Appliances in Net-Zero Energy Buildings." *Science of The Total Environment* 596–597 (October): 405–16. https://doi.org/10.1016/j.scitotenv.2017.03.107.

Hoxha, Endrit, Cédric Liardet, and Thomas Jusselme. 2018. "Measuring the Effect of Office Densification on the Energy and Carbon Lifecycle Performance".

Ilic, Alexander, Thorsten Staake, and Elgar Fleisch. 2009. "Using Sensor Information to Reduce the Carbon Footprint of Perishable Goods." IEEE Pervasive Computing 8 (1): 22–29. https://doi.org/10.1109/MPRV.2009.20.

IPCC. n.d. "IPCC – Intergovernmental Panel on Climate Change." Accessed June 18, 2018. http://www.ipcc.ch/.

ISO 9241-11. 1998 "Ergonomic Requirements for Office Work with Visual Display Terminals (VDTs)." The International Organization for Standardization 45: 9.

Jochem, Eberhard, Philipp Rudolf von Rohr, et al. 2004. "Steps towards a Sustainable Development. A White Book for R&D of Energy-Efficient Technologies." Edited by Eberhard Jochem. Novatlantis.

Kellenberger, Daniel, Hans-Jörg Althaus, Tina Künniger, Martin Lehmann, and Philipp Thalmann. 2007. "Life Cycle Inventories of Building Products: Cement Products and Processes." Final Report Ecoinvent V2.0 No.7. EMPA Dübendorf: Swiss Centre for Life Cycle Inventories. 2007.

Kelley, Kate, Belinda Clark, Vivienne Brown, and John Sitzia. 2003. "Good Practice in the Conduct and Reporting of Survey Research." *International Journal for Quality in Health Care* 15 (3): 261–66. https://doi.org/ 10.1093/intqhc/mzg031.

Kohli, Raymond, Schweiz, and Bundesamt für Statistik. 2010. "Les scénarios de l'évolution démographique de la Suisse 2010–2060." Neuchâtel: Office fédéral de la statistique.

Leaman, Adrian. 2000. "Usability in Buildings: The Cinderella Subject." *Building Research and Information* 28 (4): 296–300.

Lussault, Michel. 2009. "De la lutte des classes à la lutte des places." Paris, France: Grasset.

Myerson, Jeremy, and Jo-Anne Bichard. 2016. "New Demographics New Workspace: Office Design for the Changing Workforce." Routledge.

Office Fédéral de l'énergie OFEN. 2014. "Performance globale en éclairage – Global Lighting Performance; Final Report." Bern, Switzerland: Office Fédéral de l'énergie OFEN.

SIA 2024, Winfried Seidinger, and Martin Ménard. 2007. "SIA 2024 Cahier technique, conditions d'utilisation standard pour l'énergie et les installations du bâtiment." Zurich: SIA.

Verma, Himanshu, Hamed S. Alavi, and Denis Lalanne. 2017. "Studying Space Use: Bringing HCI Tools to Architectural Projects." In *Proceedings of the 2017 CHI Conference on Human Factors in Computing Systems*, 3856–3866. ACM.

Vohs, Kathleen D., Joseph P. Redden, and Ryan Rahinel. 2013. "Physical Order Produces Healthy Choices, Generosity, and Conventionality, Whereas Disorder Produces Creativity." *Psychological Science* 24 (9): 1860–67. https://doi.org/10.1177/0956797613480186.

⑤ Low-carbon thermal inertia

Arianna Brambilla
Cecile Nyffeler
Hugo Gasnier
Jean-Marie Le Tiec
Arnaud Misse

The research aimed at identifying possible strategies for a low-carbon design. In this chapter, we will present the steps taken to establish the guidelines for the design choices for the envelope of the future *smart living lab* building. Based on the 2000-Watt Society, the most sensitive parameters of the energy-efficient building design were analysed to understand their influence on the life cycle approach. Thermal inertia was identified as the most controversial parameter due to its positive influence on operational impacts and negative influence on embodied impacts. For this reason, we investigated compressed earth blocks as a potentially reliable solution to enhance thermal inertia benefits over the entire building life cycle.

The building envelope is the interface between the indoors and outdoors, and acts as a filter between external agents and the resulting internal environment. In cold continental climates such as that of Switzerland, the envelope must provide protection from the outdoors while preserving pleasant and healthy indoor conditions.

The building envelope must be designed using a multidimensional approach that maximizes indoor comfort and, at the same time, minimizes the use of energy. This means the envelope itself should not only be a barrier between the indoors and outdoors, but should also be able to adapt to external agents and to utilize them when they can be of benefit. In other words, the envelope must simultaneously provide indoor comfort, maximize building energy efficiency and minimize environmental impacts.

A passive design aims to maximize the use of natural sources of heating, cooling and ventilation to create comfortable conditions inside a building (Passive building design – Designing Buildings Wiki). The initial envelope design is typically need-based and must integrate an energy concept that drives all of the choices regarding the architecture, technological systems and technical installations. Passive strategies can be divided into two broad groups depending on the season: winter strategies and summer strategies [Figure 5.1].

Winter strategies aim to reduce active heating needs by capturing heat generated from other sources, like the sun (i.e. solar gains), or those already generated inside the building, like gains from lighting, electrical appliances and occupants (i.e. internal gains). Conversely, summer strategies aim to protect the interior from heat generation and to dissipate internal gains. The strategies are defined based on the actions needed to achieve the desired result [Figure 5.1].

However, the range of passive strategies is quite broad. As such, their application must be considered within a given context. Improving these strategies without taking into account criteria to counterbalance their effects could ultimately lead to even greater discomfort due to a lack of prioritization.

In this chapter, we will summarize the research process we used to define the general energy concept for the future *smart living lab* building (SLB), while focusing notably on the aspects prioritized in the investigations. This prioritization results from an iterative process based on a key question: how to store passive heat using a low-carbon strategy?

5.1 Research boundaries and assumptions

Passive thermal storage traditionally included materials and strategies with high embodied impacts. Given the *smart living lab*'s mission and values, it was essential to understand whether:
1) thermal storage is a relevant strategy in continental climates such as that of Fribourg;

Fig. 5.1 Passive strategies for winter and summer periods (Jusselme et al. 2015). Passive heat generation in a building comes from the sun (solar gains, represented by solar beams), whereas internal gains come from lighting, equipment and occupants (represented by a light bulb)

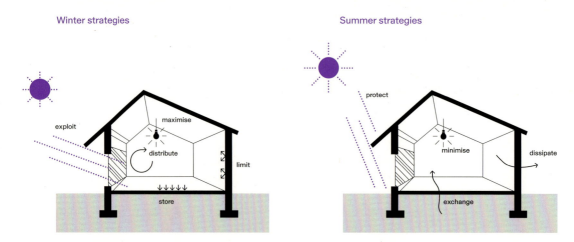

Fig. 5.2 Percentage distribution of impacts on global warming potential (GWP) indicators for macro-components. Only the insulation materials were changed in the analysis: cellulose fibre vs. polystyrene (SCBI 2006)

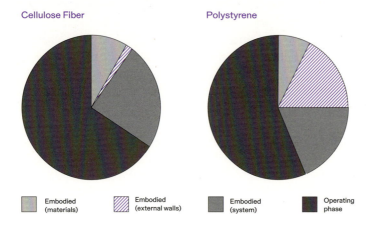

2) it would significantly contribute to energy savings and thermal comfort; and
3) it would be possible to maintain the benefits of thermal storage with lower embodied impacts and, if so, under what conditions.

The SLB has ambitious goals in terms of performance and achievement, given its aim of becoming a model building with outstanding environmental performances (Chapter ②). The preliminary research phase investigated possible strategies to help designers fine-tune their architectural proposals to meet stringent requirements in terms of life cycle performance. Life cycle assessment (Chapter ⑧) is a powerful methodology for quantifying the environmental impacts of products and processes that has been used in the construction industry since the 1990s (Ortiz et al. 2009, Scbi 2006). This method assesses a building's impacts during its operational life and embodied phase, i.e., from its manufacturing to its use in the construction of a building to its disposal (EN 156432:2011 2011, EN 15978:2011 2011). To optimize the life cycle, it is important to weigh these two aspects: that of the building's use and that of the impacts from the construction process and material choices. Nonetheless, a building's environmental impacts are intrinsically linked to its architectural design. In order to outline a general energy concept for the SLB's purposes, we had to define the boundaries and assumptions of the analysis.

The idea behind the research project was to steer the architectural concept using a few key points without limiting the freedom of the future designers. We therefore needed to understand how to balance the two components. To define the research boundaries, we referred to the above mentioned passive strategies ^(Figure 5.1) and established the key assumptions for the analysis, identifying what fell outside of our scope due to the need for architectural freedom.

These passive strategies can be divided based on the building features involved:

Exploit and **protect** as regards solar gains management. In passive design, precise management of solar penetration inside a building is essential for controlling passive heating and overheating (Olgyay et al. 2015). This essentially depends on the shading system, building orientation and optimization of solar access through the fenestration system (window dimensions/position and glazing properties). As these features are embedded within the architectural design, we considered them outside of the scope of the research phase and also assumed the optimization of these two strategies based on a southern orientation (in order to maximize solar gains) and an optimized automatic shading system (to protect from unwanted solar radiation in summer).

Maximize and **minimize** internal gains management. These strategies have to do with the actual heat produced indoors, which depends on the building's installation and occupation patterns. These patterns are often difficult to predict. Hence, we always assumed standard internal gains as defined by the building code (Seidinger and Ménard 2007).

Limit and **dissipate** refers to the thermal insulation design, which is clearly established by the MINERGIE[7] standard. The quantity of insulation determines the walls' thermal resistance, which influences the building's energy consumption by controlling its thermal performance and, ultimately, its operational impacts. The choice of insulation material, however, affects the building's embodied impacts. For this reason, we attempted to investigate this issue more closely, as described later.

Store and **distribute** refers to the natural heat storage of the building materials (Rempel and Rempel 2013), a phenomenon also known as thermal inertia (TI). Regarding insulation, while the quantity affects the operational phase, the material influences the embodied phase of a building's life. As such, we further investigated the possible influence of TI on the building's environmental performance.

5.2 Thermal insulation analysis

Thermal insulation acts as a thermal shield for buildings. The higher the level of thermal insulation, the higher the thermal resistance of the envelope, which in turn reduces heat exchange between the internal and external environment. Ideally, a hyper-insulated envelope can minimize heat losses to almost zero, allowing the building to retain solar and internal gains and warm the space passively[8]. This means that a well-insulated envelope reduces the operational impacts of the energy used for conditioning a space. On the other hand, more insulation also means higher embodied impacts due to the grey energy[9] of the products (Sartori and Hestnes 2007, Stephan et al. 2013). In the framework of the research, finding a balance between these two factors was essential. Understanding insulation's effects on operational and embodied impacts helped us define the most suitable strategy for the SLB design. At the same time, the analyses of the operational/embodied balance was guided by the Swiss building code, which requires a minimum level of thermal insulation (SIA 180 2015) for new constructions. This was the assumption we made in this investigation: as we could not consider a lower level of thermal resistance, we started with this minimum level in order to understand the resulting embodied impacts.

From here, we established the amount of insulation necessary based on two different materials: cellulose fibre, as it has extremely low embodied impacts, and polystyrene, as it is one of the most commonly used insulation materials in standard Swiss constructions.

---

[7] Minergie is a Swiss-registered quality label for quantifying the energy and environmental efficiency of new and refurbished buildings.

[8] Passively: without use of any HVAC or mechanical heating system.

[9] Grey energy represents the cumulative consumption of primary non-renewable energy (fossil, nuclear and biomass as a result of deforestation). This indicator allows for predictions regarding the efficiency of the use of resources. The greater a product's (or service's) need for primary non-renewable energy is, the less efficient the product (or service) is.

When comparing fibre- and polystyrene related-emissions for manufacturing, transport, construction and end of life, the results vary by a factor of 25 (from 0.3 to 7.5 kgCO$_2$/kg), underlining the importance of the choice of the material, which can have significant effects on a building's life cycle environmental impacts ^{Figure 5.2}.

Based on the analysis, the issue of thermal insulation was solved by combining the building code directives with a low-carbon material. The SLB scientific programme shared these results with the designers and recommended the use of low-carbon insulation materials.

5.3 Thermal inertia

During warm seasons in continental climates such as that of Fribourg, the risk of overheating is generally associated with internal gains, especially when high levels of insulation—which are mandatory in such climates due to the harsh winters—are used. In the recent past, knowledge regarding the benefits of thermal insulation and progress in terms of energy efficiency standards (such as Minergie) led to a shift in the predominant heat flux in buildings: from weather-dominated buildings, we have moved toward internal load-dominated buildings. This is especially true in the case of high internal-load buildings such as offices, where cooling loads are drastically increasing (Adnot 2003, Frank 2005).

Recent research indicates that high thermal inertia levels and adequate ventilation strategies can lead to greater indoor comfort and lower energy consumption (Gagliano et al. 2016, Givoni 1998). However, thermal inertia is a very complex phenomenon that occurs due to the interdependencies of several factors (Armstrong et al. 2006 Part I, Amstrong et al. 2006 Part II), including the building's architectural features, patterns of occupation and the context (Artmann et al. 2010, Karlsson 2012). For this reason, thermal inertia is a factor that is often overlooked in building regulations (Aste et al. 2015) in favour of a steady-state approach based on thermal insulation (Di Perna et al. 2011). While a benchmark already existed for thermal insulation (Swiss norms), we were obliged to start from scratch in order to understand whether thermal inertia would be truly beneficial in the SLB context and what impact it might have on the life cycle assessment.

5.3.1 The need for low-carbon inertia

Thermal inertia in buildings is traditionally created through the use of heavy-weight materials. Among them, the most common are bricks (Gregory et al. 2008, Pavlík et al. 2015), stone (Mariani 2018) and concrete (Orosa and Oliveira 2012). However, such materials have high embodied energy (Dodoo et al. 2012, Hacker et al. 2008), which makes it quite difficult to determine their effects on the entire life cycle (Karimpour et al. 2014). For this reason, the *smart living lab*'s research focused on the effects of thermal inertia on a building's life cycle and aimed to find a reliable, robust alternative to traditional materials to counterbalance the operational and embodied benefits of TI.

The fossil fuel crisis and high energy-efficiency requirements of new performance standards has led to a surge of natural or bio-inspired materials (Cabeza et al. 2013) with potentially lower carbon emissions (Pacheco-Torgal 2014). Among these, we focused on raw earth, which is widely available and easy to process, (Minke 2012) and has promising TI features (Mansour et al. 2016).

Among the raw earth products available (Pacheco-Torgal and Jalali 2012), compressed earth bricks (CEB) offer a good alternative to standard bricks as they are often cheaper to buy (Williams et al. 2010), less expensive to produce and have excellent TI properties (Morel et al. 2001).

Compressed earth bricks — or blocks — are a traditional construction material obtained by compressing moistened powdered soil in a mould using a press. Bricks can be prepared directly from on-site materials Figure 5.3, which greatly reduces the impacts of the manufacturing and transport phases. Notably, products that use an interlocking system allowing for dry construction based on the principle of male-female joints also exist, providing a system that is easy to dismantle and reuse.

For these reasons, compressed earth bricks were identified as one of the best materials for maximizing TI, stabilizing indoor temperatures and limiting carbon-related emissions, which were of key importance for the *smart living lab*'s building research phase Table 5.4.

5.3.2 The Experiment

After identifying the thermal inertia issue and the potential solution of compressed earth bricks, we were able to develop the following hypothesis:
- High levels of thermal inertia reduce the operational impacts of a building by reducing the cooling loads. At the same time, the use of compressed earth bricks can decrease the embodied impact of the materials.

To test this hypothesis in the context of the development of the SLB, we decided to compare different thermal inertia scenarios, from a very lightweight option to a very heavyweight one. The results in terms of heating/cooling needs and the indoor operative temperature indicate the benefits of each scenario for the operational phase. A life cycle assessment (LCA) was used to assess the various scenarios and determine their benefits for the embodied phase.

In the field of building physics, software is often used to simulate a building's behaviour based on different assumptions. In our case, thermal inertia efficiency is the result of the dynamic interactions between thermal inertia (TI), the context and the

Fig. 5.3   Manufacturing of earth bricks: a) prepare recycled earth b) mix raw materials c) compress in the mould d) assemble

Tab. 5.4   Compressed earth block properties

Properties	Value	Unit
Dry density ρ	1600–2200	kg/m³
Ambient water content w	0–5	%
Drying shrinkage	1–3	%
Vapour resistance coefficient μ	5–13	
Thermal conductivity λ_{BTC}	0.7–0.9	W/mK
Compression resistance Rc	0.4–7	MPa
Specific heat capacity c	600–1000	J/kg.K
Volumetric heat capacity C	960–2200	kJ/m³.K
Thermal conductivity λ	(0.81–0.93)	W/m.K

building. Cooling potential may vary significantly depending on the case. As such, the magnitude of its effects is difficult to predict. Hence, we needed dynamic software to create simulations that would allow us to assess the building's transient behaviour. Based on these assessments, it is possible to quickly evaluate the building performance in terms of energy consumption and thermal comfort over long periods of time. It is therefore useful having a fast, easy, user-friendly tool to help to solve the sort of complicated algorithms that govern buildings' behaviour.

Using transient simulation software called TRNSYS (University of Wisconsin 2000), we were able to assess a model building's yearly energy consumption and thus its operational impacts and thermal comfort in different situations. The iterative calculation allowed us to test different assumptions and scenarios.

However, thermal inertia's strong dependency on the interactions between several parameters and the difficulty of describing them accurately create a gap between thermal simulations and reality, wherein TI effects are often overestimated (Maile et al. 2010, Menezes et al. 2012). Results obtained in this matter would most likely be too biased for the SLB's purposes. One way to overcome this issue is to calibrate the virtual model by measuring the values in real conditions using a prototype. The assumptions and limits of the two models should be identical so that the outcomes are comparable and the virtual output can be calibrated based on the real prototype results.

For this reason, real scale experiments are necessary to define the specific potential of TI.

5.4 Testing the hypothesis: experiment set-up

Our experiment was based on a comparison of two different models, one physical and one virtual. We created a real 1:1 scale prototype and its digital twin in a virtual environment. The most important step was breaking the model down into different features that could be used in identical ways for both the virtual and the real prototype. The experimental set-up had to be clearly defined in order to understand potentially useful insight and the limitations of the study. Describing the two models used was therefore of the utmost importance.

5.4.1 The physical model

The real prototype design [Figure 5.5] was based on several key issues that served as background information. These ideas steered the concept of a fully-equipped building to be used for research purposes:
1) The prototype was needed to calibrate the virtual model. The calibration process (Raftery et al. 2011,

Fig. 5.5 Architectural section (top) and plan (bottom) of the prototype with the two identical double-office rooms. The room on the right, which has a second internal layer of compressed earth bricks, is the high inertia room. The other is representative of a lightweight wooden construction, typical of highly-efficient Swiss buildings (Brambilla and Jusselme 2017)

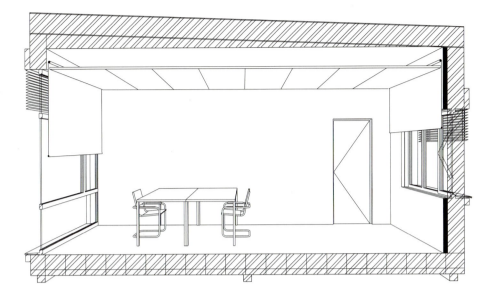

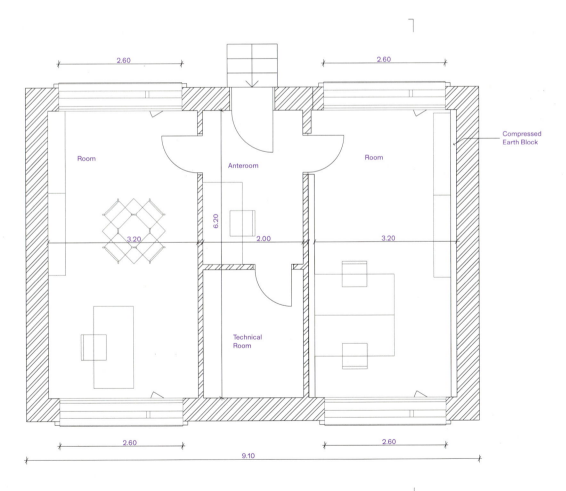

Fig. 5.6 Pictures of the prototype. On the right, the prototype during the experimental phase. The windows were completely obscured with insulated wood panels (6 mm) and a dark plastic sheet to prevent uncontrolled heat gains from solar radiation (Brambilla and Jusselme 2017)

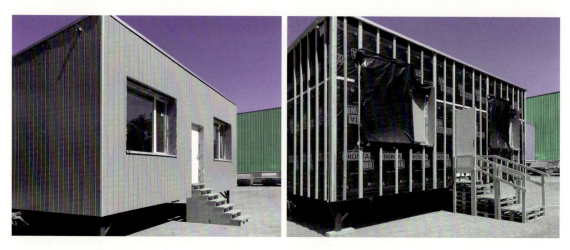

Fig. 5.7 Picture of the compressed earth brick wall

Royapoor and Roskilly 2015, Ryan and Sanquist 2012) is usually done for two extreme conditions. In our case, these conditions were lightweight and heavyweight. We thus needed to test these two scenarios on the real scale prototype. As the external climate influences the building's thermal behaviour, the ideal conditions for real scale test (which compared two simple solutions in different scenarios) had to run the two solutions contextually.

2) Thermal inertia is more effective when in contact with indoor air. Thus, we had to include thermal inertia internally.
3) The prototype had to be representative of highly efficient Swiss-standard construction.
4) The prototype had to be representative of a standard double office in terms of dimensions, internal load and building equipment.

As such, our prototype is a small building comprised of two identical rooms (18 m² each), modelling the dimensions of a typical double office based on SIA 2024 (Seidinger and Ménard 2007). The two rooms, which are side by side, are divided by a buffer zone that served as anteroom and technical space during the experiment. Each room has two windows on opposite facades, oriented on the SW/NE axis.

Thermal inertia levels are different in the two rooms. The light inertia (LI) room is a lightweight wooden construction that is insulated externally with 180 mm of polyurethane (0.15 W/m²K), per the Swiss standard for innovative, highly-efficient constructions. The heavy inertia (HI) room has an additional layer of CEB internally and a total of approximately ten tons of earthen bricks.

Figure 5.7

As described earlier, the experimental campaign aimed to compare two extreme conditions (LI vs. HI) in different scenarios, in order to obtain an initial benchmark regarding thermal inertia performance. It also afforded us the chance to calibrate a virtual model, which allowed for the integration of more scenarios with additional TI levels with longer simulation times.

The first step was to define the experiment's boundaries. Our main interest was the benefits of TI and, as such, comparing the thermal behaviours of HI and LI. Thermal inertia notably depended on the ventilation strategy used (Gagliano et al. 2016), meaning that TI's effects can be enhanced or reduced through various ventilation strategies. For this reason, it was important to compare LI and HI accordingly. The experimental campaign was designed to compare TI levels based on various ventilation management strategies to obtain reliable results, all of the other variables that typically contribute to a building's thermal behaviour had to be fixed and known. In this way, we were able to isolate the effects of TI and ventilation.

All heat sources were controlled for the experimental campaign. As discussed previously, solar and internal gains can easily lead to overheating. Moreover, they strictly depend on uncontrollable variables, such as climate and occupancy. A reliable comparison of different scenarios requires identical boundary conditions. Hence, it was necessary to reproduce the same gains each day of the experimental campaign.

To that end, windows were completely obscured ^{Figure 5.6} using black plastic foil (internal) and timber panels (external) to avoid solar gains. Internal occupancy heat gains were reproduced daily using a system of incandescent light bulbs ^{Figure 5.8}. These bulbs were connected to a timer, following the suggested SIA 2024 schedule. The monitoring lasted for twenty-one days in August 2016, (i.e., summer conditions). We changed the ventilation conditions in the two rooms every other day and monitored internal temperatures in order to analyse the effects of thermal inertia and ventilation in mitigating overheating.

The ventilation was changed during the day and at night based on three strategies ^{Table 5.9}: mechanical ventilation, natural ventilation and no ventilation. The mechanical ventilation airflow was based on SIA 2024 (Seidinger and Ménard 2007) standard recommendations for ventilation profiles for offices. Natural ventilation was achieved by opening the hopper (or tilt-turn) windows on the southeast facade at an opening angle of 5°. Night ventilation (08:00 pm – 08:00 am) and day ventilation profiles (08:00 am – 08:00 pm) were defined separately and combined to create six ventilation scenarios. The two day ventilation options were:
1) mechanical ventilation, with a flow rate of 50 m^3/h
2) completely switched off. The latter served as the worst case scenario for overheating, as heat accumulated continuously during occupied hours.

The three night ventilation options were:
1) mechanical (50 m^3/h)
2) natural
3) none

5.4.2 The virtual model

We created an identical virtual model next to the experiment room and used the results from the prototype to calibrate it to improve the reliability and robustness of the analysis. Using the virtual model, we were able to increase the number of scenarios in order to test and extend the duration of the experiment to obtain annual results.

Fig. 5.8   Left: the timed light garlands used in the experiment to reproduce internal gains. Right: internal gains profile used. The discretization of the internal gains curve into 5 steps made it easier to reproduce using an artificial internal gain source (Brambilla and Jusselme 2017)

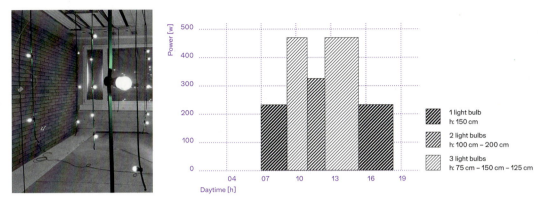

Tab. 5.9   Description of the ventilation strategy used in the experiment on the prototype

Scenario	Day ventilation 08.00–20.00	Night ventilation 20.00–08.00	Heat gains
Vp1	SIA	SIA	IGp
Vp2	SIA	natural	IGp
Vp3	SIA	—	IGp
Vp4	—	SIA	IGp
Vp5	—	natural	IGp
Vp6	—	—	IGp

Tab. 5.10 Thermal Inertia scenarios used for the analysis. TI levels were calculated using SIA380/1 (SIA 380/1 2009) and determined based on the room's heat capacity. This depended on the thermal properties of each of the surfaces delimiting the room itself. The type of construction is indicated in the table

Scenario	Longitudinal walls	Short walls	Roof	Floor	Heat capacity C [kJ/kg°K]
TI1	Light – wooden	Light – wooden	Light – wooden	Light – wooden	39.1
TI2	Wooden + synthetic rendering	Wooden + synthetic rendering	Light – wooden	Light – wooden	46.2
TI3	Light – wooden	Light – wooden	Light – wooden	Wooden + cement screed	50.4
TI4	Wooden + compressed earth bricks	Light – wooden	Light – wooden	Light – wooden	58.7
TI5	Wooden + compressed earth bricks	Light – wooden	Light – wooden	Wooden + cement screed	70.0
TI6	Concrete + internal mortar rendering	Concrete + internal mortar rendering	Concrete + internal mortar rendering	Concrete + cement screed	94.4

Tab. 5.11 Description of the ventilation strategies used in the simulation experiment

Scenario	Basic airflow	+	Mechanical ventilation	Natural ventilation
V1	46.3 m³/h during occupancy	+	—	—
V2	as reference scenario	+	46.3 m³/h from 2am to 6am	—
V3	as reference scenario	+	46.3 m³/h if Tint-Text > 2°C and Tint > 21°C	—
V4	as reference scenario	+	—	Open windows during occupied hours
V5	as reference scenario	+	—	Open windows 24/24 h

We created six different TI levels (varying from very light to very heavy) to better determine the possible solutions for use in offices. In $^{\text{Table 5.10}}$, we show the TI scenarios tested and their thermal capacity. Scenario TI1, with a very lightweight construction, was used as a reference for TI and served as the calibration prototype.

The scenarios tested in the prototype and the basic scenarios established for the virtual model $^{\text{Table 5.11}}$ account for standard, typical use of the building (internal gains by SIA). However, this is rarely the case. In reality, occupancy patterns, interactions between a building and its occupants and variations in the external climate greatly influence a building's actual behaviour.

Among the possible variables, the least controllable are window opening patterns and user-building interactions (Hoes et al. 2009, Hong et al. 2016). For this reason, four risk scenarios taken from the literature were introduced to reflect possible critical situations that might interfere with the effects of natural ventilation:

- R1   Misuse of blinds (considered 50 % open all day and night) (Office fédéral de l'énergie OFEN 2014)
- R2   A hot year in Fribourg, which Meteonorm describes as a "ten-year extreme hour" (i.e. hottest), spreading out the distribution of values while the climatological mean remains constant (Office fédéral de l'énergie OFEN 2014, Remund et al.)
- R3   Misuse of openings (manual opening), meaning natural ventilation made by users only when internal temperatures surpass 26°C (Office fédéral de l'énergie OFEN 2014)
- R4   Extreme risk scenario (combination of all risks)

The reference case for all scenarios is scenario V4 (previously defined), which represents the most basic scenario for natural ventilation. Scenarios R1 and R3 are the results of an extensive study on the effective use of movable shading devices in offices and the relative impacts of indoor lighting by the Swiss Energy Office. Scenario R2 represents potentially warmer summers in the future or a weather anomaly leading to an unusually hot summer, as defined by the climatic projections of the Intergovernmental Panel on Climate Change. The last scenario is the sum of all the previous risk factors.

5.5   Lessons learned

The experimental campaign results were analysed using a two-step approach: first, the findings and results of the experiment were highlighted and analysed; then, based on the latter, we were able to generalise the experiment for a broader context. General insight was based on specific evidence from the experiment and analysed the effects of ventilation and thermal inertia on energy needs (cooling and heating) and indoor temperature profiles.

5.5.1 Findings from the real scale prototype assessment

The first part of the experiment focused on the real scale prototype. The measurement campaign allowed us to monitor temperatures in the two rooms (high-inertia and low-inertia levels) based on the various ventilation scenarios. This was particularly useful for better understanding the actual influence of thermal inertia in a real environment.

The experiment took place from August 1–21, 2016. Temperatures at that time were somewhat lower than average [Figure 5.12]. As can be seen in the figure, the median temperature value of 17°C during this period is lower than the median for a typical meteorological year, as well as those of the Intergovernmental Panel on Climate Change's (IPCC) A1B, A2 and B1 scenarios. 2016 also saw the greatest temperature range during this period, with variations of up to 20.8°C (versus 18.4°C for a TMY) and an average of 19.1°C for the 2050 projected values.

IPCC projection scenarios A1B, A2 and B1 provide a prospective temperature profile for 2050. These three projections posit that higher temperatures are to be expected in the future. The monitored data is therefore not exactly representative of future temperature trends. However, it does offer insight regarding internal temperature changes when outdoor temperatures (which are also projected to rise in the future) are highly variable.

The experiment campaign in Fribourg shows that major fluctuations in outdoor temperatures inevitably impact the prototype's indoor temperatures as shown by the monitored temperatures over the experiment period [Figure 5.13]:

The three temperature profiles underwent fluctuations over 24 hours with lower temperatures at night and higher ones during the day. The temperature in the light inertia room varied considerably based on outdoor temperature swings, with up to 4.4°C of variability, whereas those of the HI room never exceeded 3.3°C. The CEBs in the high inertia room were able to store heat during the day and release it at night, thus mitigating temperature variations in the room.

Due to the different levels of thermal inertia in the two rooms, temperature differences varied depending on the time of day, with more marked differences during the day and less disparity at night. The type of ventilation used also influenced indoor temperatures. When natural ventilation was used at night (scenario Vp2 and Vp5), both rooms cooled down and the difference was less marked. When no night ventilation was used (natural or mechanical), as in scenarios 3 and 6, the CEBs' thermal inertia was sufficient for

Fig. 5.12 Boxplot of the outdoor temperature over the 01.08.16 – 21.08.16 period (Brambilla and Jusselme 2017)

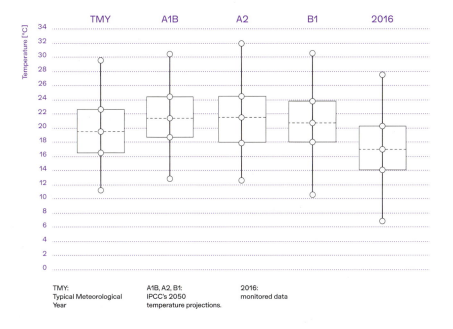

TMY:
Typical Meteorological
Year

A1B, A2, B1:
IPCC's 2050
temperature projections.

2016:
monitored data

Fig. 5.13 Hourly average temperatures of outdoor and indoor LI and HI rooms in function of time, based on different ventilation scenarios Table 5.9 (Brambilla and Jusselme 2017)

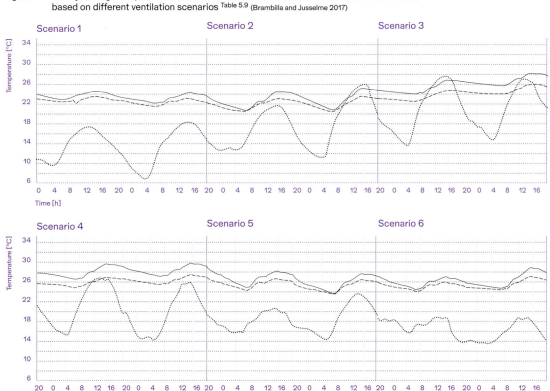

Fig. 5.14 HI and LI indoor temperatures based on the outdoor temperature Table 5.9 (Brambilla and Jusselme 2017)

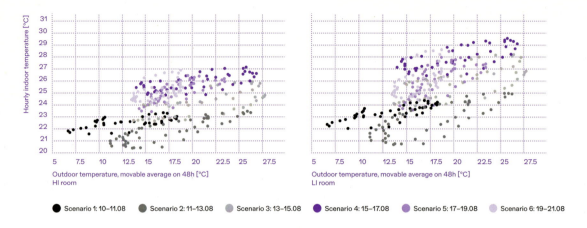

Fig. 5.15 Maximum and minimum temperatures observed for the different surfaces of the HI (light purple) and LI (light grey) rooms (Brambilla and Jusselme 2017)

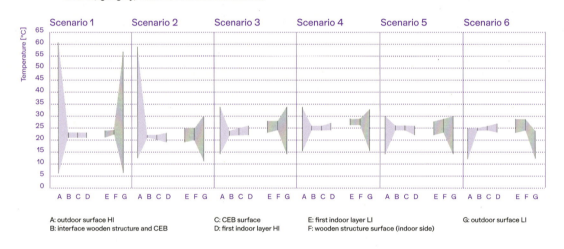

A: outdoor surface HI
B: interface wooden structure and CEB
C: CEB surface
D: first indoor layer HI
E: first indoor layer LI
F: wooden structure surface (indoor side)
G: outdoor surface LI

Fig. 5.16 Indoor temperature plotted against outdoor movable average. Comfort limits for the mechanically-ventilated scenario are in purple, and in grey for the naturally-ventilated scenario. The minimum for the naturally ventilated range (grey) coincides with the minimum for the mechanical ventilated range (purple) (Brambilla and Jusselme 2017)

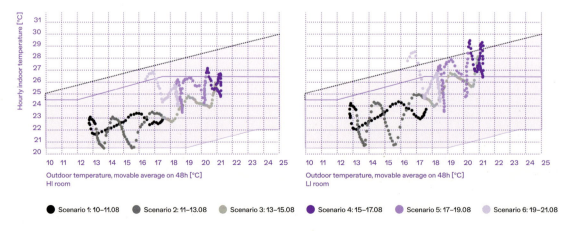

126   Exploring

absorbing heat and thus avoiding overheating conditions. Finally, the temperature differences between HI and LI also greatly depended on the outdoor temperature. Effectively, we observed the greatest temperature differences between HI and LI (up to 3°C) during the heat stress period (scenarios Vp3 and Vp4), which was when the compressed earth bricks showed their full potential by allowing for smoother, less drastic temperature variations, which is essential for user comfort. All of these facts are highlighted on ^{Figure 5.14}.

Scenarios Vp3 and Vp4 reflect the highest internal temperatures in both rooms, presumably due to the heat stress in these scenarios. The fact that either no ventilation (Vp3) or only night mechanical ventilation (Vp4) were used might have hindered sufficient cooling, which explains the rise in temperatures during this period. Scenario Vp6, whose indoor temperature values were also relatively high, measured for a somewhat colder period. As no ventilation was used in this scenario, the high temperatures were clearly a consequence of a lack of heat discharge with the outdoors. The internal gains accumulated inside the rooms thus led to higher temperatures (overheating) due to a lack of ventilation. This overheating was especially marked in the LI room (versus the HI room), where it was somewhat controlled for by the thermal inertia of the compressed earth bricks.

CEBs thus allow for more stable, less extreme indoor temperatures. They also help control temperature variations on the different surfaces of the HI room. The temperatures of the indoor surfaces of the LI room were more sensitive to indoor and outdoor temperatures ^{Figure 5.15}.

Scenarios Vp1 and Vp2 show extreme outdoor temperature values due to the sensors being placed directly on the black fabric covering the prototype. As such, false values were recorded. The sensors were then rearranged so as not to be in contact with the fabric and, starting from scenario Vp3, monitored the correct values. We nonetheless observed that the surface temperatures of the internal HI wall were much more stable than those of the LI room. This was the case for all scenarios. Moreover, the surface temperatures of the HI room were always lower than those of lightweight construction (LI room). Ventilation systems also affect surface temperatures. Natural ventilation with increased airflow led to the greater thermal variability in both rooms, as shown in scenarios Vp2 and Vp5.

This difference between the LI and HI rooms in terms of temperature behaviours (which was also recorded inside the rooms and not only on their internal surfaces) was somewhat significant. As the SIA norms state, user comfort depends on both the actual indoor temperature and its stability. A running mean of the outdoor temperature was done to assess user comfort. SIA norms are specific in terms of the conditions necessary for a room to qualify as "comfortable." These requirements differ from European Norms

(Aste et al. 2015, Di Perna et al. 2011) depending on whether mechanical or natural ventilation is used. The graph ^{Figure 5.16} helps in determining whether the prototype could be described as "comfortable" for the different scenarios:

The high inertia room respected the indoor value limits for all of the ventilation scenarios considered. Scenarios Vp1, Vp2, Vp3 and Vp5 were in the more restrictive range of mechanically-ventilated conditions. Scenario Vp6 and Vp4 somewhat exceeded natural ventilation values, which is acceptable given that scenario Vp6 was not ventilated at all and scenario Vp4 had only mechanical ventilation at night (the comfort analyses focus on occupied hours only). The low inertia room, on the other hand, exceeded both natural and mechanical ventilated comfort zone values by several points. This means that 7 % of occupied office hours were not within the comfort range, which does not meet SIA norms. Hence, the importance of having a certain degree of thermal inertia in an office room is once again obvious.

5.5.2 Findings from the virtual prototype assessment

The second step of the experimental campaign involved calibrating the virtual model based on the previous results. This procedure was crucial for creating a reliable virtual model and for further investigating the effects of thermal inertia and natural ventilation using more complex scenarios wherein we were then able to simulate the building performance for an entire year.

Energy consumption: heating and cooling needs

Here we consider the heating energy needs as a function of the thermal inertia level ^{Figure 5.17}. The energy needed to heat the facility declines as thermal inertia increases, with an average decrease of 0.2 % (TI3 to TI4) to 3.2 % (TI5 to TI6). Overall, a heavyweight construction (HI: TI6) uses up to 10 % less heating energy than does a lightweight construction (LI: TI1).

Nonetheless, the full potential of high thermal-inertia materials can be appreciated in warmer periods, when cooling is necessary. Such materials' dynamic capacity to store heat and release it at night in cooler conditions has a much higher impact ^{Figure 5.18}.

The cooling energy needs, calculated based on SIA norms (SIA 380/1 2009), decreased as thermal inertia levels increased. Mechanical ventilation systems (V2, V3) showed overall higher cooling demands than natural ventilation systems (V4, V5). This gap was particularly large for lightweight constructions and decreased for higher thermal-inertia materials. From the construction with the least thermal inertia (TI1) to the one with the most (T6), the cooling energy saved ranged between 60 % (for the mechanical ventilation system V1) and 100 % (for the natural ventilation system V5). A major decrease was also observed for the temperature gradi-

Fig. 5.17   Heating needs for different TI levels under minimal hygienic ventilation rate V1 (46.3 m³/h)

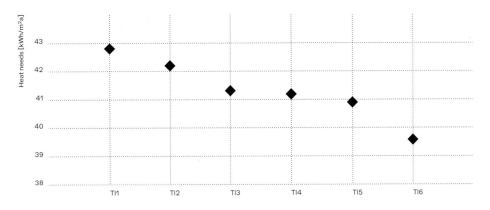

Fig. 5.18   Cooling needs of different ventilation rates for variant thermal inertia levels needed to reach the SIA comfort threshold of 26.5 °C

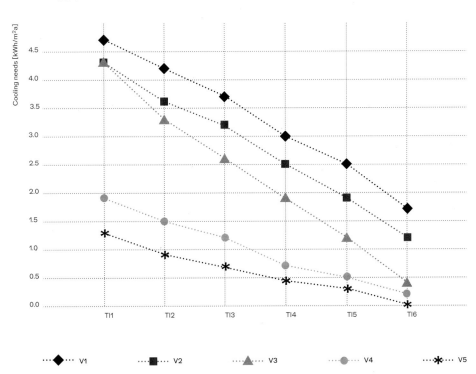

⑤ Low-carbon thermal inertia

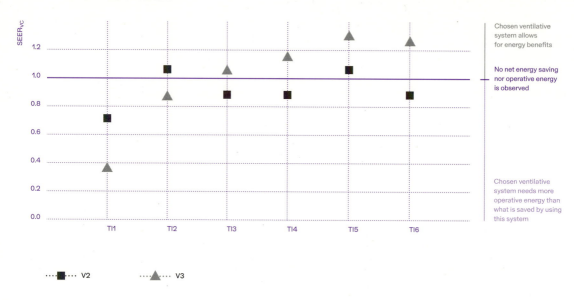

Fig. 5.19 Seasonal energy efficiency ratio for ventilative cooling (SEER$_{vc}$) applied to the ventilation scenarios V2 and V3 based on different thermal inertia conditions. For this simulation, SPI = 0.4 W/(m³/h) = 46.3 m³/h and H depend on the ventilation scenario

Tab. 5.20 Number of overheating hours (as defined by SIA based on the running outdoor mean temperature) corresponding to every combination of thermal inertia Table 5.10 and ventilation system Table 5.11

| | Ventilation Scenario | | | | |
TI Level	Scenario V1	Scenario V2	Scenario V3	Scenario V4	Scenario V5
TI1	743	712	591	25	13
TI2	689	636	493	9	5
TI3	648	592	401	4	2
TI4	666	616	326	0	0
TI5	613	544	276	0	0
TI6	533	434	128	0	0

ent-based ventilation system V3, whose cooling needs decreased by approximately 90 %. This was the only mechanical ventilation system whose performance was close to that of natural ventilation systems, with a difference of less than 0.5 kWh/m².

Energy efficiency ratio indicator for the ventilation strategy used

The seasonal energy efficiency ratio for ventilative cooling ($SEER_{VC}$) as presented in EBC Annex 62 (Karlsson 2012) was used to better assess the increased efficiency of the mechanical temperature gradient ventilation system V3, versus the mechanical time-scheduled ventilation system V2. This indicator shows the mechanical ventilation's performance associated with a specific mechanical ventilation system. It is expressed as:

$$SEER_{vc} = \frac{Q_{Cref} - Q_c}{E_{vc}} \text{ where } E_{vc} = SPI \cdot \vartheta \cdot H \quad \text{(Karlsson 2012)}$$

Q_{Cref}	Cooling need of the reference scenario (without ventilative cooling) [kWh/m²]
Q_C	Cooling need of the scenario with ventilative cooling applied [kWh/m²]
E_{VC}	Energy used to apply ventilative cooling [Wh]
SPI	Specific power input of the ventilation system [W/(m³/h)]
ϑ	Airflow rate of the mechanical ventilation system [m3/h]
H	Number of running hours of the ventilation system for cooling purposes [h]

The $SEER_{VC}$ values obtained can be interpreted in the following way:

$SEER_{VC} < 0$ The cooling needs associated with the cooling strategy are higher than those in the reference scenario. The strategy evaluated thus has a negative impact on the overall cooling demand.

$0 < SEER_{VC} < 1$ The ventilative cooling strategy might be beneficial for reducing the cooling load but requires more energy to apply than the effective savings.

$SEER_{VC} = 1$ The savings obtained on the cooling demand are nullified by the energy used to run the ventilation system.

$SEER_{VC} > 1$ The ventilative cooling strategy chosen has overall energy benefits and is effective in reducing energy needs due to cooling requirements.

The importance of the choice of the mechanical ventilation system is graphically weighted in Figure 5.19.

A time-constrained mechanical ventilation system did not provide conclusive results in terms of its energy-saving capacities. The temperature gradient ventilation system V3, on the other hand, showed effective use of energy once the thermal inertia level TI3[10] was exceeded. This means that a ventilation system that uses external and internal temperature conditions is beneficial when the envelope has sufficiently high thermal inertia.

10   TI3: Walls and roof: light – wooden; Floor: wooden + cement screed Table 5.10

11   This number varies according to the building code reference used. The Swiss building code, SIA, is one of the strictest, as it does not allow for any exemptions and requires that all occupied hours be within the comfort zone.

Indoor thermal environment

The importance of the ventilation system is once again shown in Table 5.20.

Exceeding the threshold of a certain number[11] of hours of overheating may result in health issues for room users. The purple numbers in Table 5.20 correspond to the acceptable number of hours of overheating as defined by SIA norm 180:2014 (SIA 180 2015, p.180). Greater thermal inertia results in fewer hours of overheating, regardless of the ventilation system considered.

Even natural ventilation system V5 (windows open all the time) and natural ventilation system V4 (operated during office hours) require that the people working in the office use them correctly. If a person were to close the window every time a breeze came into the room, the ventilation capacity and overall cooling efficiency might be diminished, leading to overheating. Misuse of shades or extreme climatic conditions are other potential complications that must be taken into account to effectively ensure the best possible indoor comfort for users. In order to assess the impact of such misuse and extreme weather conditions, a risk analysis using ventilation system V4 is provided hereafter Figure 5.21.

Regardless of the risk scenario considered, the impact of misuse of openings and/or climatic variations diminishes as thermal inertia increases. Heavy-duty constructions (TI6) showed almost no difference when compared with the reference scenario, whether the openings were misused (R2) (for example, by opening windows only once the internal temperature reaches 26°C instead of during the cooler morning or evening hours) or used correctly. However, considering the accumulated risks, even heavy-duty constructions showed increased cooling needs of about 80%. Educating users about how to use the equipment correctly is therefore essential and must be coupled with high inertia materials to temper the impact of different risk scenarios. If not, indoor temperatures can vary greatly Table 5.22.

Life cycle efficiency ratio indicator

Higher thermal inertia materials thus seem useful, as they allow for better performance when correctly designed. They can also help compensate for misuse of the system and inappropriate ventilation methods. However, high inertia materials (such as concrete, mortar, etc.), while beneficial during operation, may have heavier environmental impacts in terms of their production, transport, destruction, etc. A life cycle analysis thus allows us to weigh the benefits and disadvantages of high-inertia materials and their impact on the environment throughout their entire life cycle (production, use and destruction). The life cycle analysis (LCA) conducted in view of this dilemma expresses the results graphically and also required the introduction of a new indicator: the life cycle efficiency ratio (LCER). This parameter compared the operative gains

Fig. 5.21 Cooling needs for different risk scenarios and thermal inertia levels applied to ventilation system V4

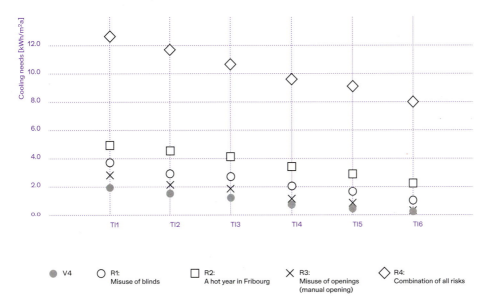

Tab. 5.22 Internal temperature of room with ventilation system V4. On left column: temperature associated with no risk; on right column: values when maximum risk is applied (scenario R4) (TI scenarios Table 5.10)

TI scenario	Tmax °C	
	V4	V4 + R4
TI1	31	40
TI2	31	39
TI3	30	38
TI4	29	35
TI5	28	34
TI6	27	32

Fig. 5.23 LCER indicator on the GWP, CED and CED$_{nr}$ LCA categories for all thermal inertia levels and ventilation systems. Thermal inertia level T1 $^{Table\ 5.10}$ serves as reference in the LCA and is thus not pictured here (Brambilla et al. 2018) $^{Table\ 5.11}$

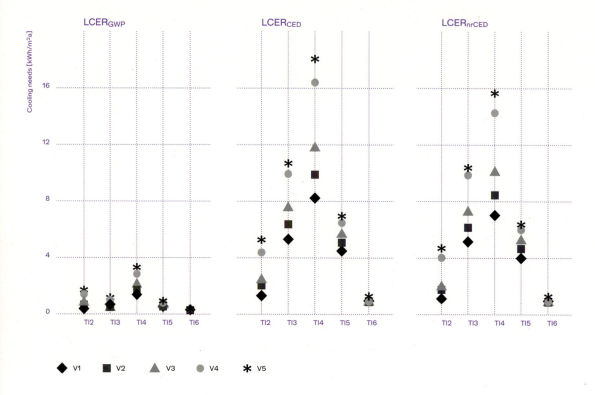

of a given scenario with those of the reference scenario, which were weighted on the difference between the embodied impacts in the two scenarios considered.

$$LCER = \frac{(OI_{ref} - OI)}{(EI - EI_{ref})}$$

OI_{ref} Operative impacts of the reference scenario (CED and CED_{nr} in $MJ_{oil\text{-}eq}$ and GWP in kg CO_2)
OI Operative impacts of the scenario analysed (CED and CED_{nr} in $MJ_{oil\text{-}eq}$ and GWP in kg CO_2)
EI_{ref} Embodied impacts of the reference scenarios (CED and CED_{nr} in $MJ_{oil\text{-}eq}$ and GWP in kg CO_2)
EI Embodied impacts of the scenario analysed (CED and CED_{nr} in $MJ_{oil\text{-}eq}$ and GWP in kg CO_2)

This indicator was applied to all thermal inertia levels and ventilation systems. A focus was then applied to three of the LCA categories: the cumulative energy demand (CED)[12], the non-renewable cumulative energy demand (CED_{nr})[13] and the global warming potential (GWP). The results are presented in Figure 5.23.

Higher LCER scores meant fewer major repercussions on the environment (embodied and operational impacts). In this respect, the materials with the highest thermal inertia levels did not score well. Concrete and cement, which were mainly present in scenarios TI5 and TI6 and helped to increase thermal inertia of the office in question, also have high energy costs and environmental impacts in their retrieval, shipment and elimination phases. Thermal inertia scenario TI4 seems the most appropriate, with the highest levels of LCER for all of the categories considered. This scenario uses compressed earth bricks (CEB) in addition to wood in the wall composition.

5.5.3 Key lessons from the virtual and real prototype assessments

The results clearly indicate that thermal inertia is a key factor in increasing a building's resiliency to ventilation strategies that underestimate misuse or changes in our initial assumptions, as shown in the risk scenarios. Thermal inertia and natural ventilation can significantly reduce energy consumption for both heating and cooling thanks to dynamic heat storage and release, resulting in more comfortable indoor thermal environments that improve occupants' health and well-being. Moreover, compressed earth bricks are a good compromise between high inertia levels and minor impacts on the environment over their life cycle.

5.6 Useful insights

The research presented here aimed at better understanding the potential role of thermal inertia in buildings in lowering CO_2 emissions in the future. The goal was to provide evidence on how

[12] Cumulative energy demand
[13] Cumulative energy demand (non-renewable)

to balance the operational and embodied impacts in terms of TI, and the use of compressed earth bricks as a possible material for improving a building envelope's thermal efficiency without using high embodied-impact solutions. To that end, we compared different levels of thermal inertia under different ventilation strategies on both a real scale prototype and a virtual model. This dual approach helped us to improve the reliability of the results by comparing the two methods and, at the same time, analyse a broader set of possible scenarios.

The results show that with a higher level of thermal inertia, it is possible to keep indoor temperatures more stable and less dependent on external conditions. This indicates that TI can provide superior indoor comfort and health conditions for occupants. Moreover, if TI can be used to stabilize indoor temperatures and to store or release heat when necessary, the need for conditioning (heating or cooling) can be diminished. Moreover, thermal comfort can be provided for 100 % of occupied hours, with a pleasant indoor environment for occupants. However, the same cannot be said for a lightweight scenario. In continental climates, thermal inertia is essential for maintaining temperatures within a comfort range and for saving energy on heating and cooling. With the prototype and the experiment, we were able to quantify the benefits of using compressed earth bricks and to test the buildability of this construction system in an office space. It took roughly a day for three non-expert workers to build the earthen walls made of approximately ten tons of materials. This observation clearly underlines the great potential of this type of brick, given that it does not require specialized skills to create, that the installation process is not energy-intensive and that embodied impacts are low.

Low-carbon, unfired earth bricks, which are easy to use and show extremely promising results, could be extremely useful in view of more stringent future low-carbon requirements.

Acknowledgements

The authors would like to thank Claude-Alain Jacot for his inestimable role as coordination and technical support in this adventure, Dr Hamed Alavi and Dr Himanshu Verma from the Human-IST laboratory at Fribourg University for their input and suggestions regarding the experiment design, Peter Hansen for his invaluable guidance in developing the methodology and all of the *smart living lab* colleagues for the fruitful, interesting discussions.

Partners

Building2050 / EPFL: Arianna Brambilla, Thomas Jusselme, Cecile Nyffeler
ESTIA: Jérôme Bonvin, Flourentzos Flourentzou
CRAterre: Jean-Marie Le Tiec, Hugo Gasnier
CARPE: Elsa Cauderay
TERRAbloc: Rodrigo Fernandez

Related Publications

Brambilla, Arianna, Endrit Hoxha, Thomas Jusselme, Marilyne Andersen. 2016. "LCA as Key Factor for Implementation of Inertia in a LOW Carbon Performance Driven Design: the Case of the Smart Living Building in Fribourg, Switzerland". *Proceedings of Sustainable Built Environment regional conference, Zurich*, 15–17 (June).

Brambilla, Arianna, Hamed S. Alavi, Himanshu Verma, Denis Lalanne, Thomas Jusselme, Marilyne Andersen. 2017. "Our Inherent Desire of Control: a Case Study of Automation's Impact on the Perception of Comfort." *Energy Procedia* 122: 925–930

Brambilla, Arianna, Thomas Jusselme. 2017. "Preventing Overheating in Offices Through Thermal Inertia Properties of Compressed Earth Bricks: a Study on a Real Scale Prototype". *Energy and Buildings* 156: 281–291

Brambilla, Arianna, Jérôme Bonvin, Flourentzos Flourentzou, Thomas Jusselme. 2018. "Life Cycle Efficiency Ratio: a New Performance Indicator for a Life Cycle Driven Approach to Evaluate the Potential of Ventilative Cooling and Thermal Inertia". *Energy and Buildings* 163: 22–33

Brambilla, Arianna, Jérôme Bonvin, Flourentzos Flourentzou, Thomas Jusselme. 2018. "On the Influence of Thermal Mass and Natural Ventilation on the Overheating Risk in Offices". *Buildings* 8(4); 47

References

Adnot, Jérôme. 2003. "Energy Efficiency and Certification of Central Air Conditioners (EECAAC), Final Report." Paris, France: D.G. Transportation Energy (DG TREN) of the Commission of the E.U.

Armstrong, Peter R., Steven Lee B., and Leslie K. Norford. 2006a. "Control with Building Mass – Part I: Thermal Response Model."

Armstrong, Peter R., Steven Lee B., and Leslie K. Norford. 2006b. "Control with Building Mass – Part II Simulation I Air Conditioning I Hvac." Scribd. 2006. https://www.scribd.com/document/47417377/Control-with-Building-Mass-Part-II-Simulation.

Artmann, Nikolai, Rasmus L. Jensen, Heinrich Manz, and Per Heiselberg. 2010. "Experimental Investigation of Heat Transfer during Night-Time Ventilation." *Energy and Buildings* 42 (3): 366–74. https://doi.org/10.1016/j.enbuild.2009.10.003.

Aste, Niccolò, Fabrizio Leonforte, Massimiliano Manfren, and Manlio Mazzon. 2015. "Thermal Inertia and Energy Efficiency – Parametric Simulation Assessment on a Calibrated Case Study." *Applied Energy* 145 (May): 111–23. https://doi.org/10.1016/j.apenergy.2015.01.084.

Brambilla, Arianna, Jérôme Bonvin, Flourentzos Flourentzou, and Thomas Jusselme. 2018. "Life Cycle Efficiency Ratio: A New Performance Indicator for a Life Cycle Driven Approach to Evaluate the Potential of Ventilative Cooling and Thermal Inertia." *Energy and Buildings* 163 (March): 22–33. https://doi.org/10.1016/j.enbuild.2017.12.010.

Brambilla, Arianna, and Thomas Jusselme. 2017. "Preventing Overheating in Offices through Thermal Inertial Properties of Compressed Earth Bricks: A Study on a Real Scale Prototype." *Energy and Buildings* 156 (December): 281–92. https://doi.org/10.1016/j.enbuild.2017.09.070.

Cabeza, Luisa F., Camila Barreneche, Laia Miró, Josep M. Morera, Esther Bartolí, and A. Inés Fernández. 2013. "Low Carbon and Low Embodied Energy Materials in Buildings: A Review." *Renewable and Sustainable Energy Reviews* 23 (July): 536–42. https://doi.org/10.1016/j.rser.2013.03.017.

Di Perna, Costanzo, Francesca Stazi, Andrea Ursini Casalena, and Marco D'Orazio 2011. "Influence of the Internal Inertia of the Building Envelope on Summertime Comfort in Buildings with High Internal Heat Loads." *Energy and Buildings* 43 (1): 200–206. https://doi.org/10.1016/j.enbuild.2010.09.007.

Dodoo, Ambrose, Leif Gustavsson, and Roger Sathre. 2012. "Effect of Thermal

Mass on Life Cycle Primary Energy Balances of a Concrete- and a Wood-Frame Building." *Applied Energy* 92 (April): 462–72. https://doi.org/10.1016/j.apenergy.2011.11.017.

EN 156432:2011. 2011. "Sustainability of Construction Works, Assessment of Buildings." Part 2. Vol. Framework for the assessment of environmental performance.

EN 15978:2011. 2011. "Sustainability of Construction Works, Assessment of the Environmental Performance of Buildings." Calculation Method.

Frank, Thomas. 2005. "Climate Change Impacts on Building Heating and Cooling Energy Demand in Switzerland." *Energy and Buildings* 37 (11): 1175–85. https://doi.org/10.1016/j.enbuild.2005.06.019.

Gagliano, Antonio, Francesco Nocera, Francesco Patania, Angela Moschella, Maurizio Detommaso, and Gianpiero Evola. 2016. "Synergic Effects of Thermal Mass and Natural Ventilation on the Thermal Behaviour of Traditional Massive Buildings." *International Journal of Sustainable Energy* 35 (5): 411–28. https://doi.org/10.1080/14786451.2014.910517.

Givoni, Baruch. 1998. "Effectiveness of Mass and Night Ventilation in Lowering the Indoor Daytime Temperatures. Part I: 1993 Experimental Periods." *Energy and Buildings* 28 (1): 25–32. https://doi.org/10.1016/S0378-7788(97)00056-X.

Gregory, Katherine, Behdad Moghtaderi, Heber Sugo, and Adrian Page. 2008. "Effect of Thermal Mass on the Thermal Performance of Various Australian Residential Constructions Systems." *Energy and Buildings* 40 (4): 459–65. https://doi.org/10.1016/j.enbuild.2007.04.001.

Hacker, Jacob N., Tom P. De Saulles, Andrew J. Minson, and Michael J. Holmes. 2008. "Embodied and Operational Carbon Dioxide Emissions from Housing: A Case Study on the Effects of Thermal Mass and Climate Change." *Energy and Buildings* 40 (3): 375–84. https://doi.org/10.1016/j.enbuild.2007.03.005.

Hoes, Pieter, Jan Hensen, Marcel Loomans, Bauke de Vries, and Denis Bourgeois. 2009. "User Behavior in Whole Building Simulation." *Energy and Buildings* 41 (3): 295–302. https://doi.org/10.1016/j.enbuild.2008.09.008.

Hong, Tianzhen, Sarah C. Taylor-Lange, Simona D'Oca, Da Yan, and Stefano P. Corgnati. 2016. "Advances in Research and Applications of Energy-Related Occupant Behavior in Buildings." *Energy and Buildings* 116 (March): 694–702. https://doi.org/10.1016/j.enbuild.2015.11.052.

Jusselme, Thomas, Arianna Brambilla, Endrit Hoxha, Yingying Jiang, Didier Vuarnoz, and Stefano Cozza. 2015. "Building 2050 – State-of-the-Arts and Preliminary Guidelines." https://infoscience.epfl.ch/record/214871.

Karimpour, Mahsa, Martin Belusko, Ke Xing, and Frank Bruno. 2014. "Minimising the Life Cycle Energy of Buildings: Review and Analysis." *Building and Environment* 73 (March): 106–14. https://doi.org/10.1016/j.buildenv.2013.11.019.

Karlsson, Jonathan. 2012. "Possibilities of Using Thermal Mass in Buildings to Save Energy, Cut Power Consumption Peaks and Increase the Thermal Comfort." Division of Building Materials, LTH, Lund University. http://portal.research.lu.se/

Maile, Tobias, Martin Fischer, and Vladimir Bazjanac. 2010. "A Method to Compare Measured and Simulated Data to Assess Building Energy Performance." 2010.

Mansour, Mohamed Ben, Ahmed Jelidi, Amel Soukaina Cherif, and Sadok Ben Jabrallah. 2016. "Optimizing Thermal and Mechanical Performance of Compressed Earth Blocks (CEB)." *Construction and Building Materials* 104 (February): 44–51. https://doi.org/10.1016/j.conbuildmat.2015.12.024.

Mariani, Silvia. 2018. "Review of Building in Historical Areas: Identity Values and Energy Performance of Innovative Massive Stone Envelopes with Reference to Traditional Building Solutions, by Federica Rosso and Marco Ferrero". *Buildings* 8 (2): 17. https://doi.org/10.3390/buildings8020017.

Menezes, Anna Carolina, Andrew Cripps, Dino Bouchlaghem, and Richard Buswell. 2012. "Predicted vs. Actual Energy Performance of Non-Domestic Buildings: Using Post-Occupancy Evaluation Data to Reduce the Performance Gap." *Applied Energy* 97 (September): 355–64. https://doi.org/10.1016/j.apenergy.2011.11.075.

Minke, Gernot. 2012. "Building with Earth: Design and Technology of a Sustainable Architecture." Walter de Gruyter.

Morel, Jean-Claude, Ali Mesbah, Michel Oggero, and Pete Walker. 2001. "Building Houses with Local Materials: Means to Drastically Reduce the Environmental Impact of Construction." *Building and Environment* 36 (10): 1119–26. https://doi.org/10.1016/S0360-1323(00)00054-8.

Office Fédéral de l'énergie OFEN. 2014. "Performance globale en éclairage – Global Lighting Performance; Final Report." Bern, Switzerland: Office Fédéral de l'énergie OFEN.

Olgyay, Victor, Aladar Olgyay, Donlyn Lyndon, Victor W. Olgyay, John Reynolds, and Ken Yeang. 2015. "Design with Climate: Bioclimatic Approach to Architectural Regionalism." New and expanded edition. Princeton: Princeton University Press.

Orosa, José A., and Armando C. Oliveira. 2012. "A Field Study on Building Inertia and Its Effects on Indoor Thermal Environment." *Renewable Energy* 37 (1): 89–96. https://doi.org/10.1016/j.renene.2011.06.009.

Ortiz, Oscar, Francesc Castells, and Guido Sonnemann. 2009. "Sustainability in the Construction Industry: A Review of Recent Developments Based on LCA." *Construction and Building Materials* 23 (1): 28–39. https://doi.org/10.1016/j.conbuildmat.2007.11.012.

Pacheco-Torgal, Fernando. 2014. "Eco-Efficient Construction and Building Materials Research under the EU Framework Programme Horizon 2020." *Construction and Building Materials* 51 (January): 151–62. https://doi.org/10.1016/j.conbuildmat.2013.10.058.

Pacheco-Torgal, Fernando, and Said Jalali. 2012. "Earth Construction: Lessons from the Past for Future Eco-Efficient Construction." *Construction and Building Materials* 29 (April): 512–19. https://doi.org/10.1016/j.conbuildmat.2011.10.054.

"Passive Building Design – Designing Buildings Wiki." n.d. Accessed July 11, 2018. https://www.designingbuildings.co.uk/wiki/Passive_building_design.

Pavlík, Zbyšek, Miloš Jerman, Jan Fořt, and Robert Černý. 2015. "Monitoring Thermal Performance of Hollow Bricks with Different Cavity Fillers in Difference Climate Conditions." *International Journal of Thermophysics* 36 (2–3): 557–68. https://doi.org/10.1007/s10765-014-1752-8.

Raftery, Paul, Marcus Keane, and James O'Donnell. 2011. "Calibrating Whole Building Energy Models: An Evidence-Based Methodology." *Energy and Buildings* 43 (9): 2356–64. https://doi.org/10.1016/j.enbuild.2011.05.020.

Rempel, Alexandra, and Alan Rempel. 2013. "Rocks, Clays, Water, and Salts: Highly Durable, Infinitely Rechargeable, Eminently Controllable Thermal Batteries for Buildings." *Geosciences* 3 (1): 63–101. https://doi.org/10.3390/geosciences3010063.

Remund, Jan, Esther Slavisberg, and Stefan Kunz. n.d. "Meteonorm."

Royapoor, Mohammad, and Tony Roskilly. 2015. "Building Model Calibration Using Energy and Environmental Data." *Energy and Buildings* 94 (May): 109–20. https://doi.org/10.1016/j.enbuild.2015.02.050.

Ryan, Emily M., and Thomas F. Sanquist. 2012. "Validation of Building Energy Modeling Tools under Idealized and Realistic Conditions." *Energy and Buildings* 47 (April): 375–82. https://doi.org/10.1016/j.enbuild.2011.12.020.

Sartori, Igor, and Anne Grete Hestnes. 2007. "Energy Use in the Life Cycle of Conventional and Low-Energy Buildings: A Review Article." *Energy and Buildings* 39 (3): 249–57. https://doi.org/10.1016/j.enbuild.2006.07.001.

SCBI, U. 2006. "Sustainable Building and Construction Initiative: Information Note." Paris, France *DTIE*.

SIA 180. 2015. "SIA 180 Isolamento termico, protezione contro l'umidità e clima interno degli edifici." Zurich: SIA.

SIA 380/1. 2009. "380/1. Sia. L'energia termica nell'edilizia. Schweizer Norm Norme Suisse Norma Svizzera. SIA 380/1:2001 Costruzione /1 - PDF." 2009. http://docplayer.it/38582525-380-1-sia-l-energia-termica-nell-edilizia-schweizer-norm-norme-suisse-norma-svizzera-sia-380-1-2001-costruzione-1.html.

SIA 2024, Winfried Seidinger, and Martin Ménard. 2007. "SIA 2024 Cahier technique, conditions d'utilisation standard pour l'énergie et les installations du bâtiment." Zurich: SIA.

Stephan, André, Robert H. Crawford, and Kristel de Myttenaere. 2013. "A Comprehensive Assessment of the Life Cycle Energy Demand of Passive Houses." *Applied Energy* 112 (December): 23–34. https://doi.org/10.1016/j.apenergy.2013.05.076.

University of Wisconsin. 2000. "TRNSYS – Transient System Simulation Program." 2000. http://sel.me.wisc.edu/trnsys/.

Williams, Colin, Steve Goodhew, Richard Griffiths, and Linda Watson. 2010. "The Feasibility of Earth Block Masonry for Building Sustainable Walling in the United Kingdom." *Journal of Building Appraisal* 6 (2): 99–108. https://doi.org/10.1057/jba.2010.15.

⑥ Low carbon building energy system: design and operation

Didier Vuarnoz
Julien Nembrini
Philippe Couty
Thibaut Schafer

This chapter aims to address the question of how to design and operate a building energy system that both minimizes its life cycle GHG emissions and respects the various energy targets of the 2000-Watt Society. To do so, we proposed a generic versatile modelling framework to assess the design of a building energy system using a multi-criteria approach, with a special focus on GHG emissions, the Cumulative Energy Demand and the Non-Renewable part of this demand.

Having a low impact on climate change is a key value of the future *smart living lab* building (SLB). Applied to the building sector (section 2.2) Figure 2.4, the Kaya identity indicates the global warming potential (GWP) of energy consumption as one of the main drivers for reducing greenhouse gas (GHG) emissions. Onsite renewable systems and energy storage are now widely used to reduce the operational impact of buildings. While the performances of these components are usually known when considered as individual elements (Hiremath et al. 2015, Peng et al. 2013), their implementation into an energy system and the resulting performances at the building level are not straightforward. In particular, one must be certain that the extra-embedded impact of on-site renewable systems and energy storage is counter-balanced by low operative impacts (Bourelle et al. 2013, Jusselme et al. 2016).

The proposed method compares simulated performances of possible building energy system scenarios, which consist of a certain number of choices in terms of the building's energy system (e.g., renewable energy system and energy storage). To better utilize the temporal variations in the primary energy and carbon footprints of the building's available energy supply sources, the modelling framework simulates the interplay and energy fluxes between the different elements that comprise the building's energy system in hourly increments. The framework is intended to help designers choose appropriate energy sources and storage systems systematically and has been tailored to accept new strategies for lowering GHG supply and / or demand. We propose two strategies: the first consists of an operating algorithm that chooses the energy supply for the building based on its GWP as measured by its $CO_{2\text{-}eq}$ emissions; the second consists in shifting part of the building's energy demand (in response to the high-carbon footprint of its energy supply) to a time when the energy supply footprint is more virtuous.

This chapter summarizes the various efforts that have been undertaken in the context of sustainable building energy systems as part of the SLB Research Program. We also exemplify the different aspects discussed in this chapter by taking the *smart living lab* building as a case study in so far as possible. The details of the modelling framework, boundaries of the building's energy system and performance indicator assessment techniques are presented in section 6.1. An operational strategy to minimize the carbon footprint of the building's energy supply is proposed in section 6.3. The building energy demand and a possible GHG emission reduction strategy by load-shift are presented in section 6.3. In section 6.4, we will discuss the various possible energy supply sources and how they should be designed to be incorporated in the modelling framework. An operational strategy to minimize the carbon footprint of the building's energy supply is proposed in section 6.5. Finally, we will apply the methodology to SLB to determine the most performant energy system relative to the 2000-Watt Society targets (Jochem et al. 2004) in section 6.5. The chapter ends with concluding remarks concerning the proposed modelling framework as a tool for designing and assessing the performance of building energy systems, and more specifically on the results obtained for the SLB project.

6.1 Modelling framework

We developed a modelling framework as a design tool, based on a systematic comparison of the life cycle performances of potential building energy systems. The procedure consisted of three successive steps: first, a number of scenarios comprised of specific combinations of building energy system elements were defined. Their performances were then assessed. Finally, the latter were compared in order to determine the most promising alternative. The key component of the modelling framework is a co-simulation platform wherein each scenario is considered. The principle functions of this platform are:

- To depict a large variety of possible building energy system configurations
- To assess the global performance indicators of a building's operational phase
- To test and assess new strategies for both the demand and supply

As shown on the opposite page Figure 6.1, the co-simulation platform considers an energy system as a set of varied elements related to one of three groups, namely the building's energy demand, the energy supply and energy storage. The following sections will provide more detailed information about the different elements represented by the pictograms Figure 6.1 and the way they must be modelled. The co-simulation platform connects the disparate components by exchanging relevant information about the operating conditions of the energy system and its elements. Except for storage, elements are modelled individually using specific tools. The secondary functions of the co-simulation platform are:

- Managing the different dynamic simulations processed by third-party softwares
- Handling the operating algorithm for the building's energy management
- Simulating the operation of the energy storage

The energy flows relative to each element were simulated at hourly increments over a one-year period to account for the various cyclic changes the system undergoes during its operation. Based on these energy flows, we then assessed life cycle performance indicators relative to the building's operational phase. Based on Swiss standards (SIA 2040 2011), a first set of indicators was chosen by which

Fig. 6.1　General concept of the building energy system modelling framework. Left: the different components available in the framework. Right: various assemblies of components depicting different building energy systems

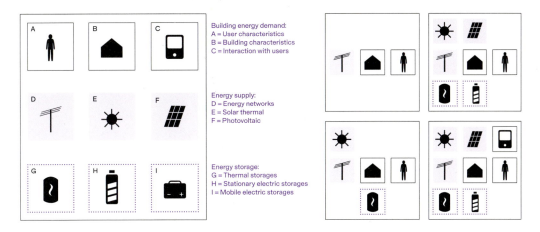

Fig. 6.2　The algorithm's principle is the delivery of electricity (purple line) from the source exhibiting the lowest GWP

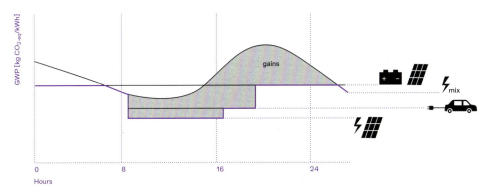

performance targets were set. This applies particularly to GHG emissions in kg $CO_{2\text{-eq}}$ /year·m^2 and the cumulative energy demand (CED) in $MJ_{oil\text{-eq}}$/year·m^2. These indicators, the overall system efficiency of the building's technical systems (HVAC installation, heat and power generation, domestic hot water supply, built-in lighting, etc.) and the fuels/energy carriers used were taken into account. Furthermore, we considered the portion of the energy requirement provided by non-renewable resources (CED_{nr}, also in $MJ_{oil\text{-eq}}$/year·m^2). Indicators were assessed at the building scale throughout their entire life cycle based on a cradle-to-grave framework (extraction of resources, manufacturing, use and final disposal of the product). They are assessed in the following manner:

$$EI_O = [\,\Sigma\,(E_{RE,i} \cdot CF_{RE}) + (E_{ES,i} \cdot CF_{ES,i}) + (E_{G,i} \cdot CF_{G,i}) - E_{RE,exp}(CF_{G,i} - CF_{exp,i})\,]\,/\,ERA$$

EI_O	Operational environmental impact under consideration (in our case, GHG emissions, the CED and its non-renewable portion CED_{nr})
E	Energy flow
CF	Conversion factor of the indicator in question
ERA	Energy reference area

Indices are used to describe:
RE	renewable energy system[14]
ES	energy storage
G	energy from grid
exp	exports
i	time interval

[14] Depending on the standard considered, the perimeter of renewable sources can vary. For example, SIA 2040 (2011) does not consider geothermal sources inside the assessment perimeter.

The benefits of implementing photovoltaic (PV) and electricity storage were assessed with CED_s, $CED_{nr,s}$ and GWP_s indicators, representing the mean annual energy and carbon footprint of each electric kWh delivered to the building. The notion of building autonomy was considered with the energy imported and exported annually [MWh/year], with the relative time of energy exchange from and to the grid [-], as well as the peak power of imports and exports during the evaluation year [kW]. A grid matching index, f_M, combines these three aspects of autonomy (Vuarnoz et al. 2018a). The described modelling framework was applied to a case study and is described in section 6.5.

6.2 Operational strategy

Most standard control systems for building energy management use electricity and its tariff as the sole criteria of choice (e.g. Loxone—smart home Miniserver[15] product, Siemens—Synco[16], and Alpiq—Gridsense product[17]). The algorithm presented in this chapter introduces the carbon footprint of energy flux as a key parameter for reducing the use of energy sources with a high global warming potential. We define the carbon footprint as the amount of associated life cycle GHG emissions (kg $CO_{2\text{-eq}}$) per unit of energy (kWh). The algorithm's working principle is presented on

[15] Loxone—smart home product Miniserver: https://www.loxone.com/enus

[16] Siemens—Synco: https://www.siemens.com/global/en/home.html

[17] Gridsense: https://www.gridsense.ch

Figure 6.2. Our algorithm aims to simulate the energy flows of a hypothetical building with defined energy requirements and to test the proposed energy management strategy over a given period. This algorithm can also be used for regulating energy flows in an existing building.

We have developed the first practical application of this operational strategy for the future *smart living lab* building. The most sophisticated building energy system uses building-integrated photovoltaic panels (BiPV) installed on the facades and roof, fixed batteries and the batteries of electric vehicles connected to the building. The algorithm makes it possible to use only parts (or none) of the available equipment and to interfere (or not) with users' activity by load shift (see section 6.3.2).

Simulations allow for the overview of an entire year's phenomena in hourly increments in just a few seconds. The scenarios presented in Section 6.5 can be introduced and compared by modifying specific parameters of the technical equipment (battery size or technology, for example). The carbon footprint of energy sources was assessed using a life cycle cradle-to-grave approach (see section 6.4).

The regulation algorithm works according to a decision tree Figure 6.3. Thanks to CF_{GHG}, we can compare the potential sources of energy that can be used to supply the building. The algorithm chooses the "cleanest" instantaneous energy source combination to meet the building's electricity demand. Based on this, a decision tree that includes all the technical equipment is created to emulate the energy system's operation. The performances of other scenarios can also be assessed by limiting the algorithm to the essential branches of the decision tree. To validate the accuracy of the algorithm, two types of tests were carried out: the first confirmed the quality of the decision tree and the second substantiated the return value (i.e. the quantity) of the simulation. Fixed weather values were considered to validate the algorithmic regulation. The algorithm's choice of recurring actions was investigated in Schafer and al. (Schafer and al. 2017).

6.3 Building energy system demand

In this section, we will define the building energy demand (BED) and how it must be assessed so as to be incorporated into the modelling framework, as well as discuss the main challenges of provisional BED assessment. In the second section, we will explore the possibility of shifting part of the building's energy demand as a potential solution to mitigate GHG emissions. This could help in reducing GHG emissions by decreasing the energy demand until phases when the energy supply footprint is more virtuous.

Fig. 6.3   Algorithm decision tree

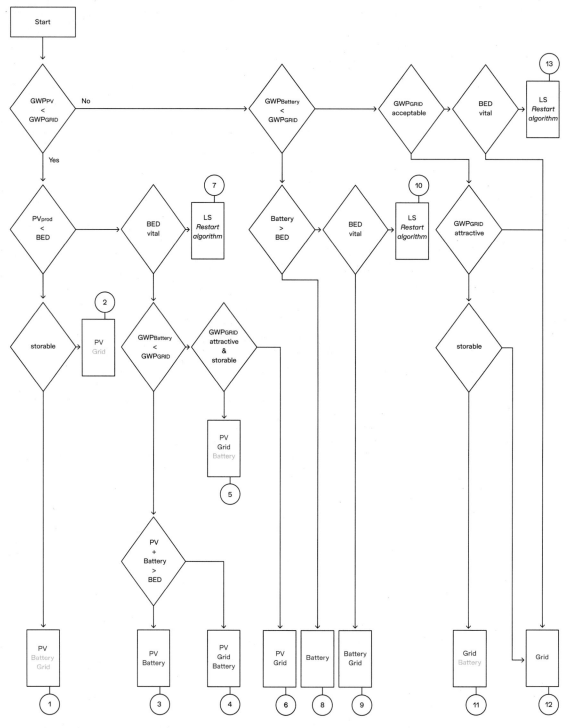

Acceptable: low (relative to a chosen threshold)
Attractive: very low (relative to a chosen threshold)
BED: Building Energy Demand
LS: Load Shift
Energy flux: from / to

6.3.1 Building energy demand

A building's energy demand is generated by various needs including appliances, lighting, heating and cooling, domestic water and ventilation[18]. To incorporate demand into the modelling framework described in section 6.1, it must be assessed during the building design stage in hourly increments over one reference year. To that aim, commercial solutions for dynamic building performance simulation (DBPS) exist (e.g. Lesosai[19], TRNSYS[20] and energyPLUS[21]). The quantity of final energy also had to be considered in order to take into account the overall system efficiency of the building's various technical systems, applied to each of the end-use sectors.

National standards are often considered as input parameters related to building usage (SIA 2024 2015, ASHRAE 90.1 2004) when sizing the energy infrastructure needed to meet energy demand for normal use of the planned building. For more accurate assessment, a multitude of other models have been developed. (Yan et al. 2015, Hong et al. 2016). However, the difficulty of accurately predicting how the building will actually be used naturally generates a gap between the assessments performed at the design phase and real energy consumption during operation.

As is the case for many modern constructions in temperate climates, several energy demand assessments based on different architectural feasibility studies for the future *smart living lab* building (Vuarnoz et al. 2016, Vuarnoz et al. 2019) confirm that electrical appliances and lighting use the most energy. Moreover, they are largely dependent on the behaviour of the building's users. As the SLB will mainly be used for academic work, we wanted to find out more about academics and the impact of their working schedules and energy demands (i.e. equipment) on the building's overall energy demand. We therefore used the results of a survey based of approximately 1500 participants from the three *smart living lab* academic partners (Maeder et al. 2015). In a second phase, we also took quantitative measurements of the occupancy rate and equipment energy use in the *smart living lab*'s temporary offices. (Verma et al. 2017, Vuarnoz et al. 2018b). The goal was to better determine occupancy rates and equipment energy use for the future SLB co-workers.

Occupancy in a given area of a building was modelled in DBPS with a nominal occupancy density P_o, represented in (p/m^2) and then multiplied by an hourly occupancy rate f_{occ} (–). The assessments of P_o and f_{occ} were evaluated for the office portion of the *smart living lab* building using two methods: the survey and the room occupancy measurement campaign. The results obtained were then compared to the values proposed in the Swiss standards SIA (SIA 2024 2015) Figure 6.4. While the survey method provides more accurate information about the time increments during the occupancy rate than do the SIA standards, the robustness of the results was still not as high as those obtained through direct measurement of room occupancy. One reason for this is that the

---

[18] In some certification procedures, the BED does not necessarily include appliances.

[19] http://www.lesosai.com
[20] http://www.trnsys.com
[21] https://energyplus.net

Fig. 6.4   Electric equipment use in office from various sources

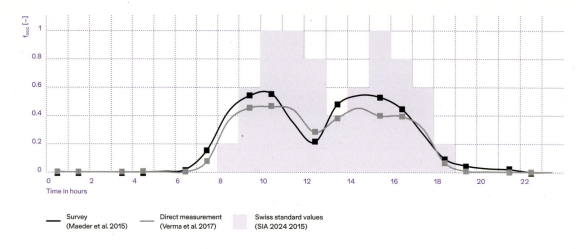

Fig. 6.5   Electric equipment profile according to the Swiss standard and the measurements at the *smart living lab* temporary offices

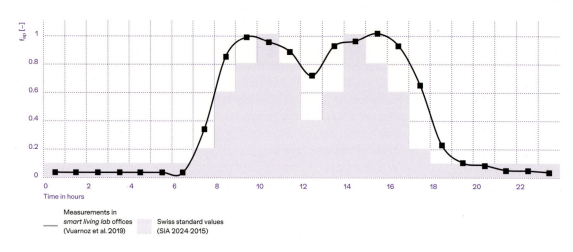

Tab. 6.6   Description of the various input parameters used for the different BED assessments presented in Figure 6.7

	Occupancy		Equipment	
	SIA	Measures	SIA	Measures
1	×		×	
2		×	×	
3	×			×
4		×		×

Fig. 6.7   Building's final energy demand resulting from the various input parameters detailed in Table 6.6

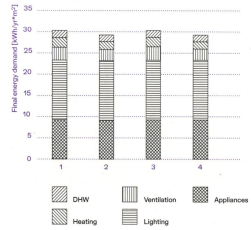

survey method considered the building as a whole. Hence, a given worker can be in the building but not necessarily in his or her office. The answers in the survey are less reliable than the direct measurements.

We dynamically modelled energy use for the equipment using a nominal energy density (P_a) in W/m² and an hourly factor (f_{ap}). For the design phase, these values were taken from Swiss standards, e.g. SIA 2024 (SIA 2015). f_{ap} was measured in the *smart living lab* temporary offices in Fribourg (Vuarnoz et al. 2019). The electric equipment were assessed using the Swiss standard and direct measurements, respectively ^{Figure 6.5}. The stand-by mode of appliances is over-estimated in the Swiss standard. However, the f_{ap} data obtained from the measurements shows generally higher figures than do the standards for non-occupancy periods. The effective nominal energy density P_a measured in the temporary *smart living lab* office was 5.34 W/m² versus 7.00 W/m² for the Swiss standard value, respectively (SIA 2024, 2015).

We next investigated the impact on the BED of using standards or measured values ^{Figure 6.7} for both occupancy rates and appliances, based on consecutive changes of the input parameter in DBPSs ^{Table 6.6}. To optimally adapt to the conditions for which the measurements were produced, we considered an office building in Fribourg, Switzerland, of roughly the same size as the SLB (ERA: 4355 m²). The full description of this case study is available (Vuarnoz et al. 2019). In this case study, no photovoltaic or solar thermal panels were considered and heat was provided by a heat pump. Thus, the main source of energy was electricity.

The building energy demand assessments ^{Figure 6.7} were obtained by changing input parameters ^{Table 6.6}. Although daily patterns of energy consumption can differ substantially, the differences over a one-year period were negligible. The refinement of the occupancy rate had a stronger impact than did the refinement of equipment use. The combination of both effects revealed a 3% decline in the final annual energy demand.

6.3.2 Encouraging users to shift electrical load based on carbon content information

In addition to infrastructure that shifts the building's energy demand away from high carbon-footprint phases, encouraging occupants to modify their individual energy demand towards more virtuous phases is also an excellent potential solution. However, this strongly depends on occupants' perception of the notion of "carbon footprint," a term that is often heard, particularly as relates to transportation, where the importance of reducing carbon emissions is generally acknowledged. However, most people only have rudimentary knowledge of how they personally can reduce carbon emissions in their daily lives, notably at home and at work.

One reason for this is that many people are simply unaware that different sources of electricity have different carbon footprints. Hence, by choosing the "right" source, they can help to lower carbon emissions. The second reason is that when discussing environmental impacts, people tend to focus on reduction, e.g. reduction of waste or lowering heating set points, which is often associated with reducing costs. Thus, many users cannot imagine they can lower their electricity carbon footprint without reducing the amount of energy they consume.

Moreover, the remote, highly dynamic nature of electricity production translates into an intangible, ephemeral notion of "virtuous" behaviour. Users must understand the dynamics and be attentive in order to positively impact their footprint. The use of automatic systems, such as those presented in section 6.1. (Costanza et al. 2014) studied the behaviour of users interacting with such systems. However, the focus in the present approach is on exploring non-automatic solutions to help people reduce their carbon footprints at home and/or work by raising their awareness of:

1) the carbon footprint of their electricity sources
2) less carbon-intensive periods in which to do certain activities
3) the overall impact of changing behaviour and routines.

In a first study, the aim was to create a prototype application that would help users identify the source of their electricity and how carbon intensive it is at any given point in the day. The objective was also to help them make decisions about how they could postpone or advance the timing of certain activities over the course of the day to lower their carbon footprint rather than reduce their activities. Examples of similar research (Kjeldskov et al. 2015), (Brewer et al. 2015, Bourgeois et al. 2014) focus on displacing ("shifting") the electricity demand. However, none have been found to directly tackle the non-intuitive notion of carbon content.

To understand how the relationship between carbon emissions and electricity consumption is viewed by energy experts, seven experts were asked to explain this relationship to three different hypothetical audiences (a seven year-old child, the person sitting in front of them on the train and an architect) using sketches. These sketches served as mental models to extract key elements that were then used in the prototype.

This prototype, named Oïkos [Figure 6.8], lets users see where electricity comes from at different times of day and how carbon-intensive it is (indicated by colour). It also allows them to create what-if scenarios in which they can place different daily activities at different times of day to see the overall impact of these changes on their carbon footprint.

In a second study, the first goal was to understand the pattern of electricity usage in a typical research office environment.

Fig. 6.8   Oikos Load-shifting prototype – carbon content, what-if (regular use and after shift)

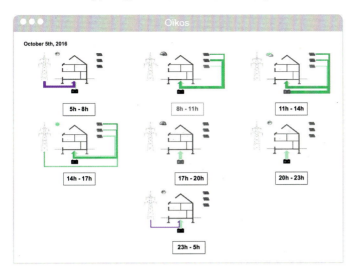
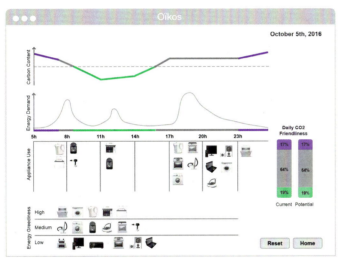
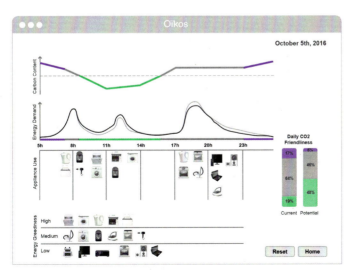

Fig. 6.9 Difference in load between baseline period and treatment period (email notification) for group 1 (mean and rolling mean). A negative value in the afternoon and a positive value in the morning indicates a shift

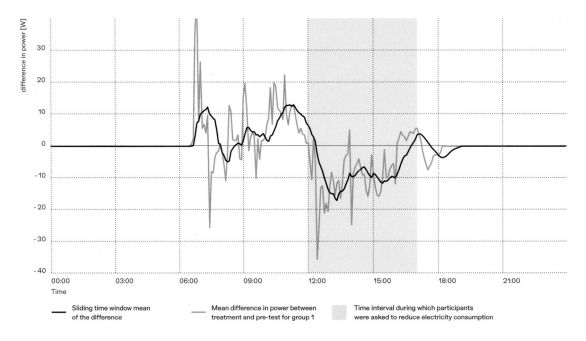

Fig. 6.10 Difference in load between baseline period and post-treatment period for group 1 (mean and rolling mean). Load shifting is less evident

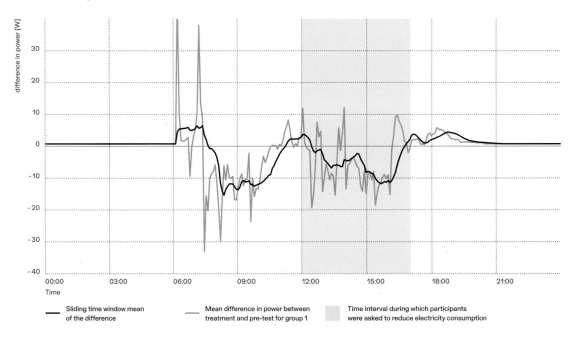

The second goal was to investigate the user-driven potential for carbon-based electricity load shifting in such a context. Similar studies involving users in Switzerland include shifting electricity demand in the housing context (Weber et al. 2016) and increasing energy consumption awareness in the office context (SME 2014). The present study differs in that it monitors individuals' electricity consumption and their reactions to notifications. It involved an eleven-week study to thirteen participants in their work context during which the power consumption of their personal devices was recorded. Users were asked to avoid electricity consumption in the afternoon (12 pm – 5 pm), which was identified as a carbon-intensive phase in Switzerland. Tips were offered to help people shift loads to other time periods. Users then received daily email information about their consumption inside and outside the carbon-intensive period. An analysis of the baseline data prior to the experiment allowed us to extract typical load profiles, which were then compared with standardized ones (section 6.3.1).

Although participants did not rate the information contained in the emails as very useful, the difference in daily load profile between the notification period versus that of the baseline shows that the emails nonetheless served as reminders to participants (for instance, raising users' awareness about powering-off equipment. Regarding the actual load shifting away from the proposed time periods, a difference was observed between the two periods ^{Figure 6.9}, but the small sample size together with great variations in the load profiles resulted in a lack of statistical significance. The load shift was clearly less important after the notification period, though the overall power load diminished ^{Figure 6.10}.

Ultimately, the development of the prototype and feedback from users stressed the fact that for users to plan their activities, an interface for carbon-based shifting must include some predictive information about carbon content (Kjeldskov et al. 2015). The use of "what if" scenarios actually depends on a reasonably accurate estimation of the evolution of the associated carbon content. Large variations in baseline load profile patterns between users, even within the same organizational unit, were translated into differing potential for carbon-based load shifting (Nembrini et al. In Prep) and should be taken into account by the interface. Such variations may be due to individual, organizational or technical reasons. The beneficial impact of periodical reminders was proven, as was the case in similar research (Hasselqvist et al 2016, SME 2014). However, negative comments from users about the semantics of the notifications highlighted the challenge of meaningfully conveying the notion of electricity carbon content.

In order to simulate the behaviour observed during the second experiment, changing the load profile by shifting load according to a percentage of the overall consumption should faithfully model best practices (decrease of 11% ^{Figure 6.10}).

However, the lack of statistical significance in the present results, along with a wide range of impacts reported by the literature, led the authors to conclude that the subject needed more attention prior to integrating it in the simulation scenarios described in section 6.5.

6.4 Supply of the building energy system

This section consists of three parts. The first focuses on the electricity grid as a possible energy network in which a building is embedded. The second considers photovoltaics as possible on-site renewable energy source. The third explores energy storage and the electro-chemical Li-Ion battery more specifically. The choice of these specific technologies as elements of the building energy system was driven by the target case study, namely the SLB (Section 1.2).

6.4.1 Electric grid

In the current life cycle impact assessment (LCIA), yearly averaged conversion factors (CFs) for a national electricity mix (Itten et al. 2014) are widely used to convert energy into potential environmental impacts. As CFs are expressed with the kWh as their functional unit, they are considered as environmental footprints. The proportion of technologies used to generate electricity constantly varies. Thus, each kWh at the consumer's disposal does not have the same environmental impact over time. To be incorporated in the modelling framework discussed in section 6.1, hourly electricity CFs for GHG emissions (kg CO_{2-eq}/kWh), the primary energy used, and its non-renewable portion (both in MJ_{oil-eq}/kWh) are compulsory data. The variation obtained in life cycle indicators, especially those related to GHG emissions, should be the pillars of the operational strategy for managing the building's energy system (see section 6.3.2 and 6.2). Moreover, LCIA involving hourly CFs is more accurate, especially when electricity demand varies with time, as is the case with buildings. At present, hourly descriptions of the life cycle impacts of electricity are only retrospective.

CFs were not available for the Swiss mix and thus were assessed within the scope of the SLB Research Program. The details of the methodology used to obtain the hourly CFs of a given grid are explained by Vuarnoz and Jusselme (Vuarnoz and Jusselme 2018b). The results are based on an attributional LCA and extensive inventories of electricity generation Figure 6.11. In this figure, CF_{GHG} was plotted as it was (lower track). However, to convey the meaning of these results in an intelligible way, we transformed CF_{CED} into the primary energy factor (PEF, centre curve). In the upper track, we converted CF_{CEDnr} into a ratio representing the amount of non-renewable energy ($r_{nr} = CF_{CEDnr}/CF_{CED}$). A summary of statistics based on an hourly CF

Fig. 6.11 Hourly variation of the primary energy factor (PEF), the non-renewable ratio (r_{nr}) and GHG emissions conversion factor (CF_{GHG}) of the Swiss electricity mix. Reference time is GMT+1 (Vuarnoz and Jusselme, 2018b)

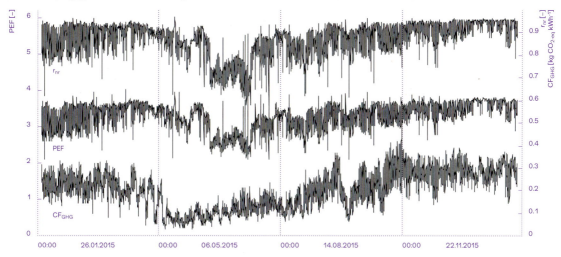

Tab. 6.12 Summary of statistics based on hourly conversion factors for the GHG emission conversion factor (CF_{GHG}), the CED (CF_{CED}) and the CED_{nr} (CF_{CEDnr}) for the Swiss mix and those of surrounding countries for a one-year period in 2015–2016 (Vuarnoz and Jusselme, 2018b)

	CF_{GHG}		CF_{CED}		CF_{CEDnr}	
Country	μ^y [kg $CO_{2\text{-}eq}$/kWh]	CV^y [–]	μ^y [$MJ_{oil\text{-}eq}$/kWh]	CV^y [–]	μ_c^y [$MJ_{oil\text{-}eq}$/kWh]	CV^y [–]
Austria	0.349	0.222	12.046	0.046	10.446	0.041
Germany	0.851	0.078	13.615	0.014	13.343	0.017
France	0.078	0.306	12.958	0.037	12.287	0.051
Swiss DP	0.040	0.389	11.412	0.149	9.7017	0.246
Swiss mix	0.206	0.410	11.859	0.109	10.458	0.181

Fig. 6.13 Hourly variation of the Swiss mix emission factor during a representative week obtained from the aggregation of a one-year assessment period (Vuarnoz and Jusselme, 2018b)

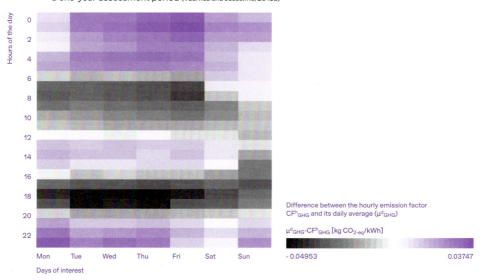

assessment is given for several countries ^{Table 6.12}. In this table, the mean annual value (μ^y) and a variation coefficient (CV^y, defined as the ratio of the standard deviation σ^y of the mean value μ^y) are given. The variation coefficients obtained indicate that Switzerland is a good candidate for $CO_{2\text{-eq}}$-based load shifting.

The hourly emission factor variation was explored based on a representative week taken from a full year of Swiss mix assessments ^{Figure 6.13}. Using a heat map, we can see a clear trend in the daily evolution of the Swiss grid $CO_{2\text{-eq}}$ footprint, which makes a "w" shape during the weekdays and whose carbon footprint is generally higher at night.

The heat map visualization technique is particularly useful for determining the best time to trigger load-shift when implementing demand-side management. Broad use of demand-based strategies changes the technology bouquet involved in electricity generation, and therefore would require an adapted approach involving marginal production.

6.4.2 Building PV integration

To incorporate PV into the modelling framework presented in section 6.1, one must consider the carbon and energy footprints (CF_{GHG}, CF_{CED} and CF_{CEDnr}) as well as the hourly energy generation rate. PV technologies can be divided into two main categories: the first, which represents approximately 90 % of the market share (Fraunhofer Institute 2017), is based on silicon-absorbing material (c-Si); the second is based on thin film technologies with a high potential for reducing embodied energy, such as amorphous silicon (a-Si), Copper Indium Gallium Selenide (CIS/CIGS), Cadmium Telluride (CdTe) and organic PV cell (OPC).

To calculate the theoretical energy production of a PV installation, the efficiency of the PV system is modelled by taking the characteristics of each of its components and the installation parameters into account and using simulation software (e.g. crmsolar[22] or PV syst[23]). The latitude, longitude and altitude of the installation location, as well as the inclination and orientation of panels on the roof and the facades should be specific to the project in question. We used hourly weather data files to perform dynamic hourly power output simulations, and we obtained an annual energy yield by totalling hourly power for a one-year period. The annual energy yield was obtained by totalling hourly power for a one-year period.

The PV life cycle is considered from "cradle to grave"—from the raw material used to make the PV panels and balance of system to the disposal and recycling of the installation. The environmental indicators CED, CED_{nr} and CF_{GHG} can be expressed per m^2 or per kWp by taking into account panel efficiency. The environmental impact factors were assessed using the EcoInvent database

[22] http://www.smarsys.com/services/gestion-de-parc-photovoltaique
[23] http://www.pvsyst.com/fr

(Frischknecht et al. 2005). Their efficiency was assessed based on the products available on the market in 2015.

Specific PV assessments must be done for each project. First, the PV layout and its dimensioning must be established. Then, hourly power output must be simulated. Finally, conversion factors must be assessed for each panel orientation. In the case of the SLB, the PV installation will be used for the roof and Building-Integrated (BI) PV for certain facades. All but one design (Alt. nb. 4) had a positive energy balance over one year. Two alternatives, Alt. nb.1 and Alt. nb. 2, show a positive balance close to zero. Alt. nb. 1 considers an equal surface of PV on the roof and BIPV on the east and west facades to increase daily production time. Alt. nb. 2 considers the entire roof area and only the necessary amount of BIPV on the west facade to obtain a net zero balance. In Alt. nb. 3, the entire available surface of the east and west facade (excluding window surfaces) and roof are covered with PV. Alt. nb. 4 considers PV on the roof surface only and thus has a negative energy load/generation balance. The various surface areas for each alternative are shown on Table 6.14.

Hourly simulations of power output were performed using crmsolar (smarsys 2017), with hourly weather data files from Meteo Suisse at Station Fribourg Posieux. The resulting annual energy balances for the four alternatives can be consulted on Table 6.15.

Our assessment of the environmental indicators per produced kWh (i.e. CF_{GHG}, CF_{CED} and CF_{CEDnr}) takes into account the building installation parameters for a thirty-year lifetime (IEA, 2015) and the installation's calculated annual energy yield in kWh/kWp. Table 6.16 gives an overview of the characteristics of the two photovoltaic technologies. As the building's orientation is not perfectly aligned with the geographic coordinates (15° shift), the obtained impact factors for the east and west panels are not the same.

6.4.3 Energy storage

In buildings, energy storage combined with intermittent renewable systems is a common solution for increasing the use of low-carbon energy produced on-site. Storage generates building energy autonomy and reduces the stress on the surrounding energy networks. Despite a large body of work on the environmental impact of energy storage considered as a single element (Hiremath et al. 2015), the impact on GHG emissions at the building level when embedded in the building energy system is relatively unexplored. The additional environmental impact of the energy undergoing the storage process should be considered, as other elements must then be added to the building energy system, each with its own embodied energy generation and losses.

A very synthetic model depicting the main features of the electricity storage operation (Vuarnoz et al. 2018a) is embedded within the co-simulation platform to mimic its operation. The model takes into account energy input/output efficiency (η) as well as the deterioration of the storage capacity over its service time in %/kwh, and depicts the GWP and amount of the stored energy at any given time. Moreover, one must consider conversion factors representing additional environmental impacts for each kWh processed by storage in order to assess the energy system in question. CFs are assessed based on an LCIA and the total energy processed during the storage system's lifetime. ^{Table 6.17} shows an example of the technology-related input parameters for a Li-Ion electrochemical battery.

Appropriate storage technology should be chosen based on the main objectives established for the building. In view of minimizing GHG emissions, this choice can be made based on the storage system's GWP. In order to do so, the GWP of the renewable energy stored and delivered by the energy storage would ideally be the sum of the CF_{GHG} of both the renewable energy and the storage, and should be lower than that of the electricity grid. The same reasoning could be applied to CF_{CED} when energy is prioritized.

When sizing energy storage capacity, building autonomy is typically an objective. Integrating electric vehicles (EVs) to enhance storage capacity during working hours is possible within our modelling framework. In this case, a cross-boundary energy valorisation was used both to manage the energy produced onsite and for mobility purposes. However, storage capacity has an effect on the performance indicators at the building level. The evolution of GHG emissions at the building level is presented when storage capacity size varies ^{Figure 6.18}. Our case study considers the architectural feasibility detailed by Vuarnoz et al. (Vuarnoz et al. 2019), Cd-Te PV technology ^{Table 6.16}, with a size that corresponds to Alt. 1 ^{Table 6.14}, and a storage battery with ideal environmental impacts (CF_{GHG} = CF_{CED} = CF_{CEDnr} = 0) and round-trip efficiency of 0.9. In both cases, the values converge at a horizontal asymptote. However, two clear tendencies appear depending on the pattern of exports, i.e., whether electricity exports to the grid are possible or not. If they are, the grid and its infrastructure are already used for electricity storage with no extra life cycle impacts. Therefore, implementing a battery storage system in a building can only make the impact balance heavier. When exporting electricity is impossible, local energy storage increases the building's autonomy and reduces GHG emissions at the building level ^{Figure 6.18}.

To have a positive impact on GHG emissions at the building level, an energy storage system should exhibit a maximum allowable GWP. The methodology used to assess the threshold at which environmental benefits occur and its application to a case study is fully detailed by Vuarnoz and Jusselme (Vuarnoz and Jusselme 2018c). The concept, which could be applied to any storage technology, in this case was applied to the GWP but could be applied to other conversion factors in a similar manner. The main outcomes are summarized

Tab. 6.14 Sizes of PV alternatives considered in this study

Alt. nb	1	2	3	4
East [m^2]	343	0	456	0
West [m^2]	343	225	445	0
Roof [m^2]	343	562	562	562

Tab. 6.15 Annual ratio of onsite renewable production divided by the building's energy consumption

	Alt. nb. 1	Alt. nb. 2	Alt. nb. 3	Alt. nb. 4
CdTe	1.00	1.00	1.48	0.80
Multi-Si	1.07	1.06	1.57	0.85

Tab. 6.16 Impact factors and efficiency of the different photovoltaic technologies considered in this study. PV panels on the roof are oriented south with a tilt of 30°

		Multi-Si (η = 15.1%)			CdTe (η = 13.5%)		
Technology	Facade	CF_{GHG} [kgCO$_{2-eq}$/kWh]	CF_{CED} [MJ$_{oil-eq}$/kWh]	CF_{CEDnr} [MJ$_{oil-eq}$/kWh]	CF_{GHG} [kgCO$_{2-eq}$/kWh]	CF_{CED} [MJ$_{oil-eq}$/kWh]	CF_{CEDnr} [MJ$_{oil-eq}$/kWh]
BIPV	East	0.132	2.297	1.956	0.094	1.522	1.406
BIPV	West	0.095	1.653	1.408	0.067	1.086	1.003
BIPV	North	0.172	2.958	2.562	0.122	1.968	1.819
BIPV	South	0.085	1.467	1.250	0.050	0.966	0.893
PV	Roof	0.059	1.017	0.866	0.041	0.662	0.612

Tab. 6.17 Efficiency, conversion factors and fading capacities factors for Li-Ion storage technologies (EV: Electric vehicle) (Vuarnoz et al. 2018a)

Alt. nb.	Technology	η [–]	CF_{GHG} [kgCO$_{2-eq}$/kWh]	CF_{CED} [MJ$_{oil-eq}$/kWh]	CF_{CEDnr} [MJ$_{oil-eq}$/kWh]	Fading capacity [%/kwh]
1	Li-Ion (graphite)	0.90	0.021	0.351	0.319	-5.65×10^{-4}
2	Li-Ion (titanate)	0.90	0.007	0.117	0.106	-3.44×10^{-4}
3	Li-Ion EV's	0.85	0.017	0.298	0.270	A) -6.00×10^{-4} B) -2.70×10^{-4}

A) Support for building purposes.
B) Support for mobility purposes.

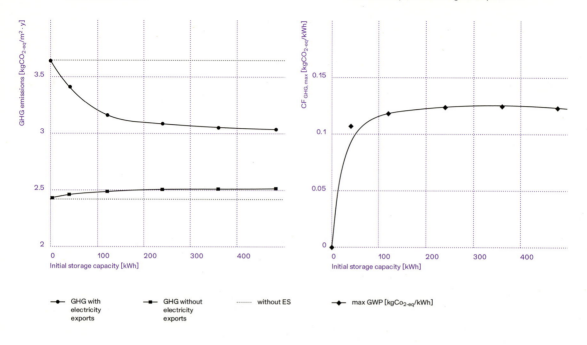

Fig. 6.18 Change in annual GHG emissions at the building level for an energy system with Li-Ion batteries of different capacities

Fig. 6.19 Maximum CO_{2-eq} footprint allowable for the energy storage to have a positive GHG emission balance when the export of overage is impossible.

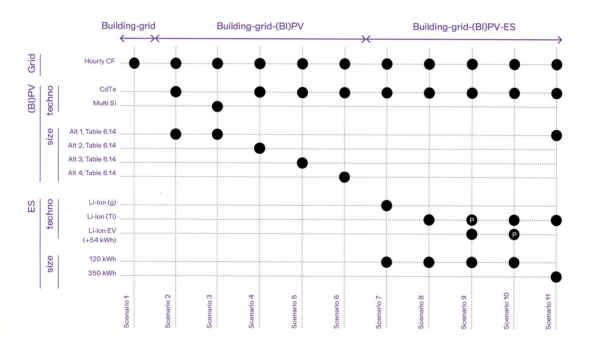

Fig. 6.20 Overview of the scenarios investigated in the study

on ^(Figure 6.19). Effectively, as seen in the previous figure ^(Figure 6.18), it is impossible to mitigate GHG emissions at the building level when exporting electricity from the building to the grid. As a result, a maximum allowable carbon footprint assessment is only possible without electricity exports to the grid. The results obtained are, of course, specific to the case study investigated.

6.5 Analysis of selected case studies

Given the ambitions as regards the performance of the future *smart living lab* building, this specific case study seems particularly relevant to the application of our modelling framework to evaluate the building's operational performance. The large body of material available for this project (e.g. hourly energy/carbon footprints of the supply sources, detailed final energy consumption rates, weather data and PV production assessment) also makes it easier to implement this case study in the modelling framework.

In this analysis, we have considered several alternative energy systems ^(Figure 6.20). However, carbon-based load shifting for GHG emission mitigation (see section 6.3.2) has not yet been assessed by computation. For all of the cases, exporting the surplus of onsite renewable energy that was not used or stored instantaneously was determined to be feasible.

Scenario 1 represents a situation wherein the grid is the building's sole electricity provider. The second group of scenarios (2–6) includes PV systems, thus allowing the building to consume its own renewable energy and export the surplus to the grid. By adding energy storage (scenarios 7–11), the building is able to become autonomous for some parts of the year instead of simply importing and exporting energy.

When considering PV panels, two scenarios can be used to compare two PV technologies (scenarios 2–3). Different sizes and orientations of PV ^(Table 6.14) were assessed for the technologies with the best life cycle performances (scenarios 4–6). In terms of energy storage, scenarios 7 and 8 compare two storage technologies with the same capacity (120 kWh). Increasing the storage capacity of the better of these two scenarios by adding electric cars provided us with scenarios 9 and 10. In scenario 9, the priority of charge is set for the stationary storage, while electric car batteries are given priority in scenario 10. Scenario 11 does not include cars but rather an increased battery capacity of 350 kWh.

6.5.1 Results and discussion

The results are summarized in ^(Figure 6.21) and consist of annual balances of selected performance indicators. A more in-depth analysis of the performance indicators obtained is available in Vuarnoz et al. (Vuarnoz et al. 2018a).

Fig. 6.21 Overview of the results obtained in the different scenarios investigated in the study. Target values given by SIA 2040 (2011) are indicated by the vertical lines in the three environmental impacts (GHG, CED and CED_{nr}). Similarly, the three vertical lines in the three energy supply indicators (GWP_s, CED_s and $CED_{nr,s}$) indicate the baseline obtained by the sole use of grid electricity Table 6.12

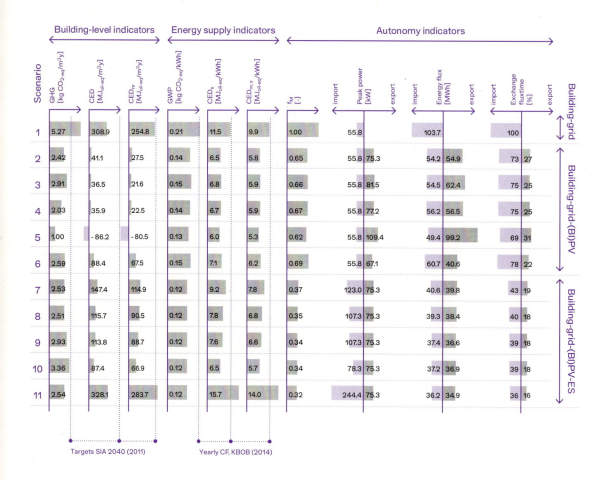

In scenario 1, which consists of a building with grid mix energy only, the GHG emission target was far from being met. Despite the fact that the CED easily met the target, the gap between the CED_{nr} performance and its target increased.

All systems with PV and a connection to a grid met the SIA 2040 targets. Implementing a photovoltaic system based on the Net Zero Energy Building (NZEB) objective makes it possible to reduce GHG emissions by a factor of at least two, and the CED by a factor of at least four, compared to scenario 1. Implementing PV in the energy system makes it possible to reduce the amount of energy imported from the grid by a factor of nearly two, and allows for electricity export during some periods of the year. These energy exports have a dramatic effect on the CED and CED_{nr}, causing them to become negative (see equation of section 6.1). As a result, scenario 5 has the best energy and GHG emission performances. When comparing the two proposed PV technologies, CdTe panels allow for better performances overall, despite the superior efficiency of the multi-Si panels $^{Table\ 6.16}$.

When considering energy systems that include a PV system, an energy storage system and a connection with a grid (scenarios 7–11), on-site use of excess renewable energy reduces the electricity imported from the grid. Compared to scenario 2, incorporating energy storage does not help in meeting better building-level performance indicators. Moreover, implementing storage with an increased energy capacity (scenario 11) actually worsens these indicators, making it impossible to meet the CED_{nr} target. In scenario 11, the energy indicators (CED_s and $CED_{nr,s}$) of the supply mix are also inferior to those obtained using the grid alone. The building's autonomy proved not to be strictly proportional to the storage capacity.

Energy supply indicators evolved in much the same way, as the building-level indicators were subject to the targets described previously; the system design that best supplies the building with good-quality energy (in terms of energies and GHG emissions) does not involve electricity storage. When a large storage capacity is implemented, the electricity mix supplied to the building has a larger cumulative energy footprint (CED_s and $CED_{nr,s}$) than the grid.

Autonomy indicators are useful for comparing the performance features of different PV and storage system scenarios. Based on the set of scenarios analysed here, f_M could be mitigated by a third, when PV is included in the energy system infrastructure. Another third can be reduced by using energy storage. The volume of electricity imported to the building is drastically reduced by the use of PV. Adding electricity storage is another way to slightly mitigate electricity imports. Autonomy has clear economic value by reducing the amount of electricity imported from the grid. The cumulative time of imports could be reduced by roughly a quarter with PV and roughly 60% with PV and storage. Export time tends to hover at approximately 25% and 18% respectively for systems that use PV and those that use both PV and storage.

The system design that best meets the 2000-Watt Society targets (GHG emissions, CED and CED_{nr}) includes PV panels but not storage. The reason for this lies in the assumption of an unrestricted opportunity for electricity exports to the grid. The highest share of renewable energy used at the building level was achieved with scenario 4 (35% of its CED) and the lowest with scenario 11 (14% of its CED), which did not respect the CED_{nr} target.

When it comes to GWP-based versus traditional energy-management procedures, a small but noticeable reduction in GHG emissions can only be achieved when energy storage is an integral part of the energy system. A 1% reduction in GHG emissions is achieved at the cost of nearly three times more primary energy (Vuarnoz et al. 2018a). Indeed, carbon-based load-levelling by grid mix storage has a strong impact on primary energy use. The battery should then be charged with a renewable source rather than with electricity from the grid.

It is important to clarify the inherent limitations of the present study. First, LCA is known to be a relevant, powerful approach for performing comparative studies. However, it also has major drawbacks when it comes to generating robust absolute values, especially in our case when dealing with construction material and uncertainties in terms of the energy source. Moreover, the use of an attributional approach in the grid mix LCA leads to the assumption that a given building's design and associated energy demand would not influence the proportion of the different means of production for the electricity mix. In the case of widespread use of renewables, energy storage and load-shifting in buildings, the electricity demand from traditional grids would diminish and therefore not be produced with the same energy mix. Thus, a consequential approach should be adopted when scaling up the assessment to a larger ensemble of buildings. Lastly, we assumed that the export of surplus electricity produced by onsite renewables can always be exported to the grid. This specific assumption is valid in the temporal and geographical context of our case study but not necessarily in other circumstances.

Synthesis

Buildings' energy demands vary over time, as does the availability of a low-carbon energy supply. Life cycle environmental impact assessments that are performed traditionally, with yearly averaged conversion factors, do not make it easy to take full advantage of these temporal variations. Therefore, in this chapter, we proposed reviewing two aspects developed in the scope of the SLB Research Program. These consisted of:
1) a versatile modelling framework to assist in the design of a building energy system, given selected environmental constraints and multi-criteria objectives
2) an operational control algorithm to ensure that the building always uses the energy source with the lowest global warming potential.

In the second part of this chapter, we tailored the modelling framework to the case of the SLB. To do so, we identified the potential technologies that could be implemented for each element. For the demand, this included the building energy consumption and carbon-based load shifting. For the supply, this included the electrical grid, an onsite photovoltaic system and energy storage systems. We applied the modelling framework and operational control algorithm to the SLB context and several plausible building energy system scenarios. The balance equation used in the modelling framework with an asymmetric weighting factor for energy export allowed us to place the building in a given grid context that could evolve over time. However, predicting electricity mixes for the medium and long term on an hourly basis is a true challenge. Based on the results obtained using the modelling framework for the different scenarios, we concluded the following points.

First, the system design that best meets the 2000-Watt Society targets (GHG emissions, CED and CED_{nr}) includes PV panels, but not storage. These sustainability targets cannot be met without renewables. Second, with a PV system based on the NZEB target, the building can operate autonomously 25 % of the time. When energy storage is added, autonomy increases to 60 %. Third, energy storage has negative consequences on the building's carbon and primary energy indicators when the exportation of renewable energy surplus is possible. Finally, when developing an innovative energy management procedure, one must be sure that the optimization of a given indicator does not negatively impact other important indicators.

Acknowledgements

The authors would like to thank Dr Hamed Alavi and Dr Himanshu Verma from the Human-IST laboratory at Fribourg University for sharing the measurement data on occupancy at the Blue Hall. We would also like to thank all our colleagues from the *smart living lab* for their participation in the office equipment measurement campaign.

Partners

Building2050 / EPFL: Didier Vuarnoz, Thomas Jusselme, Endrit Hoxha, Stefano Cozza, Margaux Peltier

Human-IST / Fribourg University: Denis Lalanne, Agnès Lisowska Masson, Julien Nembrini, Thalia Georgardou, Pierre Vanhulst

Energy Institute / HEIA-FR: Elena-Lavinia Niederhauser, Thibaut Schafer, Gabriel Magnin

References

Bourgeois, Jacky, Janet van der Linden, Gerd Kortuem, Blaine A. Price, and Christopher Rimmer. 2014. "Conversations with My Washing Machine: An in-the-Wild Study of Demand Shifting with Self-Generated Energy." In *Proceedings of the 2014 ACM International Joint Conference on Pervasive and Ubiquitous Computing – UbiComp '14 Adjunct*, 459–70. Seattle, Washington: ACM Press. https://doi.org/10.1145/2632048.2632106.

Bourrelle, Julien S., Inger Andresen, and Arild Gustavsen. 2013. "Energy Payback: An Attributional and Environmentally Focused Approach to Energy Balance in Net Zero Energy Buildings." *Energy and Buildings* 65: 84–92.

Brewer, Robert S., Nervo Verdezoto, Thomas Holst, and Mia Kruse Rasmussen. 2015. "Tough Shift: Exploring the Complexities of Shifting Residential Electricity Use Through a Casual Mobile Game." In *Proceedings of the 2015 Annual Symposium on Computer-Human Interaction in Play – CHI PLAY '15*, 307–17. London, United Kingdom: ACM Press. https://doi.org/10.1145/2793107.2793108.

Costanza, Enrico, Joel E. Fischer, James A. Colley, Tom Rodden, Sarvapali D. Ramchurn, and Nicholas R. Jennings. 2014. "Doing the Laundry with Agents: A Field Trial of a Future Smart Energy System in the Home." In *Proceedings of the 32nd Annual ACM Conference on Human Factors in Computing Systems – CHI'14*, 813–22. Toronto, Ontario, Canada: ACM Press. https://doi.org/10.1145/2556288.2557167.

Frischknecht, Rolf, Niels Jungbluth, Hans-Jörg Althaus, Gabor Doka, Roberto Dones, Thomas Heck, Stefanie Hellweg, et al. 2005. "The Ecoinvent Database: Overview and Methodological Framework (7 Pp)." *The International Journal of Life Cycle Assessment* 10 (1): 3–9. https://doi.org/10.1065/lca2004.10.181.1.

Smarsys. 2017. "Gestion de parc photovoltaïque – smarsys." n.d. Accessed December 4, 2018. http://www.smarsys.com/services/gestion-de-parc-photovoltaique/.

Hasselqvist, Hanna, Cristian Bogdan, and Filip Kis. 2016. "Linking Data to Action: Designing for Amateur Energy Management." In *Proceedings of the 2016 ACM Conference on Designing Interactive Systems – DIS '16*, 473–83. Brisbane, QLD, Australia: ACM Press. https://doi.org/10.1145/2901790.2901837.

Hiremath, Mitavachan, Karen Derendorf, and Thomas Vogt. 2015. "Comparative Life Cycle Assessment of Battery Storage Systems for Stationary Applications." *Environmental Science & Technology* 49 (8): 4825–33. https://doi.org/10.1021/es504572q.

Hong, Tianzhen, Sarah C. Taylor-Lange, Simona D'Oca, Da Yan, and Stefano P. Corgnati. 2016. "Advances in Research and Applications of Energy-Related Occupant Behavior in Buildings." *Energy and Buildings* 116 (March): 694–702. https://doi.org/10.1016/j.enbuild.2015.11.052.

Itten, René, Rolf Frischknecht, and Matthias Stucki. 2014. "Life Cycle Inventories of Electricity Mixes and Grid, Version 1.3." *Treeze Ltd., Uster, Switzerland.*

Jochem, Eberhard, Philipp Rudolf von Rohr, et al. 2004. "Steps towards a Sustainable Development. A White Book for R&D of Energy-Efficient Technologies." Edited by Eberhard Jochem. Novatlantis.

Jusselme, Thomas, Arianna Brambilla, Endrit Hoxha, Yingying Jiang, Didier Vuarnoz, Stefano Cozza. 2016. "Building 2050 Scientific concept and transition to the experimental phase". EPFL-Fribourg

Kjeldskov, Jesper, Mikael B. Skov, Jeni Paay, Dennis Lund, Tue Madsen, and Michael Nielsen. 2015. "Eco-Forecasting for Domestic Electricity Use." In *Proceedings of the 33rd Annual ACM Conference on Human Factors in Computing Systems*, 1985–1988. ACM.

Maeder, Thierry, Vincent Kaufmann, Luca Pattaroni, Derek Christie, Emmanuel Ravalet, Sébastien Munafò, and Virginie Baranger. 2016. "smart living lab: démarche de design social." EPFL.

Nembrini, Julien, Agnès Lisowska Masson, Didier Vuarnoz, Denis Lalanne. 2017. "Exploring the Potential Impacts of Shifting Energy Consumption in Work Envi-

ronments". (In prep).
Peng, Jinqing, Lin Lu, and Hongxing Yang. 2013. "Review on Life Cycle Assessment of Energy Payback and Greenhouse Gas Emission of Solar Photovoltaic Systems." *Renewable and Sustainable Energy Reviews* 19: 255–274.
PSE, AG. n.d. "Fraunhofer Institute For Solar Energy Systems ISE." *Photovoltaics Report*.
Schafer, Thibaut, Elena-Lavinia Niederhauser, Gabriel Magnin, and Didier Vuarnoz. 2018. "Development and Validation of an Intelligent Algorithm for Synchronizing a Low-Environmental-Impact Electricity Supply with a Building's Electricity Consumption." In *Proceedings of The 4th International Conference on Renewable Energy Technologies (ICRET 2018)*. IOP Conference Series.
SIA 2024. 2015. "Données d'utilisation des locaux pour l'énergie et les installations du bâtiment". Swiss Society of Engineers and Architect (Zurich) 1–152.
SIA 2040. 2011. "Efficiency path for energy". Swiss Society of Engineers and Architect (Zurich) 1–27.

SME. 2014. "Rapport 'Semaine Energie' ou comment inciter aux économies d'énergies par le changement de comportement. Bâtiment de l'hotel des Finances (HOFIN)". 13–17 janvier 2014. Service management de l'énergie de l'état (Geneva) 1-64. (Retrieved from http://ge.ch/sme/media/sme/files/fichiers/documents/rapport_se_hofin_liens.pdf)
SIA. 2011. "SIA 2040 / 2011 la voie SIA vers l'efficacité énergétique." SIA Société suisse des ingénieurs et des architectes.
Standard, ASHRAE, and Rocky Mountain Chapter. 2004. "Ansi / Ashrae / Iesna Standard 90.1-2004." *Energy Standard for Buildings except Low-Rise Residential Buildings*.
Verma, Himanshu, Hamed S. Alavi, and Denis Lalanne. 2017. "Studying Space Use: Bringing HCI Tools to Architectural Projects." In *Proceedings of the 2017 CHI Conference on Human Factors in Computing Systems*, 3856–66. ACM Press. https://doi.org/10.1145/3025453.3026055.
Vuarnoz, Didier, Stefano Cozza, Thomas Jusselme, Gabriel Magnin, Thibaut Schafer, Philippe Couty, and Elena-Lavinia Niederhauser. 2018a. "Integrating Hourly Life-Cycle Energy and Carbon Emissions of Energy Supply in Buildings." *Sustainable Cities and Society* 43: 305–316.
Vuarnoz, Didier, and Thomas Jusselme. 2018b. "Temporal Variations in the Primary Energy Use and Greenhouse Gas Emissions of Electricity Provided by the Swiss Grid." *Energy* 161: 573–582.

Vuarnoz, Didier, Thomas Jusselme, Stefano Cozza, Emmanuel Rey, and Marilyne Andersen. 2016. "Studying the Dynamic Relationship between Energy Supply Carbon Content and Building Energy Demand."
Vuarnoz, Didier, Endrit Hoxha, Stefano Cozza, Julien Nembrini, Thomas Jusselme. 2019. "Comparison between a Normative and a Reality-based Model of Building LCA." (In prep.)
Vuarnoz, Didier, Thomas Jusselme. 2018c. "Neutral Global Warming Potential Target for Electricity Storage as Threshold for Greenhouse Gas Emission Mitigation in Buildings.". *Proceedings of the PLEA 2018 conference: Smart and Healthy within the 2-degree Limit*.
Weber, Sylvain, Stefano Puddu, and Diana Pacheco. 2017. "Move It! How an Electric Contest Motivates Households to Shift Their Load Profile." *Energy Economics* 68: 255–270.
Yan, Da, William O'Brien, Tianzhen Hong, Xiaohang Feng, H. Burak Gunay, Farhang Tahmasebi, and Ardeshir Mahdavi. 2015. "Occupant Behavior Modeling for Building Performance Simulation: Current State and Future Challenges." *Energy and Buildings* 107: 264–278.

Process design

To ensure the applicability of the research developed towards helping the building take shape within ambitious performative goals, it was important not only to aim at supporting an existing design process, but also, and perhaps mostly, to support how to design the process itself. A fresh look at the iterative design process thus had to be taken, so as to make it supportive of a research-driven spirit and of an increased transparency and horizontality in decision making.

This third part introduces the dialogue-oriented approach that was developed to promote architectural quality alongside environmental performance and user satisfaction, while proposing new tools and defining specific objectives to ensure a constructive and efficient workflow from the designer's point of view.

⑦ Architecture in making

Florinel Radu

In this chapter, we argue that the desired qualities of the future *smart living lab* building are not a scientific challenge but rather a human and social one. Moreover, we posit that partial qualities linked to use, experimentation, environmental performance and context are only relevant when incorporated in the overall quality we call architecture. Their implementation depends on the capacity of various actors to get involved in a learning-by-doing process that leaves room for their divergent interests and the creation of shared values.

A research programme dedicated to the conception and realization of a building is rather rare. The *smart living lab*'s future building (SLB)[24] has given us the opportunity to explore and identify ways of influencing and supporting the process of its future construction. Fulfilling initial expectations is a key challenge when it comes to the design and realization of a building. In the case of the SLB, this challenge is paramount. In addition to the expectations of the politicians and citizens of Fribourg, the SLB must also meet the requirements of researchers in terms of its energy performance so as to serve as a research subject/object and to be a comfortable place for everyday activities. Like the goals for the project, the risks are equally high. The findings of the research programme presented in this book will be included in the design brief. The SLB vision, which is also part of the brief, states that the SLB should be "the architectural transposition of use value. It should offer a sensorial experience, connect and reassure people. It should be resilient to new uses and technology, as well as to the loss of obsolete ones... The building's performance assessment should be addressed globally and from cradle to grave. It should consider all embodied and operative impacts related to material and energy consumption, including all components in the perimeter of the building's envelope"[25].

Given the gap between academic research and practice, we must ask ourselves whether the designers, jury and builders will be able to understand and respond to this challenge? Given the SLB's role as a precursor, will the legal framework—with its myriad norms and procedures—allow for its realization? The SLB vision also states that the building "should be ready for incremental growth and the redefinition of uses". While we understand that the SLB must be designed so as to be capable of constant evolution, we wonder how this will be compatible with contemporary Swiss culture, which expects well-finished, almost perfect buildings. The SLB process involves an array of actors including politicians, administrators, researchers from various disciplines, architects, engineers and an independent jury and builders, among others. Each speaks a different language and has a different way of thinking, which limits their collaboration capacities. Is the SLB yet another attempt to build the Tower of Babel **Figure 7.1**?

There are two ways of looking at the Tower of Babel metaphor. The first is pessimistic and announces the failure to meet expectations. The second, which is optimistic, serves as a basis for our thesis: the future *smart living lab* building should be an open process wherein stakeholders strive to develop a shared understanding of the objectives and qualities and to enact them. This chapter aims to offer a conceptual framework that will facilitate collaboration between the actors during the actual process: how do actors understand the concept of architectural quality? What are their roles? How do they interact?

[24] This chapter is the result of an applied research project called "Architectural Quality and the Building Realization Process" developed between 2015 and 2016 by the TRANSFORM Institute.

[25] Excerpt from the "Vision of the *smart living lab* building" by the Scientific Committee, March 2017.

Fig. 7.1 The Tower of Babel. A metaphor for the failure of an overly ambitious plan to reach the heavens as just before God confused the builders' language (Pieter Brueghel the Elder)

In the first subchapter, we clarify the main actors' understanding of "architectural quality," which is essential for the collaboration process. For users, architecture is a building's overall quality translated into an atmosphere, an emotion triggered by their transaction with physical factors. Habits and social relationships in a work environment also contribute to the atmosphere of a place. The analogy between user comfort and atmosphere supports the idea of using a comprehensive approach to the former. For architects, architecture is also the overall quality of a building, which is known as "wholeness." To understand how architects attempt to create "wholeness," we will briefly describe "design thinking" which is their core activity and mainly qualitative. As aesthetic theories of architecture are less accessible to the public due to their specific language, we have chosen to illustrate it using several examples of well-known buildings.

In the second subchapter, we will present a theoretical framework for understanding the building realization process. In real situations versus imaginary/idealized processes, the stakeholders have different interests and understandings of the notion of architectural quality. A building's quality clearly depends on the quality of the interaction between actors. Actors are able to come to an agreement not by following legal procedures but by adhering to social norms (Epron 1981), which is a learning process (Bicchieri 2014). This means that the design phase should be conceived in such a way as to allow for the mediation of actors' divergent interests — a learning-by-doing process wherein shared values are forged.

In the final subchapter we will argue that, in order to materialize the vision of the future *smart living lab* building evoked in this introduction, collaboration is essential. We will likewise highlight the critical issues for the SLB process based on the conclusions of the previous subchapters.

The complexity of the research project required a hybrid approach combining a literature review, the framing of theoretical notions, case studies, interactions with the main *smart living lab* actors in the preparation for the actual process, and practical experiments with students in two *Joint Master of Architecture* studios at the HEIA Fribourg.

7.1   Architecture as quality

Architectural quality is a controversial notion, whose origin lies in the double meaning of the notion of quality itself. In philosophy, quality is considered as an attribute or characteristic feature of an object (Cargile 1995) (objective meaning). However, quality can also be interpreted as value (subjective meaning). For example, Jean-François Bordron considers quality as a value we can attribute to acts, objects and relationships (Bordron 2011), whereas Van der Voordt emphasizes the subjective point of view: "Quality is the extent to which a product fulfils the requirements set for it" (Van der Voordt and Wegen 2005). If we transpose these views to a building, it seems obvious that the latter has both "objective" (as a physical object) and "subjective" features based on how we judge it. Aware of this duality, Biau and Lautier stress that is difficult to reach a consensus on the definition of architectural quality (Biau and Lautier 2009). An architectural object has multiple facets; it is an object of use that can be described as functional and/or symbolic, but is also a work of art that "escapes functional comparisons." The debate on the definition of architectural quality is perpetual and crosses all historical periods.

7.1.1 Architectural quality: a lack of consensus

Many attempts have been made to define architectural quality. In their book "Architecture in Use: An Introduction to the Programming, Design and Evaluation of Buildings," Van der Voordt and Wegen (Van der Voordt and Wegen 2005) distinguish two ways of understanding architectural quality based on a thorough analysis of these definitions. The first, which is predominant in architectural discourse, is associated with perceptual qualities, cultural values and symbolic meanings. The second and more common understanding of quality defines it as a synthesis of form, function and technique. Based on these two definitions, Van der Voordt and Wegen propose another that integrates the four major sub-qualities: functional, aesthetic, technical and economic. Functional qualities refer to how spaces are adapted to users' activities ("usability") based on their organization and layout. Aesthetic qualities are linked to the atmosphere of a building and its potential to evoke meaning, which could ultimately give it cultural value. Technical qualities relate to the degree to which a building's physical properties respond to measurable requirements (structure, envelope, technical installations, energy performance, healthy indoor climate, etc.). Efficient use of financial resources and rate of return define the economic qualities. One might observe that the first three groups of sub-qualities are an updated version of the classical Vitruvian Triad, *firmitas, utilitas, venustas* (solid, useful, beautiful).

All of these definitions illustrate the fact that a building has qualities. However, the main question—that of the definition of architectural quality—remains open. Van der Voordt and Wegen talk about the synthesis and integration of these sub-qualities as a prerequisite for achieving architectural quality. However, it is not clear here who does the synthesizing and the integrating. Coming back to the idea of quality as a subjective topic, and to its dependency on fulfilling the requirements set for it, we understand that the definition of architectural quality cannot be sought in a general way; we must address it relative to the subject that produces or evaluates it. Simply put, functional and aesthetic qualities are the concern of users, historians and theoreticians. Technical qualities concern users, building owners and public administrations. Economic qualities concern investors.

We shall see how these different actors identify and evaluate these groups of sub-qualities and in what ways they are concerned by their integration.

7.1.2 User experience: pervasive quality

Regarding the architectural quality of existing buildings, it would seem that the user is the main actor of reference. In this case, we essentially consider users who occupy and utilize a building in a more or less regular way. Visitors to a building can also be included in this group, but their interest in the building is more focused. The former group performs various activities and has social relationships with other people there.

To understand how we experience a place and how quality emerges, we will take a detour through the works of John Dewey[26]. At the beginning of his article "Qualitative Thought," Dewey states that "quality lies at the heart of human experience" (Eldridge 2016) and that our ways of thinking are conditioned by the world we live in, which is primarily qualitative (Dewey 1925–1953). This means that human beings and the environment are constantly in transaction, which changes them mutually. Dewey calls this transaction an "experience," a key concept of his philosophy. According to him, our experience of reality in the fullest sense[27] is not the accumulation of distinct perceptions; rather, its origin is a "situation," a dialectical event between specific physical, biological, social and cultural conditions and the physical setting. In problematic or indeterminate situations, we tend to make connections between the different experienced elements through an "experimental inquiry," and thus transform the situation into a unified whole (Dewey 1938).

Furthermore—and this is the key point for understanding quality and architectural quality from a user's perspective—Dewey argues that a "single pervasive quality" shapes our experience by creating unity (Dewey 1925–1953). This means that we do not analyse distinct sub-qualities and then combine them; on the contrary, we have an "emotion," "impression" or "hunch" of a dominating quality in an overall situation. This emotion is the basis for subsequent thought (Dewey 1925–1953). For Dewey, this unity of pervasive quality is at once emotional, practical and intellectual (Dewey 1934). In his book "The Meaning of the Body: Aesthetics of Human Understanding," Mark Johnson claims that Dewey's understanding of experience and pervasive quality is still relevant today, and that problematic situations and the grasping of qualities even serve as the basis for scientific thinking (Johnson 2007). Tucker confirms the role of feelings and emotions in all aspects of cognition based on recent developments in brain studies (Tucker 2007). At the same time, some argue

26 John Dewey (1859–1952) was an American philosopher, psychologist, Georgist and educational reformer whose ideas have been influential in education and social reform.

27 For Dewey, "an experience is one in which the material of experience is fulfilled or consummated" (Eldridge 2016). He distinguishes it from inchoate experiences, wherein we are distracted and do not complete our course of action.

that real experiences are becoming less important in our ever-expanding digital environment. However, while our everyday tools have changed dramatically, the way we interact with the world around us is the same. The topicality of Dewey's ideas has been confirmed in the past twenty years through the key notion of user experience (UX), which was developed by specialists in ergonomics of human system interactions. The ISO 9241-210 standard specifies that emotions and behaviours are the crux of user experience throughout any process. It is worth noting that the description of UX design as a process (Interaction Design Foundation 2018) is similar to Dewey's understanding of experience. While comparing the uses of a computer and a building might seem implausible, they are both complex systems (Heylighen 2010). In fact, the conceptual basis of software design is actually architectural thinking (Perry and Wolf 1992).

Pervasive quality as atmosphere

Although Dewey does not specifically consider architecture and its qualities, we can easily discern this link through his notions of "situation" and "experience," which actually describe users' interaction with the built and natural environments. In his article "From pervasive quality to situated atmospheres," Jean-Paul Thibaud argues that the "pervasive quality" defined by Dewey is the equivalent of what we call "atmosphere" (Thibaud 2004). His description of atmosphere illustrates this analogy: an atmosphere is experienced and felt as opposed to perceived or thought. Pervasive quality (or atmosphere), he continues, can be defined as "affective tone,"[28] a term that has both objective and subjective meaning (Thibaud 2004). In this sense, the way a user experiences a place is like an aesthetic experience. However, both Dewey and Thibaud specify that there is only a difference of degree, and not of nature, between the aesthetic experience of a work of art and the experience of an everyday situation. Among the many contemporary scholars who support Dewey's concept of "continuity of aesthetic experience with normal processes of living," we find the already-cited philosopher Mark Johnson, who argues that these aspects of meaning-making are all fundamentally aesthetic (Johnson 2007).

Pallasmaa also argues for the relevance of Dewey's concept of experience in architecture and the parallel between "pervasive quality" and atmosphere in his article "Space, place and atmosphere. Emotion and peripheral perception in architectural experience" (Pallasmaa 2014). Following Dewey, he states that architectural quality results not only from visual perception but from a sensorial fusion of countless factors, i.e. an atmosphere. Pallasmaa uses the work of Peter Zumthor as an outstanding example of architecture that creates atmospheres. Zumthor himself is specific: for him, architectural quality is atmosphere (Zumthor 2006). The conceptualization of atmosphere as a key element of architecture is relatively recent. The most developed contribution comes from Gernot Böhme, another

28 "Tonalité affective" in French, "Stimmung" in German: Martin Steimann thoroughly analysed the notion of Stimmung in an architectural perspective (Lucan, Marchand, and Steinmann 2003). Another relevant example is given by Sylvain Malfroy (Malfroy 2010).

of Pallasmaa's references. While Böhme does not base his thinking on Dewey, his understanding of atmosphere as the result of experience—a "mindful physical sensation" that we can describe as elation or depression, openness, entrapment, etc.—is similar (Böhme 2013).

Atmosphere and habit: a shared experience

If experience and pervasive quality depend on an individual's transaction with a physical setting (a place), we might infer that quality is purely subjective and, as such, impossible to analyse. Nevertheless, Dewey, Thibaud and Böhme again show us that atmospheres can be shared and, moreover, contribute to social relations. As we have seen, Dewey considers pervasive quality not as an end in itself but rather a basis for further analysis, thought and development, and hence a driver of future action. Thibaud also states that our body's actions are elicited by an atmosphere, as evident in our expressions: an atmosphere can stimulate or appease, captivate or bring us down, transport or paralyze us (Thibaud 2004). Though Dewey and Thibaud offer a detailed description of the emotional dimension of an experience, they do not distinguish it from the intellectual and practical realms. A meaningful experience is fundamentally linked to action in a physical setting.

Habit is the link between individual experience and social relationships, according to Dewey and Thibaud. For Dewey, habit is acquired through past experience and directs future ones (Dewey 1921). Going further, he claims that individual habits and social customs are interdependent because they are formed in a similar way (Dewey 1921). This means that we develop our behavioural habits through exposure to other actors and that, in turn, individual habits contribute to social patterns. Thibaud makes the link between Dewey's notion of habit and atmosphere. He explains that, despite the fact that different people do not experience a given atmosphere in the same way, it can nonetheless be defined as a shared experience when it is generated by a collective dynamic. A situation can be experienced as tense or relaxed, conflicting or consensual, strange or familiar (Thibaud 2004).

Atmosphere and comfort

Going further, we argue that atmosphere is not only a relevant concept for our everyday lives, but that it should be considered in conjunction with the notion of user comfort. As we have seen, Dewey's discourse focuses on the notion of pervasive quality in meaningful experiences. However, such events are quite rare, as everyday life is largely comprised of casual experiences. These "inchoate experiences," as Dewey calls them, are incomplete and express diffuse feelings (Dewey 2005). However, that does not hinder our transaction with a given environment or impact our feelings towards it. Pallasmaa argues that our interaction with a place is influenced by countless factors (Pallasmaa 2014), and that the diffuse, general ambience of a given setting determines our feelings towards it. Böhme calls these countless factors "generators of atmosphere" and divides them in three interdependent groups (Böhme 2015). In the first group he includes the configuration of materials, spatial proportions, the aging of materials, how materials relate beetween each other and to a place, rhythms, light, etc. Synesthetic[29] properties that affect several senses form the second group. The third group consists of social characteristics.

Exploring the notion of comfort, we find that it is similar to the notions of experience and atmosphere. For De Looze et al., who developed the De Dear and Brager thermal adaptive model (De Dear and Brager 1998), comfort is subjective; it is a reaction to an environment and is affected by physical, physiological and psychological factors (De Looze et al 2003). Vischer outlines three dimensions of comfort: physical, psychological and functional (Vischer 2004). Ortiz et al. describe the way users attempt to establish comfort. In order to find a stable state when stress appears, users either manipulate the environment or adapt their behaviour under the influence of emotions and attitudes (Ortiz et al 2017). Though we find different terms in all of these descriptions, the overall meaning is the same: our experience of the environment is subjective and our transaction with (or reaction to) physical factors generates emotions/atmospheres that have an impact on how we behave, which, in turn, is conditioned by habit. This points to the fact that comfort is ultimately a feeling, a qualitative notion, and that quantitative factors — temperature, humidity, natural and artificial light, acoustics — which are often studied separately, should be approached in a global way.

7.1.3 Design thinking: in search of quality

So far, we have discussed architectural quality from a user's perspective. We will now explore architectural design, the way architects imagine buildings by trying to bring out quality.

For a long time, designing architecture was seen as a purely creative activity without conceptualization. In the past fifty years, scientific researchers have nevertheless attempted to show "how designers design." The most accurate example of this is the concept of "design thinking." Its basis lies in the works of several researchers: Herbert Simon in the sciences (Simon 1969), Robert McKim in design engineering (McKim 1973) and Bryan Lawson in architectural design (Lawson 1980). The most significant development in this area can be found in Peter Rowe's book, "Design Thinking," (Rowe 1986) where he investigates several theoretical and practical positions to reveal an underlying structure of inquiry common to all design.

Rowe considers heuristic reasoning based on Herbert Simon's "bounded rationality," as a key element of design thinking. Heuristic reasoning is a process wherein the steps necessary for solving

---

[29] Sensation produced in one modality when a stimulus is applied to another modality, as when hearing a certain sound induces the visualization of a certain colour.

"wicked problems" are not known beforehand. The final decision, the solution, is made only once the line of reasoning has been completed (Rowe 1986). Rowe considers the type of problems characteristic to architectural design as "wicked problems," resuming and developing Churchman's (Churchman 1967) and Rittel's (Rittel 1972) concept. "Wicked problems" do not have a definitive formulation or an explicit basis for ending the problem-solving activity. The solutions proposed for wicked problems are not necessarily correct or incorrect (Rowe 1986). Lawson points this out that, given that problem formulation and idea generation (solution) are intertwined in heuristic reasoning (Lawson 2009).

In order to describe the architect's position as regards these "wicked problems," Rowe uses Merleau-Ponty's concept of situation (Merleau-Ponty 1962), wherein an individual is totally immersed in a problem and identifies him or herself with it in order to understand it (Rowe 1986). Rowe argues that various aspects of the design process can be considered as "problematic situations," as architects must overcome their novelty and make sense of them. During the design process, they simultaneously reflect and act (Schön 1987). The architect selects the information and explores and identifies seemingly relevant themes for a given situation. He or she thus begins with a "move" that, following development and evaluation, is partially reformulated (Schön 1987). This first "move" is essential to the process, as it expresses an idea in sketch form, a specific type of hypothesis that enables architects to give shape to their ideas and thus fulfil their main role. This iterative, incremental approach preserves and takes advantage of the ambiguous nature of the design situation (Plattner et al 2011).

Nowadays, the use of computers challenges this traditional design process. In his chapter "Intention to Artifact," Bernstein discusses the potential of Building Information Modelling (BIM) for integrating design, production and project management into a single digital workflow. In the case of "parametric design," architects, aided by computers, systematically generate formal alternatives. According to Schumacher, architects no longer manipulate forms but rather scripts[30] (Schumacher 2012). We could argue that this does not change their traditional role, as it is they who design the scripts that lead to formal operations and decide when computer-generated forms actually become architecture. Moreover, architectural design and software design are similar. Fred Brooks (Brooks 1975) suggests that the architecture of a software system reflects an overall vision, and that software architects must assume the role of "vision keeper" and preservers of "conceptual integrity." Software design is quality-driven, as put forth in the concept of user experience (ISO 9241-210 2015) mentioned earlier. The similarity between the two also lies in their use of an identical, incremental, iterative approach for dealing with the complexity of a given situation. The foundations of architectural design and software design are based on the same

[30] In Digital Technology, a script is "an executable section of code that automates a task." (www.dictionary.com)

heuristic reasoning. Thus does Bernstein use Rowe's definition to show that parametric design is "generated only through the 'heuristic reasoning' of scripting" (Bernstein 2012).

To summarize the characteristics of design thinking—a problematic situation, the combination of reflection and action, an iterative approach and various media—we can conclude that design thinking is by and large qualitative.

7.1.4 Global and partial architectural qualities

What is the quality architects look for? As we saw previously with Van der Voordt and Wegen, in an attempt to solve the client's "wicked problem," architects try to design buildings that integrate functional, aesthetic, technical and economic qualities. Many architects use the term "wholeness" to describe the result of this integration (Herzog & de Meuron 2006, Zumthor 1996). What this wholeness (Johnson 1994) means and how it can be achieved is a permanent debate that has followed architectural discourse throughout its history, with terms like unity, harmony between parts, coherence, identity, character, integrity, presence and "universal" or "contingent" beauty [31]. Instead of entering this endless theoretical debate, we prefer to move forward in our understanding of the "perceptual qualities, cultural values and symbolic meanings" that comprise aesthetic qualities (Van der Voordt and Wegen 2005) by using examples of famous buildings.

Van der Voordt and Wegen use the controversial Jewish Museum in Berlin Figure 7.2, designed by Daniel Libeskind, as an example of emphasis on symbolic meaning. The oppressive atmosphere of the Holocaust is generated by a series of architectural devices (a puzzling path, dead ends and the black ceiling) (Van der Voordt and Wegen 2005). In contrast, Costello argues that this symbolic meaning is linked to "visitors' experience as dialogic interaction" (Costello 2013). The experience is anything but comfortable, just as Libeskind intended it (Libeskind 2015). Visitors agree. Referring to the Garden of Exile Figure 7.3 with its pillars emerging at oblique angles, Howard Jacobson says: "Nothing is as it should be here. Every perspective nauseates us. The ground won't stay still and the sky itself appears displaced" (Jacobson 2007). Combining these two perspectives confirms Dewey's idea that feeling and meaning are correlated. The spatial configurations and materiality of the Jewish Museum generate an atmosphere, in this case one of discomfort, nausea, disorientation and panic, and in this way express "the oppressive atmosphere of the Holocaust."

At the Museum Insel Hombroich Figures 7.4, 7.5 in Neuss, Germany, the combination of art, architecture and nature is designed to enhance the visitor's experience. Sculptor Erwin Heerich and landscape architect Bernhard Korte created a series of pavilions and landscapes that form an unusual setting for art exhibition. The

[31] In November 2014, the British Royal Academy held a debate on the question "Is beauty an essential consideration in architecture?" https://www.royalacademy.org.uk/article/debate-is-beauty-an-essential-consideration-in-architecture. This debate was held in a way that echoes the 17th century "Quarrel of the Ancients and the Moderns."

Fig. 7.2 Jewish Museum Berlin: the openings of the zinc-clad facade evoke a body full of scars

Fig. 7.3 The Garden of Exile, with its pillars emerging at oblique angles, creates a sensation of nausea

Fig. 7.4 Museum Insel Hombroich: A framed natural landscape seen from inside

Fig. 7.5 Museum Insel Hombroich: The works of art are exhibited without any information

Fig. 7.6   Bruder Klaus Field Chapel: Traces of burned trunks used to cast the reinforced concrete walls

Fig. 7.7   Bruder Klaus Field Chapel: A monolith that dominates the landscape

Fig. 7.8   The Barcelona Pavilion: Absence of use that leaves the pavilion open to interpretation

outdoor climate pervades the interior of the door-less pavilions, without air conditioning or artificial light. Visitors experience the works in a direct way, as they are exhibited without title or author to emphasize the experience of the work itself.

Presence is the global quality that Peter Zumthor also seeks. For him, a building should "not represent anything, just being" (Zumthor 2010) and thus elicit feelings through its spaces and materiality. The Bruder Klaus Field Chapel ^{Figures 7.6, 7.7} he designed on a farm near Wachendorf in Germany is a compelling example. With its open roof and lack of plumbing, bathroom, running water or electricity, visitors are exposed to natural elements, which heightens the experience of the interior atmosphere. Zumthor says that despite his attempts to avoid "premature meaning" during the design process, meaning, ultimately, is unavoidable (Zumthor 2013). This might very well be the case, for the Bruder Klaus Field Chapel is a monolith that sits on the edge of a field, or, as Simon Unwin argues, "the erect monolith stands at the origins of architecture" (Unwin 2016). It is an archetype that can have many meanings—marking a place, indicating an alignment with some cosmic event, dominating a landscape, embodying the power of a religious creed, partaking in a picturesque composition or evoking stories about distant pasts and peoples (Unwin 2016). Intentionally or unintentionally, Zumthor's Chapel might convey some of these meanings[32].

Historians and architecture critics play a major role in giving meaning to architecture. Looking at one of the most analysed and debated works in architecture, the Barcelona Pavilion ^{Figure 7.8} designed by Mies van der Rohe, the many interpretations and theories "explain less about what Mies made than they do about what others have made of his making" (Dodds 2005). Their analysis is anything but neutral, as Godber shows by using two opposing interpretations (Godber 1998). While Giedion sees it as "standing quiet but firm in its enlightened modernity, as night descended around it" (Giedion 1954), José Quetglas considers the pavilion's "useless, silent, marmoreal vacant qualities" as premonitory of Prussian militarism. Giedion and Quetglas' words illustrate that, in this case as well, meaning comes after feeling (Quetglas 1988).

These examples allow us to conclude that architecture is nothing other than the global quality of a building. Paradoxically or not, architecture is an adjective. However, a building must also have what we can call "partial qualities" such as stability, health, security, accessibility, energy efficiency, fire safety, an outdoor view, etc. These qualities, which concern all users, are expressed in standards and norms and are, as such, a mandatory part of building design.

We find similarities when we compare an architect's position relative to a building's architectural quality and to that of its users. The "pervasive quality" of a building or a place felt by users is global, as is the architectural quality the architect aims to create. Both are the result of similar processes, as both users and archi-

32 Unwin gives several 20th- and 21st-century examples of architecture that "allude[d] to the standing stone and employ[ed] its timeless architectural powers" and shows that they are mainly in relation to religion.

tects face problematic situations to which they attempt to ascribe meaning and, thus, live an experience. Users' experiences take place in a physical setting that they feel as a whole, while the architect's experience reflects his or her total immersion in the subject, framework and means. John Dewey already made this parallel between the user's position versus that of the architect. For him, the perceiver's activities are comparable to those of the creator (Leddy 2016). We can better understand this relationship if we consider the link between Dewey's key concepts (experience, situation and pervasive quality) and those of architectural theorists. Rowe's description of design thinking is based on Herbert Simon's heuristics, which draws on Dewey's pragmatic tradition (Barone et al 1997) and Merleau-Ponty's notions of "experience" and "situation" (likewise borrowed from Dewey) (Gibson 2016). In the late twentieth century, Jonathan Hill clearly expressed the same understanding. For him, architecture is produced by the architect through design, and by users through inhabitation and use. Hence, even users play a creative role (Hill 1998). This may explain Pallasmaa's observation that even buildings that are not designed by an architect can provoke "a sensorially rich and pleasant atmosphere," (Pallasmaa 2014). It is users' inhabitation that turns a "specific materiality, scale, rhythm, colour or formal theme with variations" into an atmosphere Figure 7.9.

Taking into account the previous reasoning, we can conclude that architectural quality—like emotion—is context-sensitive, plural (relative to the many individuals who experience it), both global (the building as a whole) and local (the spaces that comprise the building), processual (linked to the daily interaction of users and places) and a continuum between positive (quality, in common language) and negative (unacceptable constraints) extremes.

7.2 In search of an agreement

Architects and users are not the only actors who make architecture. The realization of a building always entails a series of phases involving different stakeholders: a client formulates a brief outlining the qualitative and quantitative requirements. Based on this, designers (architects, engineers and other specialists) create a concept and schematic design that (for public buildings) is then submitted for competition. Architects then must develop all the constructive aspects that one or several construction companies will build, and that users will then occupy. Sometimes, a building's life cycle continues with its transformation. In other cases, its life ends with its demolition and possible recycling or reuse of some of its parts. This generic description of the architectural process highlights its key phases: a brief that establishes the objectives and criteria for evaluation, several actors/stakeholders performing various tasks using their own methods, means/tools and a schedule of activities.

Fig. 7.9   Users appropriating a public space to create a popular atmosphere in the Vallon neighbourhood, Lausanne

7.2.1 The building realization process

In most countries, the building realization process is regulated by a procedural framework that is strongly influenced by specific laws and practices. For example, comparing building procedures in the United Kingdom[33] and Switzerland[34], we can distinguish five similar phases:

1) Exploration
2) Programme and requirements
3) Design
4) Commissioning and construction
5) Use and management

However, what none of these procedures takes into account is how the various actors behave during this process, or how each one's role is goal-oriented according to their appraisal of the situation (Wilson and Shpall 2016). Frankfurt mentions that actors identify themselves with a desire while performing (Frankfurt 1998). This desire can be intentional, goal-oriented or subconscious, which leads us to the concept of agency. Agency is an actor's capacity to act in a given environment. For Doucet and Cupers, transposing the concept of agency to architecture raises a number of important questions (Doucet and Cupers 2009), for instance, how many agents should we take into account? How do they operate? Most importantly, why and with what purpose do agents perform their tasks? As we saw earlier, a building's qualities seem to be the obvious, generic answer to the last question. In this respect, Biau and Lautier underline that working with "quality actors" during the realization process is a prerequisite for architectural quality, and that actors' interactions are decisive to the quality of the result (Biau and Lautier 2009).

To emphasize the roles of actors, Tombesi organizes the workflow based on the output of each work stage (Tombesi 2012). He links each of these outputs with an actor, user, client, professional, builder or manufacturer, highlighting the importance of iteration during certain stages, which reflects how actors collaborate. Tombesi claims that design can not only provide answer to a given problem, but can also help in formulating "ways to organize the necessary means to achieve such a solution" (Tombesi 2012). Tombesi therefore proposes an analytical framework that shows the "multi-faceted, socially heterogeneous nature of design in buildings" (Tombesi 2012). This framework specifies several groups of categories that must be determined[35] and that define "a system of design production" (Tombesi 2012). Further on, he argues that, based on this framework, the design should and can be treated as a "complex network of sub-domains, specialized design contributions as well as negotiated practices" (Tombesi 2012). Here, he raises a critical question: "Who should design the project (and not simply the building)?" Without answering it directly, he suggests that use of digital infrastructures could be one way to design projects (Tombesi 2012).

---

33 RIBA Plan 2013 and the Generic Design and Construction Process Protocol Model, BIM Enabled MEP Coordination Process, IDP: Integrated design process.

34 SIA, KBOB/IPB Standard.

35 The groups of categories Tombesi proposes are:
1. Project definition and control: procurement, operations and coalition
2. Building opportunity generation: goals, stakeholders and resources
3. Building scope formulation: programme, spatial/visual, performance and specification
4. Building manufacturing: materials/systems, tectonics and fabrication
5. Building erection: testing, assembly and site
6. Building use and maintenance: use, maintenance and change

While these arguments in favour of a comprehensive design approach of the construction process are compelling, their transfer to practice is problematic. In reality, the construction process is an ad-hoc effort that involves public and private actors. The latter are obliged to respect the legal framework that defines their rights and obligations but not the way they interact, which is based on culturally-established common models. It is therefore difficult to imagine them engaging in a design process in which their roles are questioned and redefined. First and foremost, this would entail understanding the meaning of design in general and the design process more specifically. However, as we have seen, these complex concepts require at the very least basic architectural knowledge that most actors do not have. The implementation of a theoretically-based design process must bridge the gap between scientific knowledge and practice—in other words, a long-term objective.

7.2.2 Builders' and architects' analogue positions

In his somewhat older but nonetheless relevant book, Epron stresses that the act of building cannot be an ideal process, as it is always the result of a "circumstantial and non-systematic encounter between heterogeneous elements belonging to five domains" (Epron 1981): the architectural doctrine, the architectural institutions to which the professionals involved belong, the economy and/or political structure, the technical aspects of the building process (objects, elements and procedures) and the education system.

After thoroughly analysing historical building processes, Epron identifies their characteristic features, which are similar to those of design thinking discussed above. As building activity is "situated," the builder must define the problem to be solved, as "the terms of constructive problems are not given" (Epron 1981). Consequently, Epron defines building activity as "the art of formulating problems" and considers technical problems as "the mediation by which building activity is related to its conditions" (Epron 1981). As the characteristics of a given context do not emerge in an objective way, the builder must begin by formulating a hypothesis and choosing methods. To formulate this hypothesis, the builder, like the designer, must refer to his or her knowledge of construction and construction processes, which provides him or her with a set of solutions. Construction activities usually involve several builders whose positions differ depending on their role, the task at hand and the course of their actions. As such, these positions are inevitably "conflicting" (Epron 1981).

The building process is a place for discussion of these conflicting positions. During these discussions, the builder tries to either maintain conditions that favour his or her position, or change them in order to gain an advantage (Epron 1981). Tense on-site discussions between architects and builders is but one obvious example. This helps us in understanding why the building process cannot be completely rationalized and should instead be understood as "a patient or authoritarian search for an agreement between the participants" (Epron 1981). Epron's main point here is that the actors are less united by respect of legal norms and standards than by their adherence to a social norm, what Epron calls "rule." Bicchieri offers a new argument in favour of Epron's understanding by showing that social norms do not result from planning but rather from unforeseen interactions between individuals (Bicchieri 2014). He points out that the creation of social norms is a learning process through which actors "internalize the common values embodied in the norms." The potential conflict between individual desires and collective goals can be resolved only if they succeed in establishing a common value system (Wilson and Shpall 2016) through cooperation.

This means that conflict between actors' values and interests occurs within both the design and building processes, and that the decisions made are the outcome of this conflict. The design and building processes mediate divergent interests, and the debates to which they give rise actually have to do with how each understands architectural quality. The building owner (the client) also plays a decisive role in this debate. The client, as Biau and Lautier show, seeks the "quality of the thing sold" (Biau and Lautier 2009) in conjunction with the needs and desires of its users. For the owner, architectural quality is a combination of price, uses, technical quality and comfort. As we have seen, architects also search for a compromise between the client's requirements and their own way of understanding and approaching architectural quality.

7.3 Collaboration for shared qualities

In this final subchapter, we will compare the reasoning and conclusions discussed previously in light of the SLB case in order to identify critical issues and to make recommendations for addressing them.

Generally speaking, the fact that different actors have different perceptions of architectural qualities combined with the desired innovative, experimental nature of the SLB supports the hypothesis presented in the introduction: the need for its realization to be an open process. Consistency can only be guaranteed when actors and stakeholders engage in a learning process and share their points of view.

7.3.1 The involvement of actors

Actors' and stakeholders' involvement in this kind of iterative approach affords them the opportunity to find optimal solutions through the mediation of their different or even divergent interests. Involving users in the design process is an almost commonplace procedure in urban planning in Switzerland. However, the former are seldom involved in the architectural design process. As the other chapters of this book demonstrate, the *smart living lab* building is exemplary in this sense. Surveys on users' preferences and levels of satisfaction regarding working conditions in the Blue Hall, the "user environment" experiment and the involvement of researchers and laboratory directors in defining the vision for the building are examples of user involvement in preparation for the future design brief. The involvement of the *smart living lab* researchers throughout the entire process was essential for several reasons. To begin, they were able to take part in the materialization of their vision. It also gave them an opportunity to offer their expertise in various domains. Finally, as future users, they helped to define their preferred atmospheres.

First critical issue: the gap between the atmosphere proposed by designers and what users actually experience

This first issue is critical in the sense that there is always a gap between the atmosphere proposed by designers and what users actually experience. The interior perspectives, which are usually drawn in the preliminary design stage, offer only partial information regarding the future setting and lack both the effects of environmental factors (light, temperature, ventilation, noise, etc.) and social interactions, which are key factors for generating atmospheres.

As we saw, actors' adherence to social norms is necessary for reaching an agreement. For example, involving construction companies at an early stage could allow the builder to enter into the negotiations. The "Alliance Contracts in Australia" is an example of one such attempt to create a legal consensus between actors to align commercial interests with project outcomes (Noble 2010).

7.3.2 Initial stage

By looking at several cases[36], we learned that most important decisions are made in the initial stages. As we saw earlier, the definition of the "wicked problem" sets the tone for the rest of the process. This corresponds to the formulation of the preliminary design brief, which establishes the objectives and the programme. For the SLB, the objectives were expressed in the aforementioned "Vision of the *smart living lab* building." However, they are ambiguous in nature and open to interpretation. Moreover, they are not easily understood by designers because of the inherent complexity of academic language.

Second critical issue: translation of the vision into operational objectives

The second critical issue is translating the vision into operational goals. The brief should be generic in order to give designers ample room to interpret the problematic situation and, at the same time, formulate innovative solutions. In light of the previous

36 Case studies: Blue Hall in Fribourg, NEXT 21 Complex project in Osaka City (Japan), Research Center ICTA-ICP · UAB and Media-ICT building CZFB in Barcelona, Sino-Italian Ecological and Energy Efficient Building, Tsinghua University, Europa Building in Brussels and NEST in Dübendorf.

discussion, we would like to suggest that the objectives expressed in the Vision could be divided into four simple groups of qualities linked to use, experimentation, environmental performance and context. However, approaching them globally, which is necessary for reaching the main objective, i.e. the sought-after architectural quality, raises design issues. Environmental performance objectives, for instance, are specific relative to other performance objectives because of their quantitative nature: "The building will have to reach the objectives of the SIA Energy Efficiency Path guidelines (SIA 2040)." Their inclusion in the preliminary design brief might be problematic because the evaluation of these objectives depends on a high level of architectural detail that is not available in the preliminary design. We recommend translating them into qualitative requirements, which must be integrated into an environmental concept and correlated with the overall architectural concept. The legal obligation to respect comfort norms—which is part of the usability objectives category—is problematic in the case of the SLB. The norms consider an "average" user and ignore the subjective nature of comfort and its link with atmosphere described above. The study of comfort in office environments in correlation with energy consumption is currently one of the research themes of the *smart living lab*. Again we encounter the paradox presented in the introduction: the fact that the SLB is intended to embody qualities that require entirely new know-how.

Third critical issue: programme definition

Defining a programme is the problematic third critical issue. The *smart living lab*, the research centre that will occupy the building, is not a homogenous entity but rather a horizontal union of researchers from three institutions. Although currently operating in a temporary building[37], the *smart living lab* is a young academic consortium whose collaboration has only just begun. As such, it is still not clear how the researchers from various institutions and laboratories will work together, nor where the various research groups wish to be located. If they have separate spaces, how and where will they exchange ideas? Most importantly, how do they understand the *smart living lab* and its building? We propose that the programme be defined in a generic way so as to give the designers the freedom to interpret the given problematic situation and formulate innovative solutions accordingly. User involvement in the preliminary design stage could provide the necessary feedback for this.

7.3.3 Preliminary design stage

All of the previous considerations led to the idea of defining an iterative brief that would allow for a gradual attunement of users' requirements and designers' responses. However, the legal procedure is usually sequential, which as such does not favour an iterative

37   Since 2015, the Blue Hall, which is located in the blueFACTORY site, next to its future location, has been home to the *smart living lab*.

approach. As the SLB is a publicly-funded building, its design stage must respect the rules of public markets. In other words, the preliminary design must be chosen by open competition, which makes involving actors in the co-construction of the design impossible.

Fourth critical issue: type of procedure

This raises a fourth critical issue: that of implementing a procedure that facilitates collaboration between users, stakeholders, designers and experts. For this, we suggest transposing the "Parallel Studies Commission" model (in French "Mandat d'études parallèles – MEP"). An approach often used in Switzerland for urban design competitions, MEP are useful in projects that require a direct dialogue between an expert panel and participants, as in the SLB case. However, even in this case, the decision is ultimately made by an independent jury.

Fifth critical issue: jury selection

The fifth critical issue is the jury selection. The jury should be selected based on the SLB's objectives. In other words, its members should have skills in the areas of use, experimentation, energy efficiency and architecture. At this point it is important to come back to the actors'—in this case, the jury members'—subjective view of architectural quality; this means that the organizers of the MEP must clearly present their intentions to the jury members to allow for a comprehensive understanding of the SLB case.

Sixth critical issue: decision-making procedure

The sixth critical issue is how the jury makes its decision. Based on the interpretation of architectural quality presented here, the evaluation process cannot depend on an "averaging" of partial qualities (i.e. checklist), as some might give rise to contradictory situations. For example, concerning the experimental aspect, the vision states that the building "should be designed for incremental growth and redefinition of use." Hence, the designers must provide technical and construction solutions that will allow for this type of transformation. However, transforming part of a building is likely to affect users' typical behaviour and comfort. Consequently, adequately assessing the situation should take the form of a critical debate between jury members that considers both the qualities desired for the SLB and the jury members' points of view (Hanrot 2005). Their decision at the end of the preliminary design stage is critical.

Seventh critical issue: targeting architectural and life cycle environmental qualities

One particular aspect of the SLB project is linked to the goal of creating a building that has both architectural and lifecycle environmental qualities. This is a seventh critical issue, as buildings that are environmentally performant tend to lack architectural qual-

Fig. 7.10　A clinical atmosphere reigns in the offices of the 2226 Building

ities and lead to user discomfort (Ortiz et al 2017). One of the main reasons for this is the idea that environmental performance is merely a technical issue, which leads to myriad high-tech devices and systems and ultimately stereotypical solutions imposed by various standards and labels. However, as we have already seen with Epron, the technical problem is not an objective one, as the act of building is always circumstantial and depends on a specific context and the available resources. Complying with the requirements of a "green" label is not enough to create sustainable architecture if the building is not conceived of as a whole, in other words, if environmental objectives are not considered relative to other objectives. The fact that the architectural concept is often developed prior to the environmental concept is another reason buildings often lack both architectural and environmental qualities.

Eighth critical issue: lack of collaboration between architects and engineers

The eighth critical issue is usually a result of architects' and engineers' failure to collaborate during the design process. We can resume this long-debated issue by highlighting the fact that their approaches and thinking as regards design differ greatly. Architects have an incremental, iterative approach that focuses on qualitative aspects, whereas engineers solve "well-defined" problems that generally target a building's quantitative aspects. Of course, architects work on quantitative aspects as well. By defining a building's spaces, they position and dimension its material elements (structure, partitions, envelope, equipment, etc.). In reality, there is an intrinsic connection between qualitative and quantitative architectural elements, as Bordron argues is the case for the relationship between quality and quantity in general (Bordron 2011). This means that environmental engineers should also work on qualitative aspects and, most importantly, that the architectural and environmental concepts should be developed simultaneously. The collaboration between Jürgen Stoppel and Lars Junghans (Baumschlager Eberle Architekten) in the initial stage of the design process for the "2226" building ^Figure 7.10^ in Lustenau, Austria, is a notable example of this. This passive building—which has neither a heating nor a cooling or ventilation system—uses the thermal inertia of its thick walls made of efficient bricks (Baumschlager Eberle 2017).

As mentioned at the beginning of the chapter, the discussions regarding architectural quality and the building realization process cannot and do not provide definitive answers. For better or for worse, real architectural processes are open to unforeseen events. Instead, these discussions offer a framework and a set of questions that, in the case of the *smart living lab*'s future building, will hopefully improve a shared understanding and facilitate collaboration between the actors involved. How can we ensure collaboration? How can we implement a legal procedure to facilitate it? How can we create shared qualities? How can we involve designers and important decision makers in this adventure? How will designers and other actors materialize the SLB vision into an actual building with architectural qualities and atmospheres that will stimulate interdisciplinary exchanges between researchers? How will architects and engineers work together to develop coherent architectural and environmental concepts? How to involve all of the stakeholders throughout the entire process? These are the challenges designers, decision makers and users will face from this point on. Ultimately, an optimistic interpretation of the Babel tower metaphor hinges on collaboration that itself depends on creating trust and mutual respect between actors. This is not so much a scientific challenge as a human and social one that is rarely met in practice.

Acknowledgements

The Joint Master of Architecture students who contributed to the experiments are Pierre Burgener, Christophe Borne, Maeva Bortoluzzi, Loic Buyck, Francisco Calvo Arce, Pintusorn Chantranuwat, Simon Clément, Nicolas Maeder, Yvana Manini, Gilles Ottet, Nathita Panawat, Frédéric Pires, Kim Pittier, Axel Rabassa and Gaëtan Simko.

Partners

TRANSFORM / HEIA-FR, HES-SO: Florinel Radu, Chantal Dräyer François Esquivié
Building2050 / EPFL: Yingying Jiang

References

Baumschlager Eberle Architekten. 2013. "2226 / Baumschlager Eberle Architekten." ArchDaily. November 26, 2013. http://www.archdaily.com/451653/2226-be-baumschlager-eberle/.

Jessica Mairs. 2015. "Architecture Should Not Be Comforting Says Daniel Libeskind." Dezeen. November 19, 2015. https://www.dezeen.com/2015/11/19/daniel-libeskind-architecture-should-not-be-comforting-memorials-ground-zero-masterplan-jewish-museum-berlin/.

Gili Merin. 2013. "Peter Zumthor: Seven Personal Observations on Presence In Architecture." ArchDaily. December 3, 2013. http://www.archdaily.com/452513/peter-zumthor-seven-personal-observations-on-presence-in-architecture/.

The Interaction Design Foundation. Accessed December 6, 2018. "What Is User Experience (UX) Design?" https://www.interaction-design.org/literature/topics/ux-design.

Barone, David F., James E. Maddux, and Charles R. Snyder. 1997. "Social Cognitive Psychology." The Plenum Series in Social/Clinical Psychology. Boston, MA: Springer US. https://doi.org/10.1007/978-1-4615-5843-9.

Bernstein, Phil. 2012. "Digital Workflows in Architecture: Design–Assembly–Industry." Edited by Scott Marble. Vol. Intention to Artifact. Birkhäuser Basel.

Biau, Véronique, François Lautier, Réseau activités et métiers de l'architecture et de l'urbanisme, Plan urbanisme construction architecture (France), and Architecture et maîtres d'ouvrage (Association), eds. 2009. "La qualité architecturale: acteurs et enjeux." 1re éd. Cahiers Ramau 5. Paris: RAMAU, Réseau activités et métiers de l'architecture et de l'urbanisme: Editions de la Villette.

Bicchieri, Cristina, and Ryan Muldoon. 2014. "Social Norms." In The Stanford Encyclopedia of Philosophy, edited by Edward N. Zalta, Spring 2014. Metaphysics Research Lab, Stanford University. https://plato.stanford.edu/archives/spr2014/entries/social-norms/.

Böhme, Gernot. 2015. "Constructing Atmospheres: Test-Sites for an Aesthetics of Joy." Edited by Margit Brünner. Vol. Atmosphere as an Aesthetic Concept. AADR – Art, Architecture, Design Research. Baunach: Spurbuchverl.

Böhme, Gernot. 2013. "Atmosphere as Mindful Physical Presence in Space – PDF." Accessed June 19, 2018. http://docplayer.nl/23311131-Atmosphere-as-mindful-physical-presence-in-space.html.

Bordron, Jean-François. 2011. "Trois ordres de la valeur selon la qualité, la quantité et la relation." *Semen. Revue de sémio-linguistique des textes et discours*, no. 32 (October): 35–52.

Brooks, Frederik. 1975. "The Mythical Man-Month" Reading, Mass: Addison Wesley. *Essays on Software Engineering*.

Cargile, J. 2005. "The Oxford Companion to Philosophy." Edited by Ted Honderich. 2nd ed. Vol. Qualities. Oxford; New York: Oxford University Press.

Chevrier, Jean-François. 2006. "Ornament, Structure, Space [A conversation with Jacques Herzog]". Herzog & de Meuron 2002–2006, El Croquis, no. 129/130, p. 33.

Churchman, C. West. 1967. Guest Editorial: Wicked Problems. JSTOR.

Costello, Lisa A. 2013. "Performative Memory: Form and Content in the Jewish Museum Berlin." *Liminalities: A Journal of Performance Studies* 9 (4): 9–4.

De Dear, Richard, and Gail Schiller Brager. 1998. "Developing an Adaptive Model of Thermal Comfort and Preference."

De Looze, Michiel P., Lottie F.M. Kuijt-Evers, and Jaap Van Dieen. 2003. "Sitting Comfort and Discomfort and the Relationships with Objective Measures." *Ergonomics* 46 (10): 985–997.

Dewey, John. 1938. "Logic: The Theory of Inquiry." Holt, Rinehart and Winston, New York.

Dewey, John. 1925–1953. "The Later Works." Ed. J. A. Boydston, 17 vol., Carbondale and Edwardsville, Southern Illinois University Press, 1981–1990.

Dewey, John. 2005. "Art as Experience." Penguin.

Dewey, John. 2007 (first edition 1921). "Human Nature and Conduct: An Introduction to Social Psychology." *Cosimo Classics Philosophy*. Kindle edition.

DIS, ISO. 2009. "9241-210: 2010. Ergonomics of Human System Interaction-Part 210: Human-Centred Design for Interactive Systems." International Standardization Organization (ISO). Switzerland.

Dodds, George. 2005. "Building Desire: On the Barcelona Pavilion." Routledge.

Doucet, Isabelle, and Kenny Cupers. 2009. "Agency in Architecture: Reframing Criticality in Theory and Practice." *Footprint*, 1–6.

Epron, Jean-Pierre. 1981. "L'architecture et la règle: essai d'une théorie des doctrines architecturales." Vol. 15. Editions Mardaga.

Frankfurt, Harry G. 1988. "The Importance of What We Care about: Philosophical Essays." Cambridge University Press.

Gibson, Grant Wellington. 2016. "Experience, Education and Subjectivity: A Comparison of John Dewey's and Maurice Merleau-Ponty's Conceptions of Experience and Their Implications for Education." PhD Thesis.

Giedion, Sigfried. 2008. "Space, Time and Architecture: The Growth of a New Tradition." Harvard University Press.

Godber, Ben. 1998. "The Knowing and Subverting Reader." *Occupying Architecture*. London: Routledge.

Hanrot, Stéphane. 2009. "La qualité architecturale. Acteurs et enjeux." Edited by Véronique Biau and François Lautier. Paris, Éditions de La Villette.

Heylighen, Ann. 2000. "In Case of Architectural Design. Critique and Praise of Case-Based Design in Architecture."

Hill, Jonathan. 2005. "Occupying Architecture: Between the Architect and the User." Routledge.

Jacobson, Howard. 2007. "Great Modern Buildings: Howard Jacobson on the Jewish Museum, Berlin." *The Guardian,* October 11, 2007, sec. Art and design. https://www.theguardian.com/artanddesign/2007/oct/11/architecture.berlin.

Johnson, Mark. 2005. "Dewey's Zen: The 'Oh' of Wonder" n.d. Accessed December 6, 2018. http://www.philosophy.uncc.edu/mleldrid/SAAP/USC/DP17.html.

Johnson, Mark. 2008. "The Meaning of the Body: Aesthetics of Human Understanding." Paperback edition. Chicago London: The University of Chicago Press.

Johnson, Paul-Alan. 1994. "The Theory of Architecture: Concepts Themes & Practices." John Wiley & Sons.

Lawson, Bryan, and Kees Dorst. 2009. "Design Expertise" *(Vol. 31)*. Architectural Press, Oxford, UK.

Lawson, Bryan. 1980. "How Designers Think." *Westfield, NJ: Eastview Editions.* Inc.

Leddy, Tom. 2006. "Dewey's Aesthetics." September. https://plato.stanford.edu/archives/win2016/entries/dewey-aesthetics/.

Lucan, Jacques, Bruno Marchand, and Martin Steinmann. 2003. "Matière 6: Actualité de la critique architecturale." Presses polytechniques et universitaires romandes. https://infoscience.epfl.ch/record/85685.

McKim, Robert H. 1972. "Experiences in Visual Thinking." Monterey, Calif: Brooks/Cole Pub. Co.

Malfroy, Sylvain. 2010. "Atmosphère." Faces n° 67.

Merleau-Ponty, Maurice. 1962. *"Phenomenology of Perception"* [Phénoménologie de la perception]. Routledge & Kegan Paul.

Nobel, B. 2010. "Alliance Contracts in Australia." *Mainroads Western Australia* 4.

Ortiz, Marco A., Stanley R. Kurvers, and Philomena M. Bluyssen. 2017. "A Review of Comfort, Health, and Energy Use: Understanding Daily Energy Use and Wellbeing for the Development of a New Approach to Study Comfort." *Energy and Buildings* 152: 323–335.

Pallasmaa, Juhani. 2014. "Space, Place and Atmosphere. Emotion and Peripheral Perception in Architectural Experience." *Lebenswelt. Aesthetics and Philosophy of Experience*, no. 4.

Perry, Dewayne E., and Alexander L. Wolf. 1992. "Foundations for the Study of Software Architecture." *ACM SIGSOFT Software Engineering Notes* 17 (4): 40–52.

Plattner, Hasso, Christoph Meinel, and Larry Leifer, eds. 2011. "Design Thinking: Understand – Improve – Apply." *Understanding Innovation.* Berlin: Springer.

Quetglas, Jose. 1988. "Fear of Glass: The Barcelona Pavilion" in: *Architecture Production, Colomina, B. and Ockman, J.* New York, NY, Princeton Architectural Press.

Rittel. 1984. "Second Generation Design Methods I Design Methods I Cost–Benefit Analysis." n.d. Scribd. Accessed December 7, 2018. https://www.scribd.com/document/223709722/Rittel-1984-Second-Generation-Design-Methods.

Rowe, Peter G. 1994. "Design Thinking." 5th print. Cambridge, Mass. London: MIT Press.

Schon, Donald A., and Vincent DeSanctis. 1986. "The Reflective Practitioner: How Professionals Think in Action." Taylor & Francis.

Schumacher, Patrik. 2012. "On Parametricism: A Dialogue between Neil Leach and Patrik Schumacher." *Time+ Architecture* 5.

Simon, Herbert A. 1969. "The Sciences of the Artificial MIT Press." Cambridge, MA.

Thibaud, Jean-Paul. 2004. "De la qualité diffuse aux ambiances situées." *Raisons Pratiques*, no. 14: pp–227.

Tombesi, Paolo. 2012. "What Do We Mean by Building Design?" *Digital Workflows in Architecture: Designing Design – Designing Assembly – Designing Industry.* Edited by Scott Marble. Vol. Basel: Birkhäuser.

Tucker, Don M. 2007. "Mind from Body: Experience from Neural Structure." Oxford University Press.

Unwin, Simon. 2016. "The Ten Most Influential Buildings in History: Architecture's Archetypes." *R*outledge.

Vischer, Jacqueline C. 2003. "Designing the Work Environment for Worker Health and Productivity." In *Proceedings of the 3rd International Conference on Design and Health,* 85–93.

Voordt, Dorotheus Johannes Maria van der, Theo J. M. van der Voordt, and Herman B. R. Wegen. 2005. "Architecture in Use: An Introduction to the Programming, Design and Evaluation of Buildings." Routledge.

Wilson, George, and Samuel Shpall. 2016. "Action." In *The Stanford Encyclopedia of Philosophy,* edited by Edward N. Zalta, Winter 2016. Metaphysics Research Lab, Stanford University. https://plato.stanford.edu/archives/win2016/entries/action/.

Zumthor, Peter. 1996. "Thermal Bath at Vals." Architectural Association.

Zumthor, Peter, Maureen Oberli-Turner, Catherine Schelbert, and Hélène Binet. 2006. "Thinking Architecture." Vol. 113. Boston: Birkhäuser.

Zumthor, Peter. 2006. "Atmospheres: Architectural Environments – Surrounding Objects." Basel: Birkhäuser.

⑧ A data-driven approach for life cycle performance

Thomas Jusselme
Endrit Hoxha
Stefano Cozza
Raphaël Tuor
Renato Zülli
Nicolas Henchoz
Denis Lalanne

While a life cycle assessment (LCA) is a powerful method for assessing the environmental performance of a building, the early design stage is crucial for establishing its primary characteristics. As such, using life cycle assessments beforehand or in the early stages can be extremely useful for helping designers implement performance targets. However, an LCA requires a great deal of detailed information about the building, which is obviously not available in the early stages. This chapter describes a new, data-driven method designed to overcome this problem.

To tackle the issue of climate change and decrease greenhouse gas (GHG) emissions, Switzerland is proposing the new Energy Strategy 2050 policy (based on the 2000-Watt Society), as detailed in the previous chapters. These ambitious objectives must be implemented by architects and engineers in the early stages of the design process, as it is easier to change a project earlier than later, once construction has begun. This raises the key question of how to integrate environmental targets in the early design stage, an objective that is undoubtedly complex for a number of reasons.

First, we must consider a building's environmental impacts over its entire lifetime based on the life cycle assessment (LCA) and by considering operating (i.e. usage consumption) and embodied impacts (i.e. grey energy). This drastically increases the data that must be collected for the environmental assessments. Second, the early design stage is, by definition, the stage at which the project is the least detailed. Thus, there is a major gap between the level of detail available and the level of detail required for environmental impact assessments. Third, the early design stage entails numerous and rapid exchanges between design and performance assessments. This iterative process results in the need to develop rapid feedback techniques that can keep pace with the design process. Finally, the impact assessment must be understood, discussed and shared by an interdisciplinary team of architects, engineers, experts and real estate developers, who are the typical stakeholders involved in every building project. If these criteria are not met, the LCA results cannot be used to inform the building design.

In this chapter, we will begin by looking at current best practices and the state of the art: how has this issue been handled so far? We will then propose a new approach for addressing it. Finally, we will discover a prototype called ELSA (Exploration tooL for Sustainable Architecture), the first application developed to apply this method.

8.1   Regarding the current use of LCA
8.1.1   Life cycle performance in practice

In order to understand how practitioners integrate environmental objectives such as primary energy consumption and greenhouse gas emissions, we conducted a survey of nearly 500 architects, engineers and real estate developers across Europe (Jusselme et al. 2018a).

60% of respondents declared they often or very often considered life cycle performance during building design [Fig. 8.1], a surprisingly high rate that indicates practitioners' keen interest as regards this issue.

Almost 80% of the respondents who said they assessed life cycle performance did so because it is part of their best practices, versus only 40% who did so at the client's demand. This shows that LCA is mainly based on a voluntary approach, which limits the

Fig. 8.1   Practitioner awareness of life cycle performance (Jusselme et al. 2018)

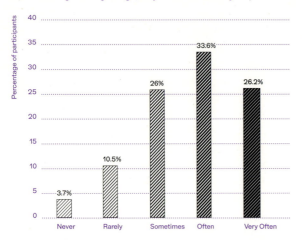

Fig. 8.2   Methodologies and tools used by practitioners (Jusselme et al. 2018)

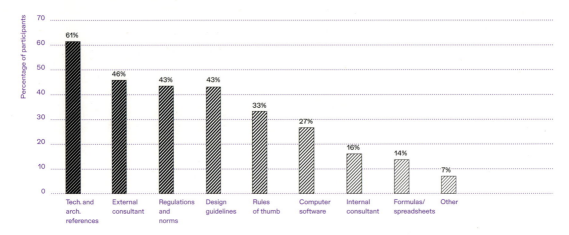

resources that can be used to this end. Consequently, only 27 % used computer software for this type of assessment at the conceptual design stage, whereas 59 % used qualitative approaches, such as technical and architectural references ^{Figure 8.2}.

Another surprising finding was that 49 % of respondents were unaware of new European Union regulations that will oblige every new building to produce more energy than it consumes starting in 2020 (EU–EPBD 2010). Given that the survey targeted EU practitioners (for whom the survey's theme is particularly relevant) this awareness rate seems quite low, given that issue at stake will completely change the built environment.

To conclude, the survey demonstrates practitioners' interest in life cycle performances but a lack of demand from clients. In addition, the life cycle approach was addressed qualitatively rather than based on a quantitative assessment (i.e. computer software). We assumed that this qualitative approach was less costly in terms of time and resources, and also better adapted to the early design stage (i.e. cheaper and facilitated faster exchanges).

8.1.2 Previous research

On the importance of LCA

In the past decades, the built environment's operating consumption has significantly improved as a result of successive regulations. Consequently, new buildings have lower energy demands, are more energy efficient, and are starting to produce clean, renewable energy. However, it is also by dint of additional materials and techniques (e.g. heat recovery mechanical ventilation, high thermal insulation qualities, photovoltaic panels, etc.) that such improvements are possible. Thus, buildings' embodied impacts are greater due to the increase in terms of relative and absolute weight. For example, a building that reaches the 2050 intermediate objectives of the 2000-Watt Society should have a 50 % – 50 % balance for operational and embodied impacts (Hoxha and Jusselme 2017).

Thus, it is essential that an impact assessment consider the building's entire lifetime from cradle to cradle (Dixit et al. 2012). This is the specific aim of an LCA, which is based on ISO-14040 that defines the method's four major phases:
1) defining the goal and scope of the study
2) perform a life cycle inventory of all environmental fluxes through this scope
3) convert these fluxes into environmental impacts
4) interpret the results.

Today, most building environmental certifications (e.g. Leed v4®, HQE, BREEAM, DGNB, etc.) are based on or inspired by the LCA approach. In France, an LCA will be mandatory for every new building starting in 2020. This means that the design phase must be monitored based on a project's compliance with life cycle performance targets as early as possible.

Exploration over assessment

While an LCA is often mandatory for current labels and will become compulsory in future regulations, it is far from being common practice, as we will see in the next section. One explanation for the infrequency of use has to do with the time-consuming, highly-detailed nature of the approach, which is necessary for producing robust information. However, as such detail is not available at the early design stage, an LCA cannot support the design process in an effective way. A promising technique for increasing its usability is the parametric approach (Hollberg and Ruth 2016). Using LCA combined with computer-aided design (CAD) tools with new Building Information Modelling (BIM) techniques allows for performance analysis in real time by measuring the effects of making changes in the drawings. Producing variants and assessing their relative environmental impacts is also facilitated. However, this still does not solve the problem of detail resolution. Energy simulation tools raise similar issues. Researchers in this field have created a new, promising set of techniques called exploration methods (Miyamoto et al. 2015, Naboni et al. 2013, Ritter et al. 2015). Instead of simplifying the performance simulation (in order to keep it on par with the project detail at the early stage) and addressing the issue of time-consumption, the idea is to create a database of design alternatives with thousands of variants of the building design at the early stages. A data visualization technique comprised mainly of Parallel Coordinate Plots (PCPs) will then allow users to explore the database by filtering the design alternatives based on their desires and constraints (Jusselme et al. 2017) ^{Figure 8.6}. The "exploration mode" is a proactive way of providing designers with rapid feedback, since they are most aware of the architectural and technical consequences of environmental targets hidden behind the assessment algorithms. So far, this method has a compatible computational cost with an energy model limited to seven variables, whereas with an LCA up to twenty variables are necessary to accurately describe a building's components and systems. Given that an LCA also considers embodied impacts, we must also study all of the potential building materials. Hence, the computational time-cost of assessing the billions of combinations derived from these twenty variables is not compatible with the design process timeline. One way of potentially reducing the computational cost is by using a sensitivity analysis, as explained further in the following section.

Sensitivity analysis for simplification

When an assessment model is too complex or involves a large set of variables, determining which ones are important to the design process, i.e. which ones impact environmental performance the most, can be useful. Sensitivity analysis is a way of addressing this issue. This tool, which is already used by building designers, ranks the parameters qualitatively or quantitatively. For our case, a fringe benefit was the sampling method to assess sensitivity. As it is based on the assessment of a sample of parameter combinations, it limits computational costs by calculating sensitivity based on a sampling of all the possible parameter combinations. Moreover, it provides a database of design alternatives that screens the design space and can be explored using PCPs. We chose the Sobol method (Saltelli et al. 2012), as it ranks parameter sensitivity quantitatively and offers low-discrepancy sampling that evenly combines the parameters within the design space.

8.2 A new data-driven approach
8.2.1 Coupling techniques for a new method

The previous section highlights the low use of LCA tools by practitioners, despite their stated interest in life cycle performance. The state of the art and recent research highlight the possibility of using and combining several techniques to overcome the challenges that LCA use raises, namely its time-consuming nature and detail resolution mismatch. The popular practice of integrating several techniques into a single workflow (Østergård et al. 2016) provides a knowledge database to support the design process. The techniques involved in the workflow are then used to create and explore the database and to gain meaningful insight into the design.

In this project and based on the previous state of the art, we decided to create a new LCA-based data-driven approach by coupling the following techniques and their related benefits:
- LCA: for the environmental impact assessment;
- Parametric analysis: to automate the impact assessment of design alternatives;
- Parallel Coordinates: to explore the multi-dimensional design space;
- Sensitivity analysis: to simplify the exploration of the design space by considering only the most sensitive design parameters.

The idea behind this workflow was to generate a personalized database for a single building project, i.e. one that takes into account the shape of the building, the local climate and geographical context and use (with appropriate occupation scenarios). Based on this information, the sensitivity analysis screening method generates a sampling of thousands of parameter combinations, which are also considered as design alternatives. An LCA is performed for each alternative. The parameter combinations and their associated assessments are embedded in the knowledge database, which the sensitivity analysis can then use to rank the parameters and the PCPs can explore the design space with.

This combination of techniques still has two major drawbacks. For one, it does not allow the designer to explore the design space with products or systems that were not considered as variables when the database was generated. Moreover, as they are specific to a single context, the results are not applicable to other building projects. As such, we added a final technological brick called "target cascading" that addresses these two issues.

8.2.2 The target cascading process

Optimizing complex systems such as buildings involves a large number of design variables and multidisciplinary analyses. Generally, iterations between design and impact assessments are conducted in order to successfully develop low-carbon projects. This process is time-consuming and requires efficient coordination of actors.

In fields like mechanical engineering, the design process is geared towards optimal objectives by breaking the system down into subsystems and components. For buildings, this can also be done by identifying targets at the component scale. The definition of target values serves several purposes:

- To highlight the components with the highest impacts;
- To allow architects and engineers to work simultaneously on different building components by reducing the interdependencies of sub-systems.

A two-step process, combining top-down and bottom-up approaches, is applied for the evaluation of impact targets at the component and system scale of the building. While the top-down approach aims to define the targets buildings must meet in terms of environmental impacts, the bottom-up approach aims to define the impact targets for building components and systems.

In our case, we defined building targets for 2050 (based on the 2000-watt Society vision) using a top-down approach. All human activities considered, these targets are 3500 Watts (2000 renewable and 1500 non-renewable) of primary energy and 3.5 t of greenhouse gas equivalent per Swiss capita. A linear, top-down breakdown of these targets enables us to define targets for all sectors (transport, consumption, infrastructure, food and building). Our chart ^{Table 8.3} includes data for primary energy (renewable and non-renewable) and global warming-potential indicators for three building typologies.

Tab. 8.3   Impact targets for the three main building typologies (Kellenberger et al. 2012)

	Primary energy (MJ/m²)	Non-renewable primary energy (MJ/m²)	Global warming potential (kg CO_2-e/m²)
Residential buildings	530	330	11
Offices	750	430	14
Schools	510	290	11.5

Fig. 8.4   Illustration of the target cascading approach (Poncety et al. 2016)

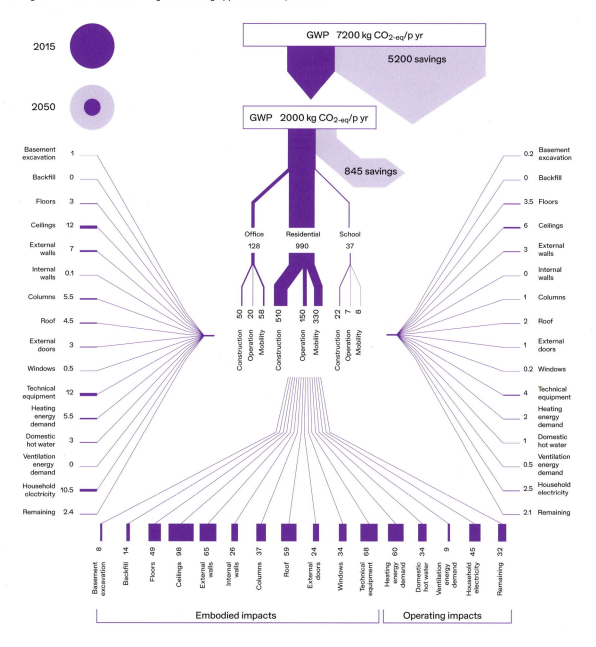

The aim of the bottom-up approach, however, is to define impact targets for building components and systems using the following equation:

$$I_f = \sum_{i=1}^{n} m_i \cdot k_{f,i} \cdot \left(\left[\frac{LB}{LM_i} \right] + 1 \right) + \sum_{k=1}^{p} C_t \cdot k_{f,t}$$

where:
- I_f Environmental impact f of the building
- n   Number of components and systems the building is broken down into
- p   Number of different types of energy demands
- m_i Mass or quantity of component or system i
- $k_{f,i}$ Environmental impact f associated with the life cycle of one unit mass or quantity i
- $[LB/LM_i]$ Largest integer not greater than LB/LM_i
- LB   Lifetime of the building
- LM_i Lifetime of the component or system i
- C_t Energy consumption in the exploitation phase of the building
- $k_{f,t}$ Environmental impact f for the unit energy t

(European Committee for Standardization 2011, Hoxha 2015).

Using the parametric approach previously described, the environmental impacts of components and systems of thousands of design alternatives are rebalanced linearly upward to the target defined in the top-down approach. This approach allows us to define average targets at the system or component scale using a design alternative database. Moreover, these average targets can be dynamically set according to a database subpopulation to specify objectives based on design constraints. For example, the target cascading approach performed on a database subpopulation for a concrete structure allows us to determine the expected impact of windows to satisfy the overall building objectives. ^{Fig. 8.4} provides an illustration of the target cascading concept applied to the 2000-Watt Society and GWP objectives for three different building typologies (offices, residential buildings and schools) per person per year.

8.2.3 Presentation of the new workflow

This target cascading approach was adapted to the built environment in complement to LCA, parametric assessment, sensitivity analysis and data-visualization. Using this combination of techniques, we developed a five-step methodology ^{Fig.8.5} according to Jusselme et al. (Jusselme et al. 2018b)

The project is described so as to be specific to a given context. Next, the parameters to be used as variables in the parametric approach are qualified and quantified. The parameters are sampled using the sensitivity analysis method. Each combination of parameters represents a design alternative that is then assessed using energy simulations and a LCA. Three complementary methods use the resulting knowledge database to gain insight about the design project. The PCPs can be used to explore the database via a filtering process. The sensitivity analysis identifies the most relevant parameters based

Fig. 8.5　Description of the new LCA-based data-driven design method (Jusselme et al. 2018b)

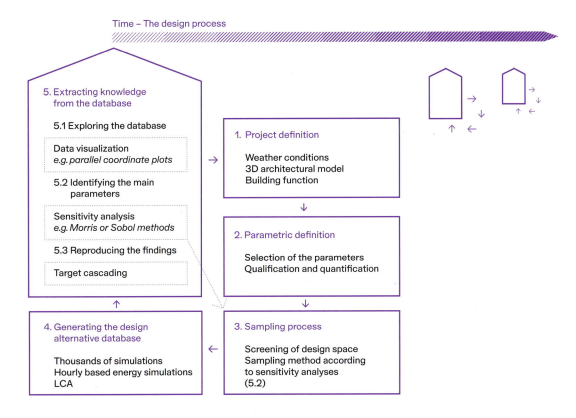

Fig. 8.6　Workflow with the software and tools utilized for the initial ELSA prototype.

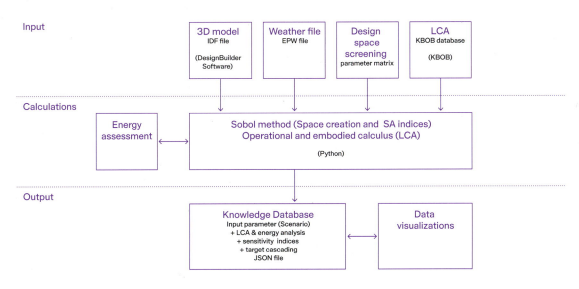

on a performance objective and then reduces the number of potential variables. Finally, the target cascading process breaks the building impacts down into components, allowing engineers and architects to set reliable, reproducible targets independently, following an overall design strategy that is specific to and compliant with the building's performance objectives. The Building2050 research group recently filed a patent for the EPFL based on this methodology (Jusselme 2016).

8.3   ELSA: an initial prototype
8.3.1 Description of the calculation workflow

An initial prototype named ELSA (Jusselme et al. 2016) (Exploration tooL for Sustainable Architecture) was created following the definition of the methodology. The prototype consists of a graphical interface (available online at elsa.epfl.ch) and an automated workflow combining all of the techniques to provide a knowledge database. Figure 8.6

We used the EnergyPlus dynamic simulation engine to generate performance data. EnergyPlus is an entire building energy simulation programme that models consumption for heating, cooling, ventilation, lighting, office equipment and water use in buildings (Crawley et al. 2001). EnergyPlus is free and open-source, and the U.S. Department of Energy's (DOE) Building Technologies Office funds its development. The LCA was done following ISO 14040 and ISO 14044 guidelines and used the KBOB database (KBOB 2014) to evaluate the environmental impacts of building elements and components.

The 3D model information was embedded in an IDF file created using DesignBuilder (DesignBuilder 2016) within a modelling environment. This software offers advanced modelling tools in an easy-to-use interface and is compatible with the EnergyPlus simulation engine. A weather file in EPW format was used in accordance with the building project's climatic context. Design space screening was done using the Sobol sensitivity analysis screening method, which defines a unique combination of variables. Each combination is considered a design alternative that a Python script can then use to modify the IDF file accordingly and conduct the LCA and energy performance for each alternative. The Python script then calculates the Sobol sensitivity indices using all of the results as input. Finally, the impacts of each alternative are linearly regressed so as to match the overall building objectives. This final operation is later used for the target cascading process. The LCA, energy simulation and target cascading results are then compiled in a JSON file, which serves as the knowledge database to be uploaded in the online Graphical User Interface (GUI).

8.3.2 From a database to a dynamic graphical interface

Interaction sciences and design research

Two Labs joined forces to make this methodology, developed by the Building2050 research group, a reality for building designers. The University of Fribourg's Human-IST research institute studies Human-Computer Interaction Science, with a special focus on information visualization for this project. The EPFL+ECAL Lab Design Research Center explores scenarios of use, visual expression and interaction design. The purpose of this joint venture was to provide architects and engineers access to the knowledge database through a GUI at the early design stage, an objective that raised several issues:

Simplification of the complexity: The tool gathers a complex set of data. How to make the interaction more intuitive and provide clear understanding to non-engineers?

A tool for inspiration: Common practices assess the energy performance of a designed building. ELSA works the opposite way by allowing building designers to play with the different parameters from the outset in order to understand which ones are crucial and their relationship when considering the various solutions.

Freedom, not judgment: Environmental issues are often seen as limiting creativity. ELSA must not be perceived as yet another limitation. On the contrary, it specifies key parameters and relationships, which offers more leeway on many other, less important features.

Using means effectively: Architectural competitions usually generate stress and costs for offices. ELSA must offer more than just efficiency and impact; it must be exciting and help to fuel the creative process.

Data visualization, often called information visualization, "is the use of computer-supported, interactive, visual representations of abstract data to amplify cognition" (Card et al. 1999). In this project, the aforementioned issues raise the following challenges for designing effective visual representations:

Reducing visual complexity: With large data sets, data visualization often implies visual cluttering. Techniques such as filtering, jittering, overview/details and sampling are necessary to provide meaningful information to users.

Highlighting correlations and discriminant dimensions: In the information visualization field, various data visualization techniques exist to highlight patterns (e.g. clusters, trends, correlations). In this project, the visual representation chosen in combination with data mining should highlight correlations as well as discriminant dimensions and choice impacts.

Data heterogeneity: While most visualization techniques are designed for continuous data, the ELSA project mainly manipulates categorical data, which involves adapting state-of-the-art techniques or creating new ones.

Gaining insight versus decision making: The major goal of information visualization is to gain insight, i.e. gain knowledge while exploring the data. The ELSA project has a somewhat complementary objective: to support decision making in the context of parametric design.

Two initial approaches

To tackle these multiple challenges, we started with two different approaches, each of which provided specific features in terms of interaction and data visualisation for the building designers. The first uses the principle of Parallel Coordinates, which is one way of interacting with the manifold relationships between the parameters. The second is reminiscent of the building-block principle in that it allows users to add one parameter after another. We turned these approaches into prototypes and tested their impacts with users. The results were then used to establish the tool's final design.

1. Parallel Coordinates: This visualization method ^{Figure 8.7} empowers the designer with data analysis capabilities, which are important in the early stages of building design (Attia et al. 2012, Huot 2005, Østergard et al. 2017). Each graduated vertical axis represents one parameter. Each tick represents a value. A design alternative is represented by a polyline that crosses all of the axes at the corresponding parameter values. This method allows users to assess the level of similarity between different design alternatives and between parameters. Colour coding is applied to polylines according to their environmental performance, which helps users assess the viability of each design alternative and detect patterns. Brushing interaction allowed us to reduce the number of design alternatives displayed to obtain a clearer overview.

2. Building Blocks: In addition to the work on Parallel Coordinates, we spent time in architecture studios exploring the creative process of building design. How could the tool be used to fuel inspiration in the early stages? This led to the creation of a second proposal ^{Figure 8.8} whereby users could add one parameter after another to see their impact; in other words, not only how each parameter affects building performance, but also how it reduces the number of solutions for all the other choices to come. Using the database, the interface proposes the solution with the most effective impact but always leaves freedom to the building designer. The pre-calculated solution for each parameter is made visible in order to provide a clear view of the system. When enough parameters have been selected, complete solutions can then be compared in a chart. User experience was designed to make the tool efficient for use on tablets as well by also allowing for interactions between several people in different situations.

Fig. 8.7   Parallel coordinates

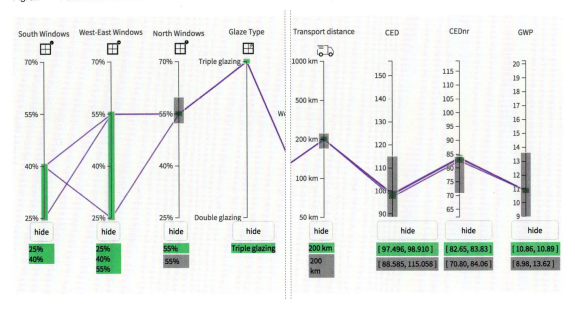

Fig. 8.8   Building blocks

221   ⑧ A data-driven approach for life cycle performance

Learnings from the initial prototypes

At the end of the first stage of development in November 2016, we decided to perform User Testing (UT) among the Master's level architecture students from the School of Engineering and Architecture of Fribourg. The goal was to gather information for the following stages based on the initial feedback. We agreed on certain goals for this UT:

1) to determine ELSA's usefulness;
2) to see if it helped the architects improve their project performance (e.g. less CO_2 emissions);
3) to learn about how it influenced the architects' knowledge; and, most importantly,
4) to see how the two visualizations compared.

To evaluate the feedback, we set up specific tests that the students (who were divided into two groups each with a different visualization technique) had to complete.

The UT started with an emotional test, the Self-Assessment Manikin (SAM) (Morris 1995), to measure their emotional response to using the tools. This was followed by a ten-question knowledge test in multiple-choice format (e.g. "Which of the following parameters can have a greater impact on a design alternative's CO_2 emissions, taking into account both the construction and the usage phase?") to better estimate the students' knowledge of the subject. The goal of the UT was to perform specific tasks wherein users had to do different practical activities using only the tool. The tasks were classified as:

- Exploration, to reveal patterns and insights from the database
- Configuration, to introduce and evaluate their own project
- Frequency, to create a project following specific constraints
- Improvement, to reduce the total environmental impact of the project

We then asked them to redo the knowledge test to find out if there were any changes after trying the software. We then moved on to a formal evaluation of the GUI with a User Experience (UX) Questionnaire based on the System Usability Scale (SUS) (Brooke 1996), to answer questions such as: "How much did you trust the information?" and "Would you use it on a regular basis?" Finally, we concluded with a focus group discussion wherein users were free to express their opinions and evaluate the overall experience.

After analysing each test, we were able to use both the quantitative and qualitative results. The first showed general satisfaction with the two visualization options in terms of usability (good results for SUS and SAM test) and, in both cases, a decrease in the knowledge test error rate after using ELSA. The outcomes of the qualitative results from the group discussion were even more beneficial and constructive. Notably, it strengthened our perception of the actual usefulness of such a tool based on early users' comments, such as:

- "We would use it because, even without any detail about the building's performance, we are able to make some smart choices"; or
- "It's really useful to be able to see the impact of the different parameters in a simple overview and to easily understand the consequences of a selection."

Moreover, we were able to use specific suggestions to improve our prototype. For example, for the question "What do you think of the interface design? What could be improved?" they answered: "It's easy to see the track from left to right (each polyline)," as well as "It's overwhelming and looks complicated" (for the parallel coordinates). Regarding the building block visualization, the same question received this answer: "We like it because we can add parameters as we want, progressively, and according to our logic and inspiration."

These results were combined with discussions with experts to define the final tool concept. Although the number of users involved, the working conditions and the user profiles did not provide quantitative results for actual use situations, the data and insight did indicate a clear path for enhancing the tool. In short, the analyses indicated that the building block approach provided a better understanding of the tool, parameters and process. Feelings seemed to be consistent, though users had more of a black-box feeling and felt the tool was quite time consuming, especially when it came to adding more parameters. Parallel Coordinates allowed for more interactivity, flexibility and excitement because all of the alternatives were visible and included from the outset. Rather than choosing between two options, the results indicate the need to find a way of combining their unique qualities. This eventually led to a breakthrough in data visualisation and interaction.

8.3.3 ELSA: a new concept and real tool

By combining the key features of the two initial prototypes, ELSA opens new horizons for data interaction and perception. However, obtaining the best of both worlds is easy in theory but more difficult in practice. We based our approach on three major concepts:

Focus on the "playground": Usually, users do not play with all of the parameters simultaneously. Therefore, we divided the full representation of Parallel Coordinates into three areas: the left column is a list of untouched parameters (no value or solution has been chosen; all solutions are still available); the playground (which shows all of the parameters under consideration) is in the centre and the right column has the selected values (the user has chosen one specific value for each parameter in this area). The playground is located in the centre of the screen. If the user wants to see all of the Parallel Coordinates, he/she can switch to EXPLORE mode [Figure 8.9].

Build the solution: Users start with all of the solutions that the system has pre-calculated. To build their own vision, the user adds the parameters to the playground one by one [Figures 8.10–8.12]. In terms of understanding each parameter and its impact, the process is the same as that of the building block prototype. However, the interaction offers a higher level of excitement as well as the efficiency of Parallel Coordinates.

Complex information becomes intuitive: The system provides a great deal of information in a visual way as simply as possible by focusing on perception rather than detailed values. For instance, the size and proportion of red and green colours show the potential impact of each choice. If building designers cannot find the desired option for a given parameter, they can select a target value and use any product listed under this value in their project. Users can also begin by selecting a target in terms of impact in order to focus on solutions that will be compatible with their goals.

This new way of interacting with Parallel Coordinates (which includes a building block approach) raised technical and scientific considerations with regard to implementation.

8.3.4 Key challenges

As mentioned in the introduction, information visualisation generally aims to explore data in order to gain insight. The approach and solution proposed open new perspectives for the field of data visualisation as a way of supporting decision making in parametric design. This implies the creation of new, goal-oriented visualisation techniques and interaction paradigms that allow users to alternate between exploration and selection and, at the same time, support their creativity and design choices. This could lead to mixed initiative solutions involving both computational tools and human intelligence (Pu and Lalanne 2002).

The tool needed to be usable with a wide range of devices and by a variety of users. We thus opted for web technologies (Javascript, HTML, CSS), which ensure great flexibility in terms of development, maintenance and simplicity, as they do not require software installation.

With a database that can propose thousands of design alternatives in rapid succession, it became clear that the tool needed to be capable of handling a large number of data items simultaneously. ELSA displays aggregates of data items scaled according to

Fig. 8.9   Explore mode
The parallel coordinates display all of the parameters. All of the available variables are listed on the left, the central area displays only active values and the user makes a decision on the right: only one path is left

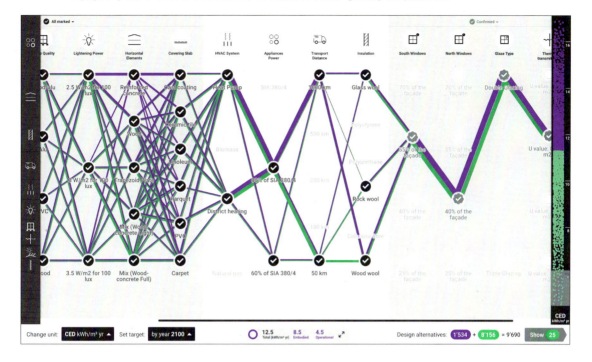

Fig. 8.10   Build mode
The build mode shows an identical diagram. However, the unchanged parameters are now listed only in the left column and the defined ones in the right. Users can focus on the parameter(s) of interest in the playground (centre)

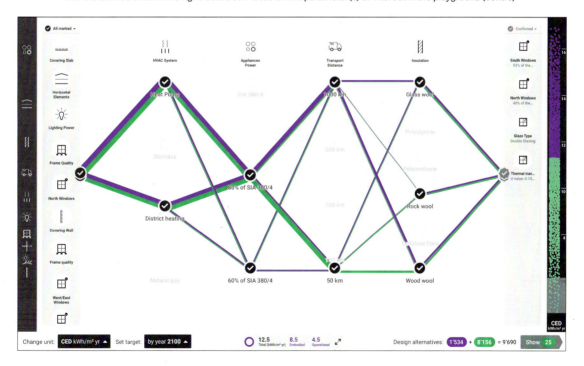

Fig. 8.11   Build mode: first and second step
Users start by selecting a first parameter of interest and eliminating some of the solutions proposed by the system. Users can add more parameters and observe their interactions by selecting or deselecting specific values

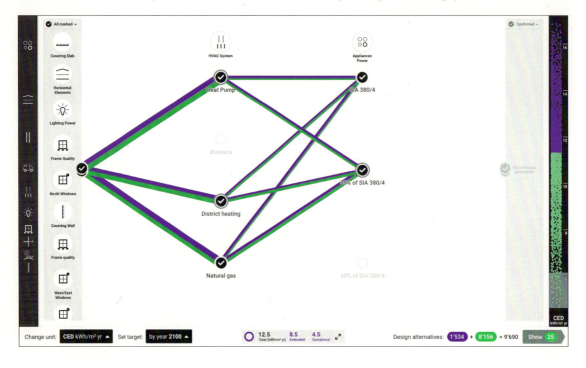

Fig. 8.12   Build mode: third step
Once they have chosen a final value, users can put the parameters in the right column

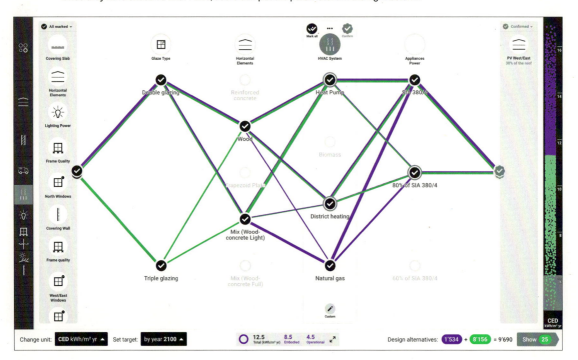

226   Exploring

their frequency, as opposed to individual polylines (as do Parallel Coordinates). This guarantees good scalability, even with a larger database.

Close collaboration between scientists, engineers and design researchers made ELSA suitable for use for the *smart living lab* building architectural competition in 2018. The competitors will use it in the preliminary design phases to develop design strategies based on the expected environmental threshold. Further developments include longitudinal testing to monitor use by end users and its impact on their practice, as well as the application of design and human-computer interaction to other content and contexts to validate the approach beyond a specific field.

8.4 The *smart living lab* building as a case study
8.4.1 Processing of an initial database

We chose the preliminary architectural feasibility study of the *smart living lab* building (SLB) as a case study. This feasibility study, which is in keeping with the urban context and regulations, is representative of the volume to be used as a starting point by the future designers. The parametric approach breaks these volumes down into real design alternatives by specifying the design parameters as detailed hereunder. We expected two main benefits from the case study. First, we wanted to test our workflow in order to identify meaningful insights and patterns in the generated database. Second, the resulting knowledge database will be useful to the future building designers for reaching the ambitious intermediate 2000-Watt Society targets. The case study is an L-shape ^{Figure 8.13} with an office area of 943 m^2, an educational area of 279 m^2, a cafeteria space with a kitchen (109 m^2) and technical rooms (WC, corridors and service rooms)[38].

All of the spaces were based on the Swiss norm SIA 2024 (SIA 2015), which defines all of the internal conditions (usage schedule, temperature, appliance electrical consumptions, etc.) for each use. A list of eighteen parameters was also drawn up to provide detailed information on the future building design alternatives. This list is the fruit of a review of the state of the art and best practice cases in the building sector (Cozza 2015, Jusselme et al. 2015).

We divided the eighteen parameters into five groups, each describing technical and architectural energy solutions affecting building performance:

Windows: This macro-group is composed of five different parameters. Three control the dimension of the windows on the various facades (window to wall ratio). The other two relate to the windows themselves (glazing type and frame quality).

PV panels: In this macro-group, users can change the dimensions of the photovoltaic panels in the different orientations and positions (facades and roof).

38 This building description does not represent the definitive *smart living lab* brief of the smart living lab, and *should* be considered only as an example within this case study.

Fig. 8.13   A simplified architectural model was used to create the 3D volume of the SLB in the ELSA workflow

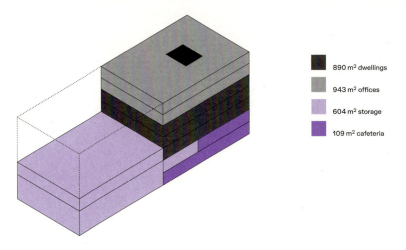

- 890 m² dwellings
- 943 m² offices
- 604 m² storage
- 109 m² cafeteria

Tab. 8.14   List of parameters combined to generate design alternatives

1.	**Windows**		
	South windows	☐ 70 % of the facade has windows ☐ 55 % of the facade has windows ☐ 40 % of the facade has windows ☐ 25 % of the facade has windows	
	East/West windows	☐ 70 % of the facade has windows ☐ 55 % of the facade has windows ☐ 40 % of the facade has windows ☐ 25 % of the facade has windows	
	North windows	☐ 70 % of the facade has windows ☐ 55 % of the facade has windows ☐ 40 % of the facade has windows ☐ 25 % of the facade has windows	
	Glazing type	☐ Double glazing – Uw value: 1.3 W/m²K ☐ Triple glazing – Uw value: 0.8 W/m²K	
	Window frame	☐ Wood/Aluminium ☐ Aluminium ☐ PVC ☐ Wood	
2.	**Photovoltaic panels**		
	PV South facade	☐ 0 % of the facade has photovoltaics ☐ 10 % of the facade has photovoltaics ☐ 20 % of the facade has photovoltaics ☐ 30 % of the facade has photovoltaics	
	PV East and West facade	☐ 0 % of the facade has photovoltaics ☐ 10 % of the facade has photovoltaics ☐ 20 % of the facade has photovoltaics ☐ 30 % of the facade has photovoltaics	
	PV Roof	☐ 0 % of the facade has photovoltaics ☐ 30 % of the facade has photovoltaics ☐ 60 % of the facade has photovoltaics ☐ 100 % of the facade has photovoltaics	

3.	Systems		
	Heating system	☐ Heat pump ☐ Biomass boiler ☐ District heating ☐ Natural gas boiler	
	Lighting power	☐ 2.5 W/m² for 100 lux ☐ 3.0 W/m² for 100 lux ☐ 3.5 W/m² for 100 lux	
	Office equipment power	☐ Appliances as SIA 380/4 ☐ Appliances as 80% of SIA 380/4 ☐ Appliances as 60% of SIA 380/4	
4.	Horizontal Elements		
	Horizontal structure (roof, slab, floors)	☐ Reinforced concrete ☐ Wood ☐ Trapezoid plate ☐ Mix (wood-concrete Light) ☐ Mix (wood-concrete Heavy)	
5.	Envelope & Structure		
	Vertical structure (columns and walls)	☐ Concrete block ☐ Fired clay block ☐ Cellular concrete block ☐ Reinforced concrete wall ☐ Wood Full ☐ Wood Light	
	Insulation type	☐ Glass wool ☐ Polystyrene ☐ Polyurethane ☐ Rock wool ☐ Cellulose fibre ☐ Wood wool	
	Thermal transmittance (average for the building)	☐ U value: 0.1 W/m²K ☐ U value: 0.15 W/m²K ☐ U value: 0.20 W/m²K ☐ U value: 0.25 W/m²K	
	Floor covering	☐ Cast coating ☐ Ceramic tile ☐ Linoleum ☐ Parquet ☐ PVC ☐ Carpet	
	External wall covering	☐ Cement panels [1 cm] ☐ Cement plaster [1 cm] ☐ Wood siding [2 cm] ☐ Zinc [0.1 cm] ☐ Steel [0.1 cm] ☐ Organic coating [1 cm]	
6.	Transport		
	Material transportation	☐ 50 km ☐ 100 km ☐ 200 km ☐ 500 km ☐ 1000 km	

Systems: This group contains the definitions of all electric appliances and thermal equipment. For example, it is possible to select different heating and lighting systems.

Envelope and structure: This group contains all of the parameters used to describe the building's structure and envelope in order to describe their thermal and physical characteristics. For example, users can select the composition of the walls and slabs, or change the type of insulation used.

Transport: This group contains only one parameter, which is the average distance the materials must travel to arrive at the construction site.

Each of these groups is composed of different design parameters, each of which can vary within certain limits. It is a combination of these parameters that makes what we called a design alternative. A comprehensive list of these parameters and options is given on the opposite page ^{Table 8.14}.

Using the Sobol method, the combination of all of the parameters allows us to assess 20 000 design alternatives. Using the workflow previously described ^{Figure 8.6}, these 20 000 alternatives were used to found a knowledge database specifically for the SLB context. The average time needed to calculate a given alternative was 1.5 minutes for one Central Processing Unit (CPU). We were able to calculate the full database in two days using eleven CPUs of a single computer. This duration can be shortened to a few hours or even minutes thanks to cloud computing and by using several CPUs in parallel.

As the SLB targets the 2000-Watt Society objectives, the three main indicators—the cumulative energy demand (CED), the non-renewable cumulative energy demand (CED_{nr}) and global warming potential (GWP)—were analysed. The CED indicator includes all forms of energy extracted from nature to supply energy to, for instance, a heat pump ^{Figure 8.15}. The final energy consumption is used to satisfy the building's energy demand, which is the result of its energy losses and comfort threshold.

8.4.2 Sensitivity analysis results

The Sobol sensitivity analysis used for this study aimed to understand how various building parameters affect their environmental impact. The question reads: "Which one of the input variables influences the model's output variance the most?" For our case, we posed the question as follows: "Which one of the design parameters influences the building's environmental performance the most?"

The results of the sensitivity analysis for the GWP, CED and CED_{nr} based on the total order of sensitivity indices are shown in ^{Figure 8.16}. First, looking specifically at the GWP, the SLB's most performance-influencing parameter in terms of CO_2 emissions is the heating system, with 37 % variance, followed by the dimension

Fig. 8.15   The three types of energy considered in the study.

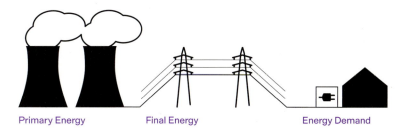

Fig. 8.16   Sobol total order indices for Global Warming Potential (GWP), Cumulative Energy Demand (CED) and its non-renewable portion (CED$_{nr}$). In this graph, the design parameters are ranked in decreasing order according to their impact on the GWP

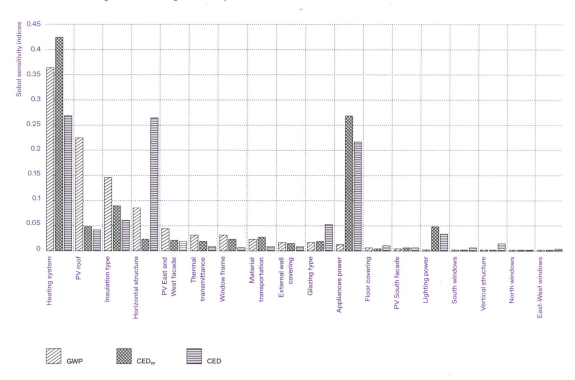

Fig. 8.17 Target cascading from the overall 2000-Watt building objective to average impact targets per component and system

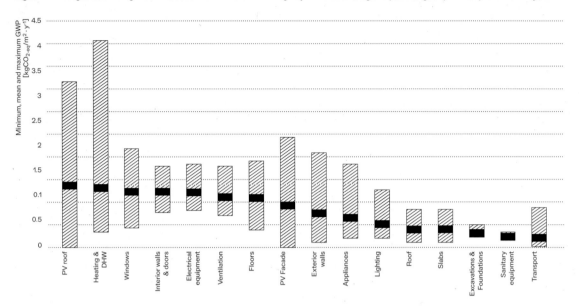

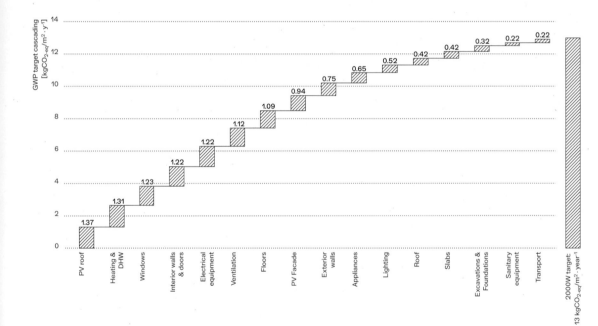

Exploring

and existence of PV roof panels (22 %), insulation material (15 %) and the horizontal structure (9 %). Note that these four parameters, representing only 22 % of all parameters (4 out of 18), account for 80 % of the variance. The Pareto principle and its 80/20 rule, which states that 80 % of effects come from 20 % of causes, thus follows. It is therefore crucial that designers focus specifically on managing these parameters, which are those that most affect the building's performance.

One also notes a correlation between the CED, CED_{nr} and GWP Sobol indices, except for two parameters: electrical appliance power and horizontal structure. For electrical appliances, this can be explained by the notable difference between energy impacts and Swiss grid CO_2 emissions, whose carbon content is low (GWP conversion factor = 100g $CO_{2\ eq}$/kWh$_{FE}$), but whose primary energy content is relatively high (CED conversion factor = 3 kWhPE/kWhFE). As electrical appliances are the largest consumer of electricity in offices, the differences between conversion factors greatly affect the Sobol indices. We also observed a lack of correlation between the CED and CED_{nr} Sobol indices for the horizontal structure. This is due to CED and CED_{nr} impacts for wood, which differ considerably due to the renewable energy embedded in this material.

It is interesting to note that the window size parameter has a very low Sobol index [Figure 8.16]. When considering environmental impacts only (and not comfort), variations in window size do not greatly affect the CED, CED_{nr} or GWP. In fact, the impact of one square meter of external wall is roughly the same as that of a window. Thus, increasing the external wall and reducing window size does not change the overall building performance. Moreover, as the study concerned office buildings with high internal heat gains, the impact of window size variations was lower due to solar heat gains and heating demands.

These somewhat surprising results require two clarifications. To begin with, the sensitivity indices highlight the influence of environmental impacts, not their absolute environmental weight. For example, windows have low Sobol indices but high environmental impacts [Figure 8.17]. Second, the whole building life span is considered, which radically changes the scope of the analysis and conclusions of the study (versus how engineers usually work, i.e. focusing only on the operational phase). That is why the choice of materials is so relevant, for both their thermal properties and their embodied energy.

8.4.3 Target cascading results

Impact targets for the SLB context and for the global warming potential indicator are presented further in this section [Figure 8.17]. Even though photovoltaic panels have a positive influence, when also considering their electricity production, their embodied impacts have the heaviest carbon weight for a 2000-Watt building.

Indeed, the electrical consumption of the other parameters counteracted the environmental benefits of PV production and simultaneously reduced their environmental footprint. The second impact in the database was heating and Domestic Hot Water (DHW) system (mainly due to the gas boiler), which was kept as an option. It is interesting to note that, in our ranking system, every building component had an impact of between 1% and 10% of the entire building. This led to the conclusion that even when the difference between the influence of the parameters was great (as demonstrated previously with the Sobol indices), all of the components must be considered without the Pareto principle when it comes to evaluating the performance of a building.

The presentation of targets in the form of intervals with mean, minimum and maximum values (instead of single values) illustrates the range of choices designers have for achieving 2000-Watt building targets. However, the technical proposal developed by building actors should have lower impacts than the average values presented, especially for components or systems with higher targets. In conclusion, developing buildings component-by-component with solutions that respect targets should result in the design of projects with lower environmental impacts. It is also interesting to note that the target cascading approach might be useful for companies that want to develop building components based on the 2000-Watt Society objectives. For example, a window manufacturer should target a carbon performance of 1.22 kg $CO_{2\text{-eq}}/m^2 \cdot year^{-1}$ for its window to be compliant with the 2050 market.

8.5 Exploration at the early stages: Towards a new paradigm

In this chapter, we proposed a new method to support the early stages of the design process. We used this method to create an initial prototype known as ELSA (Exploration tooL for Sustainable Architecture), which we call an LCA-based data-driven method. The tool addresses two key issues that prevent practitioners from integrating life cycle performance objectives early on in the design process. These two issues were highlighted through an extensive online survey of nearly 500 engineers and architects. The survey points to the fact that the latter were willing to consider life cycle performance in building projects, but lacked design support methods for employing it in the early design stages. The life cycle assessment methodology is now considered a robust, relevant technique for evaluating the environmental impacts of buildings. However, it requires highly detailed information, which is obviously not available at the conceptual design phase. Thus, as the latter is the easiest in which to impact the design, it is crucial to develop a new method that takes into account the constraints of low resolution details at the early design stage. The second key issue lies in the lack of time for performing environmental assessments and the need to develop an iterative process involving multiple assessments in the same building design phase. Hence, it is also important to develop a method that is not time-consuming and feeds this iterative process.

Based on this contextual understanding, ELSA proposes an interdisciplinary, innovative workflow that allows building engineers and architects to interact with a knowledge database by combining various techniques from the building sciences, statistical sciences, mechanical engineering, environmental sciences and human-machine interaction sciences. The database is created for a specific building project, takes into account the local climate as well as the building functionalities and volume, and embeds numerous design alternatives with different architectural and technical characteristics. The environmental performance of each alternative is assessed based on the LCA methodology and KBOB environmental impact database. Operating energy consumption is also assessed using the EnergyPlus simulation model. The Sobol method is then used to calculate the sensitivity indices, which helps designers focus on the parameters with the highest impact contribution.

Other design parameters, on the contrary, are considered unimportant, thus simplifying the designer's task of managing a range of elements. The resulting knowledge database can be explored thanks to powerful data visualization techniques originating in the field of human-computer interaction research. This allows designers to better understand the insight and design mechanisms that can be used to develop low energy/carbon buildings. The graphical user interface improves designers' knowledge of the possible impacts of life cycle targets on architectural and technical solutions, so as to establish the creative boundaries within which the building stakeholders must work. Finally, the target cascading approach provides interesting targets at the system and component levels, enabling designers to use a component-by-component approach that will be instrumental in respecting the overall building targets.

The outcome of this research opens new perspectives for engineers and architects. First, it suggests that exploration brings more added-value in the early design phase than a traditional evaluation process. Effectively, low-resolution details inevitably lead to inaccurate evaluations, whereas hypotheses fuel exploration. Secondly, it provides technology that is fast-paced enough to keep up with the iterative process. Though computationally intensive, once the knowledge database is created, it is highly interactive and provides immediate feedback. Finally, it is more than a simulation tool; it is also a communication tool that provides useful insight for both experts and non-experts by dint of its data-visualization capacity. Thus, this dynamic graphical interface is a powerful communication tool for people with different interests and backgrounds; it allows them to discuss performance metrics within the design process, whereas existing complex and static simulation reports fail to grab non-experts' attention. ELSA may inspire LCA researchers and software developers to move towards a new generation of design-supporting tools that go beyond existing assessment techniques, as the latter do not resolve the fundamental constraints practitioners face at the early design stage.

Prototyped based on the SLB case study, ELSA had three main objectives:
1) to validate the robustness of the prototype,
2) to deliver a knowledge database that could be used by the future SLB designers and
3) to assess ELSA's usability for practitioners in real situations.

This last objective must still be reached during the SLB's operational design phase, which will start in 2019.

Acknowledgements

The authors would like to thank Prof. Florinel Radu and his Joint Master students of HEIA-FR for testing the ELSA prototype, the professional engineers and architects for their help in understanding their issues regarding LCA, and the members of the Building2050 research team, for their valuable inputs through enlightening discussions.

Partners

Building2050 / EPFL: Thomas Jusselme, Endrit Hoxha, Stefano Cozza, Pedro Antunes Fernandes
EPFL ECAL lab / EPFL: Henchoz Nicolas, Renato Zülli, Andreas Koller, Andreas Sonderegger, Jasmine Florentine
Human-IST / Fribourg University: Denis Lalanne, Raphaël Tuor, Florian Evequoz
LAST / EPFL: Emmanuel Rey
LIPID / EPFL: Marilyne Andersen
Tokiwi services: Léonard Stalder

References

Attia, Shady, Elisabeth Gratia, André De Herde, and Jan L. M. Hensen. 2012. "Simulation-Based Decision Support Tool for Early Stages of Zero-Energy Building Design." *Energy and Buildings* 49 (June): 2–15. https://doi.org/10.1016/j.enbuild.2012.01.028.

Brooke, John. 1996. "SUS – A Quick and Dirty Usability Scale." *Usability Evaluation in Industry* 189 (194): 4–7.

Card, Stuart K., Jock D. Mackinlay, and Ben Shneiderman. 1999. "Readings in Information Visualization: Using Vision to Think." *The Morgan Kaufmann Series in Interactive Technologies*, 686. https://doi.org/10.1002/wics.89.

Cozza, Stefano. 2015. "Technical and Architectural Energy Strategies for the *smart living lab*, a Sustainable Building with Reliable Environmental Objectives." https://infoscience.epfl.ch/record/214954?ln=en.

DesignBuilder. 2016. "DesignBuilder Software Ltd – Home." 2016. https://designbuilder.co.uk/.

Dixit, Manish K., Jose L. Fernández-Solís, Sarel Lavy, and Charles H. Culp. 2012. "Need for an Embodied Energy

Measurement Protocol for Buildings: A Review Paper." *Renewable and Sustainable Energy Reviews* 16 (6): 3730–43. https://doi.org/10.1016/j.rser.2012.03.021.

EU – EPBD. 2010. "Directive 2010/31/EU of the European Parliament and of the Council of 19 May 2010 on the Energy Performance of Buildings (Recast)." *Official Journal of the European Union* 18 (06): 2010.

European Committee for Standardization. 2011. "EN 15978:2011 – Sustainability of Construction Works. Assessment of Environmental Performance of Buildings. Calculation Method."

Hollberg, Alexander, and Jürgen Ruth. 2016. "LCA in Architectural Design – a Parametric Approach." *The International Journal of Life Cycle Assessment* 21 (7): 943–60. https://doi.org/10.1007/s11367-016-1065-1.

Hoxha, Endrit. 2015. "Amélioration de la fiabilité des évaluations environnementales des bâtiments." Phd thesis, Université Paris-Est. https://pastel.archives-ouvertes.fr/tel-01214629/document.

Hoxha, Endrit, and Thomas Jusselme. 2017. "On the Necessity of Improving the Environmental Impacts of Furniture and Appliances in Net-Zero Energy Buildings." *Science of The Total Environment* 596–597 (October): 405–16. https://doi.org/10.1016/j.scitotenv.2017.03.107.

Huot, Stéphane. 2005. "Une nouvelle approche pour la conception créative: de l'interprétation du dessin à main levée au prototypage d'interactions non-standard." Université de Nantes.

Jusselme, Thomas. 2016. Method of identifying technical design solutions: US Patent App. 15/638,985 / EP20160178041, issued July 2016.

Jusselme, Thomas, Arianna Brambilla, Endrit Hoxha, Yingying Jiang, Didier Vuarnoz, and Stefano Cozza. 2015. "Building 2050 – State-of-the- Arts and Preliminary Guidelines." EPFL – Fribourg.

Jusselme, Thomas, Stefano Cozza, Endrit Hoxha, Arianna Brambilla, Florian Evequoz, Denis Lalanne, Emmanuel Rey, and Marilyne Andersen. 2016. "Towards a Pre-Design Method for Low Carbon Architectural Strategies." In *PLEA 2016*. Los Angeles, USA.

Jusselme, Thomas, Emmanuel Rey, and Marilyne Andersen. 2018a. "Findings from a Survey on the Current Use of Life-Cycle Assessment in Building Design." *Proceedings of the PLEA 2018 conference: Smart and Healthy within the 2-degree Limit*.

Jusselme, Thomas, Emmanuel Rey, and Marilyne Andersen. 2018b. "An Integrative Approach for Embodied Energy: Towards an LCA-Based Data-Driven Design Method." *Renewable and Sustainable Energy Reviews* 88 (May): 123–32. https://doi.org/10.1016/j.rser.2018.02.036.

Jusselme, Thomas, Raphaël Tuor, Denis Lalanne, Emmanuel Rey, and Marilyne Andersen. 2017. "Visualization Techniques for Heterogeneous and Multidimensional Simulated Building Performance Data Sets." *Proceedings of the International Conference for Sustainable Design of the Built Environment*, 971–82.

KBOB. 2014. "Eco-Bau – Données Des Écobilans." 2014. http://www.eco-bau.ch/?Nav=20.

Kellenberger, Daniel, Martin Ménard, Stefan Schneider, Madis Org, Katrin Victor, and Severin Lenel. 2012. "Réhabiliter des friches industrielles pour réaliser la société à 2000 watts. Guide et exemples." Switzerland: Projet conjoint de Stadt Zürich, Zürich ewz, Confédératioin Suisse. http://www.2000watt.ch/

Miyamoto, Ayu, Tam Nguyen Van, Damien Trigaux, Karen Allacker, and Frank De Troyer. 2015. "Visualisation Tool to Estimate the Effect of Design Parameters on the Heating Energy Demand in the Early Design Phases." https://doi.org/10.13140/RG.2.1.1515.2085.

Morris, Jon D. 1995. "Observations: SAM: The Self-Assessment Manikin; an Efficient Cross-Cultural Measurement of Emotional Response." *Journal of Advertising Research* 35 (6): 63–68.

Naboni, Emanuele, Yi Zhang, Alessandro Maccarini, Elian Hirsch, and Daniele Lezzi. 2013. "Extending the Use of Parametric Simulation in Practice through a Cloud Based Online Service." In *IBPSA Italy-Conference of International Building Performance Simulation Association, Bozen, Italy*. http://m.e3lab.org/upl/website/publication11111/IBPSAitaly13.pdf.

Østergård, Torben, Rasmus L. Jensen, and Steffen E. Maagaard. 2016. "Building Simulations Supporting Decision Making in Early Design – A Review." Renewable and Sustainable Energy Reviews 61 (August): 187–201. https://doi.org/10.1016/j.rser.2016.03.045.

Østergård, Torben, Rasmus L. Jensen, and Steffen E. Maagaard. 2017. "Early Building Design: Informed Decision-Making by Exploring Multidimensional Design Space Using Sensitivity Analysis." *Energy and Buildings* 142 (Supplement C): 8–22. https://doi.org/10.1016/j.enbuild.2017.02.059.

Poncety, Amélie, Arianna Brambilla, Endrit Hoxha, Didier Vuarnoz, Stefano Cozza, Vanda Costa Grisel, Cédric Liardet, and Thomas Jusselme. 2016. "Graphical Representation of the Smart Living Building Research Program." Gruyères, Switzerland.

Pu, Pearl, and Denis Lalanne. 2002. "Design Visual Thinking Tools for Mixed Initiative Systems." *Proceedings of the 7th International Conference on Intelligent User Interfaces – IUI '02*, 119. https://doi.org/10.1145/502721.502736.

Ritter, Fabian, Philipp Geyer, and André Borrmann. 2015. "Simulation-Based Decision-Making in Early Design Stages." In *Proceedings of the 32rd International CIB W78 Conference, Eindhoven, Netherlands*. http://www.cms.bgu.tum.de/publications/2015_Ritter_CIB.pdf.

Saltelli, Andrea, Marco Ratto, Stefano Tarantola, and Francesca Campolongo. 2012. "Update 1 of: Sensitivity Analysis for Chemical Models." *Chemical Reviews* 112 (5): PR1–21. https://doi.org/10.1021/cr200301u.

SIA. 2015. SIA 2024 – "Conditions d'utilisation standard pour l'énergie et les installations du bâtiment."

⑨ Lessons learned from a living lab research process

Thomas Jusselme
Didier Vuarnoz

This chapter aims to summarize key findings in the form of operational recommendations in order to encourage professionals in the construction business to develop comfortable, low-carbon buildings. The key drivers of a living lab research process are also highlighted to help those who are or will be involved in a living lab to improve its usability.

The material presented in this book involved roughly twenty-five researchers over a three-year period, and led to more than thirty scientific publications. It is the result of a research programme with a single focus: the *smart living lab* building (SLB). This unique experiment has had two key outputs. The first is the research findings, which will help in the design and the construction of the SLB. The second is the initial living lab experiment, whose objective was to conduct research on the SLB environment itself. These conclusions have been summarized in this chapter to assist the SLB's development in terms of design and construction, as well as to enhance its usability as a future research object. They might also prove useful for those working in the fields of architecture, engineering, construction, or living lab development. As it is a summary, some simplifications have undoubtedly been made. Given that each project has a specific context with drawbacks and advantages, the following statements should be carefully considered before attempting to transpose them to other case studies. However, each notion developed hereafter is described in depth in the previous chapters of this book, providing for a better understanding of the scientific background behind these statements.

9.1 Operational recommendations

In total, twenty-three operational recommendations have been listed and divided into six themes:
- A) Process and Brief
- B) Comfort
- C) Energy Strategy and Systems
- D) Construction Technologies
- E) Internal Layout
- F) Building Interface

Each recommendation is included in at least one of the proposed themes. A summary of these recommendations is presented in a graphical representation Figure 9.1 where each recommendation has been associated with keywords, whose spatial position indicates their relationship to the given themes.

A Process & Brief

A1 Legal procedure: The legal procedure chosen should facilitate collaboration between stakeholders, designers and experts. Approaches for managing mishaps and changes in performance targets should be incorporated at the beginning of the construction process.

A2 Objectives of the brief: The brief should be generic so as to allow designers to interpret a given issue and, at the same time, specifically formulate innovative contextual solutions. The brief should contain a series of objectives that correspond to the building's vision: quality of use, environmental quality, contextual quality, etc. The architectural quality refers to the integration of various partial qualities into a single vision.

A3 Collaboration between main actors: The main actors (users and decision makers) should be involved throughout the design phase. A participatory commission to discuss the various choices and building features with future users should follow the design process. A building design that aims for a holistic approach requires collaborative action and planning. Architects and engineers should work together to jointly develop the building's architectural and environmental design. Construction companies should also be involved early on in the process.

A4 Integration of renewables: A net-Zero Energy Building incorporates numerous systems to produce renewable energies. These systems must be sized and integrated by designers early in the design process, as incorporating them into the architectural project at a later time is more difficult.

A5 Commissioning process: The implementation of technical installations and appropriate components should be monitored via a commissioning process during the construction phase, as such oversight is instrumental in achieving the target performance levels. Each building, with its technical installations, etc., is unique and therefore requires an initial setting (set-point temperatures, aeraulic and hydraulic balancing, etc.) to ensure optimal performance.

B Comfort

B1 User control: Though the building should incorporate the highest standards of energy efficiency, users want to have maximum control when it comes to managing light, temperature, ventilation, blinds and the option to open windows. However, buildings' best operational practices are often not communicated to users. A good understanding of how to use the building is essential for achieving operational efficiency.

B2 Passive night cooling: To ensure comfort in summer in less-densely occupied spaces passively and without air-conditioning, natural night ventilation (passive night cooling) of the premises is very efficient in temperate climates, regardless of the building's inertia (and all the more so if the building inertia is mid-range).

B3 Choice of colours and materials: The materials, colours, and the presence of plants inside the building are three key contributors to comfort for the majority of building users. As such, designers should consider them carefully.

C Energy strategy and systems

C1 Performance indicators assessments: A wide variety of assessment methodologies based on different standards, labels and norms exists. These methodologies differ, particularly

Fig. 9.1   Mind map of the different operational recommendations

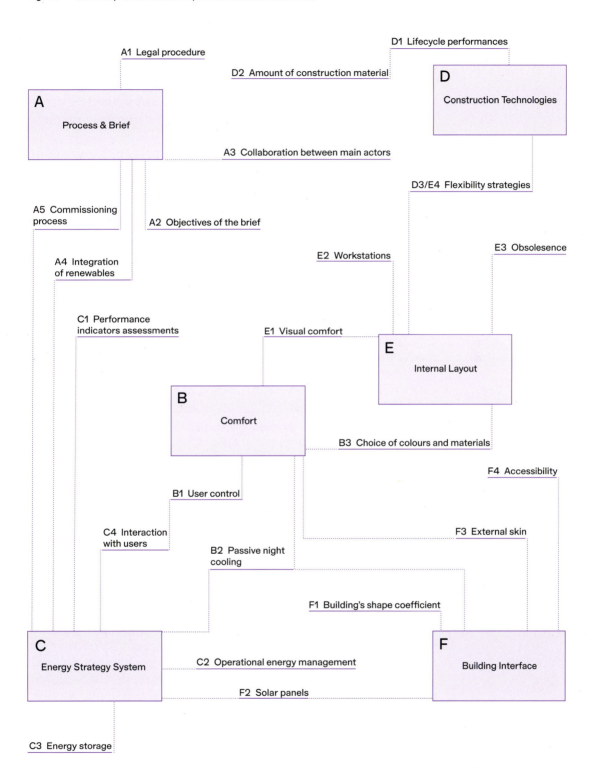

with regard to how surplus renewable energy is used in the energy and impact assessment. Therefore, a common assessment approach should be defined and used by all stakeholders. Moreover, the life cycle analysis should incorporate accurate energy conversion factors and surplus energy exports.

C2   Operational energy management: The benefits of developing new operational energy management systems must be assessed annually based on life cycle indicators for the entire system. Special attention must be paid when assessing the gains such new systems offer versus traditional ones by considering both greenhouse gas (GHG) emissions and primary energy use. Minimizing GHG emissions should not supplant the importance of cumulative energy demand (CED) and non-renewable cumulative energy demand (CED_{nr}).

C3   Energy storage: Energy storage should be integrated into the building's energy system to increase the onsite use of renewable energy and the building's energy self-sufficiency. However, autonomy has both environmental and financial costs; hence, oversizing storage capacity should be avoided. Appropriate capacity of the storage energy system should be set out in clear and explicit objectives (e.g. Net Zero Energy Building (NZEB), building autonomy), and its positive impact must be validated by a LCA at the building scale.

C4   Interaction with users: Environmentally-friendly behaviour should be suggested and encouraged, rather than imposed. A dynamic load shift requires access to hourly grid mix emission data. Offices have a lower potential of GHG emissions and primary energy mitigation by load shift than do dwellings, with winter being the optimal period. Communication and interaction with building users is essential for enabling load shift and should take place via existing devices (e.g. mobile phone, tablet, computer) to minimize embodied impacts.

D   Construction technologies

D1   Life cycle performance: Each building component must be designed and justified in terms of its life cycle performance. For instance, thick insulation *decreases* heating needs but *increases* the embodied impact of buildings, and potentially the overall environmental footprint. The same reasoning can be used with regard to thermal inertia; the more efficient the HVAC system, the less thermal inertia is needed to reduce heat consumption. Thus, low-tech materials such as rammed earth have great potential because their benefits outweigh their embodied impact.

D2   Amount of construction material: Less material means less impact. One way to limit the amount of material used for buildings is to reduce the wall layers by avoiding finishes, drop-ceilings and raised-floors, and using materials that fulfil multiple functions. Separating functional layers makes it possible to replace or transform them without compromising the overall construction system and ensuring that the components are recyclable at the end of their use-life.

D3   Flexibility strategies: As part of the building will often be used as rental units for business activities (i.e. offices and commerce), the designers should use scalable construction and technical solutions allowing for its many transformations. These solutions should also minimize disruptions for current users. Flexibility strategies should include appropriately increasing both the accessibility of vertical service ducts and the bearing capacity of the structure's components.

E   Internal Layout

E1   Visual comfort: Natural light should be favoured in the building, and primary workstations should always have an outdoor view. Collaborative activities should be done in areas with high visual openness, whereas individual tasks that require concentration should be done in areas with visual privacy.

E2   Workstations: Given the importance of being able to isolate oneself in order to concentrate on intellectually demanding tasks, workstations (especially primary ones) should provide shelter from noise and other disturbances. These workstations can be grouped into modular systems for one to five people. As such, architects and interior designers may need to rethink working conditions at intermediate scales, i.e. neither individual offices nor open space designs.

E3   Obsolesence: Functional spaces should be scalable to resist obsolescence and remain highly resilient to programmatic changes throughout the building's lifespan. Professional workspaces must be adaptable to quickly and easily meet the needs of future users. Some flexibility strategies include increasing the building's potential functions and neutralizing space units with multiple functions.

E4   Flexibility strategies: It is preferable to use universal spatial dimensions for the floor layout and equilateral, regular shapes in the building's overall layout. Increasing story height to accommodate service ducts and increase the building's usable space or surface without the aid of columns enables a greater degree of flexibility.

F   Building interfaces

F1   Building shape coefficient: Particular attention must be paid to the building shape coefficient, which corresponds to the ratio between the envelope surface and the energy reference surface. The envelope and its components have a high energy density (structure, insulation, glazing, coatings, etc.). The higher this ratio is, the more impact the materials used will have. Thus, one of the strategies for low-carbon buildings is to reduce the amount of material used.

F2   Solar panels: The energy and carbon footprint of the electricity produced by solar panels is a function of its capacity to harvest solar irradiation over its lifetime. These values must be compared with those of the grid mix when implementing photovoltaic panels, in order to generate renewable energy with lower carbon and energy footprints than electricity generated by a standard network.

F3   External skin: Increasing the independence of a building's external skin resolves the issue of renewing the individual components according to their specific lifespan, performance or changes in the usage of the building.

F4   Accessibility: To facilitate soft mobility, the creation of pleasant footpaths (i.e. to avoid main roads) from the nearest transport hub to the building's various entrances should encourage walking and the use of public transportation. Pedestrian entrances and access routes should be appropriately signposted.

9.2   Key drivers of a living lab research process

In the past decades, massive research and development efforts have been made to improve the energy efficiency of building components and architectural strategies, resulting in design advances such as passive buildings, low energy buildings, and net zero energy buildings. However, post-occupancy evaluation campaigns have highlighted the performance gap in terms of comfort and consumption between the prediction models used at the design stage and the post-construction reality. This serves as a reminder that we build to meet human needs, and that a building cannot be efficient if humans (i.e. users, builders, maintenance personnel, etc.) are not considered key factors in its success or failure. Recent developments in smart controls help facilitate human-building interactions but must nonetheless be based on a deep understanding of human behaviour. A fully automated building is no guarantee of comfort and performance, and could even be uncomfortable for users given the lack of human control. In Chapter ③, for example, we showed that, of hundreds of survey respondents, 94 % wanted to be able to control lighting, window opening, blinds, and doors.

Consequently, a user-centred approach is useful and highly recommended for rapidly handling real-life situations in the research and development process (Liedtke et al., 2012). This is where the *smart living lab* idea comes in, as an "R&D concept that aims to create innovations in a multi-contextual, real-world setting" (Konsti-Laakso et al. 2012). According to Bergvall-Kåreborn et al. (2009), the concept of a living lab can be attributed to Prof. William Mitchell at MIT, who developed the idea in order to observe user behaviours in a "smart/future" home for a given period. The model has spread across the globe since the early 2000s, and in 2018, an organization like the European Network of Living Labs (www.openlivinglabs.eu) had more than 400 living labs around the world. Though the literature on living labs is emerging, there is still a lack of feedback (Schurman et al., 2015). As this research programme has been used to initiate the *smart living lab*'s activities, the first three years of user-centred research have allowed us to identify key drivers to be considered by researchers aiming to develop both living and live-in lab research processes, as briefly discussed in Chapter ①. Each of the key drivers in question is presented below with a title, a statement and clarification.

- Shared culture
  The cognitive distance between living lab members is a source of innovation only if a shared culture is built over time.

Lab members can trigger innovation, thanks to their different backgrounds and ways of thinking (Konsti-Laakso et al. 2012). However, these differences are generally the source of communication issues. Using references as metaphors is a simple way to illustrate ideas. These references could be norms, products, buildings, etc. However, in an interdisciplinary team, these references may not initially be shared and thus cannot be used. Hence, time and effort are required to discover, understand, and integrate the research fields of the other lab members. Moreover, a common language is also necessary for presenting, describing, and communicating the core ideas of a research project. Building these common references is crucial in an interdisciplinary team, and requires both specific skills and time, which are frequently underestimated. In the framework of this research programme, a full visual representation of the findings has been painstakingly produced (Poncety et al. 2016). Summarising our findings graphically was extremely useful for a better understanding of the different research contexts, and the resulting poster provided us with a precious communication tool.

Thus, time and communication are two key ingredients for enhancing interdisciplinary collaboration. This was also observed by Bergvall-Kareborn et al. (Bergvall-Kareborn et al. 2009), who described the continuity principle as important, "since good cross-border collaboration, which strengthens creativity and innovation, builds on trust, and this takes time to build up."

- Common research objects
  Collaboration between living lab members must be stimulated by common research objects and proximity.

One of the flagship projects of the *smart living lab* is the development of its own building to support the experimental activities of researchers. Developing a research programme based on this objective has provided a common research subject, and thus allowed for collaboration on research questions from a variety of perspectives. This has been crucial in fostering the living lab spirit, by creating synergies and proximity through the experiments carried out in the temporary offices. According to Konsti-Laakso et al. (Konsti-Laakso et al. 2012), geographical proximity triggers social proximity, even if it does not automatically lead to innovation. However, this proximity is necessary for spontaneity, one of the key principles identified by Bergvall-Kareborn et al. (Bergvall-Kareborn et al. 2009): "In order to succeed with new innovations, it is important to inspire usage, meet personal desires; (…) it becomes important to have the ability to detect, aggregate, and analyse spontaneous users' reactions and ideas over time." One of the underlying issues of proximity is the critical size of a living lab and the physical presence of its members to ensure a minimum density, which is also necessary for creating social proximity.

- Experimental willingness
  The members of a living lab should have a strong and similar desire to carry out their research activities through experimentation and user-centred approaches.

Though this statement seems obvious, significant disparity in the desire to experiment results in frustration for lab members in the long term. Indeed, as a living lab is also a work-in or live-in space, those desirous to fully utilise the lab for experimentation will feel frustrated if others are disturbed by frequent experiments. Finding the right balance between live-in/work-in and experimentation is crucial for the well-being and satisfaction of all stakeholders. The "Empowerment of users" (Bergvall-Kareborn et al. 2009) is a key principle of live-in labs, and may be impacted by occupants' desire to experiment.

- Ethical issues
  Ethical rules should not be neglected by the living lab, and vice versa.

A live-in lab aims to use activity monitoring, people tracking, surveys, audio and video recording, data acquisition from sensors, etc. for experimental purposes. All experiments involving humans must comply with specific ethical procedures defined by different regulatory bodies. An effective balance between this ethical framework and human research must then be found. The gap between monitoring and ethics lies in the fact that living labs combine both work-in and live-in activities and experiments. It is therefore crucial to establish policies, procedures, and toolboxes that support human experimentation without compromising ethical rules. Given the restrictive nature of these rules, it is important to find ways to implement them more easily in order to ensure a high level of usability of the living lab.

- **Scientists as research objects**
The user-centred approach in live-in labs has a major bias, as the research environment is not representative of the real world.

Indeed, the actual context of the objects researchers investigate is not naturally present in a lab. However, one of the key features of a live-in lab is its close-to-real-world setting. Regarding the sustainable building research field, for instance, whereas dwellings are major contributors to climate change and energy consumption, labs do not usually serve as dwellings. Moreover, the lab population is quite specific (in this case, highly educated, international, young, etc.). However, it would be utopian to think that a living lab could be representative of the real world. Thus, the right balance must be found between the lab members' research fields and the lab's functionalities. Mixed use of the building (including functionalities other than the lab) and temporary facilities would increase the range of potential research topics that could be investigated.

9.3 Synthesis

This chapter summarizes the main findings of the research programme in the form of operational recommendations and key criteria for a living lab. The diversity of the findings highlights the holistic approach developed in this programme and extends the range of potential disciplines (which might include building physics, environmental engineering, statistics, social sciences, mechanical engineering, architecture, construction law, human computer interactions, computer sciences, etc.). This interdisciplinarity is fostered by the unique nature of the *smart living lab* based on two key criteria: the proximity between the researchers (i.e. physical, cognitive, organizational, etc.) and the common research object (i.e. the *smart living lab*'s future building).

Acknowledgments

The authors would like to thank all of the researchers and partners who helped us develop these key recommendations based on this research programme and living lab experience.

References

Bergvall-Kareborn, Birgitta, Marita Hoist, and Anna Stahlbrost. 2009. "Concept Design with a Living Lab Approach." In *System Sciences, 2009. HICSS'09. 42nd Hawaii International Conference On*, 1–10. IEEE.

Bergvall-Kåreborn, Birgitta, Carina Ihlström Eriksson, Anna Ståhlbröst, and Jesper Svensson. 2009. "A Milieu for Innovation : Defining Living Labs." In *DIVA*. http://urn.kb.se/resolve?urn=urn:nbn:se:ltu:diva-31540.

Konsti-Laakso, Suvi, Timo Pihkala, and Sascha Kraus. 2012. "Facilitating SME Innovation Capability through Business Networking." *Creativity and Innovation Management* 21 (1): 93–105. https://doi.org/10.1111/j.1467-8691.2011.00623.x.

Liedtke, Christa, Maria Welfens, Holger Rohn, and Julia Nordmann. 2012. "LIVING LAB: User-Driven Innovation for Sustainability." *International Journal of Sustainability in Higher Education* 13: 106–18. https://doi.org/10.1108/14676371211211809.

Poncety, Amélie, Arianna Brambilla, Endrit Hoxha, Didier Vuarnoz, Stefano Cozza, Vanda Costa Grisel, Cédric Liardet, and Thomas Jusselme. 2016. "Graphical Representation of the Smart Living Building Research Program." Gruyères, Switzerland.

Conclusion

Marilyne Andersen
Emmanuel Rey

These multidimensional research explorations conclude with a lot of promises. Throughout nine chapters, some of the key challenges inherent to the ambition of a project like the *smart living lab*'s future building have been defined and researched so as to propose tangible solutions or promising leads towards them.

In Part I, Chapter ① was an invitation to read the story behind the genesis of the *smart living lab* and what it aims to become. Chapter ② laid the foundations of the research programme supporting the development of its dedicated building, and defined the overarching principles from which the experiments were built. Chapter ③ addressed the user perspective, by investigating who will ultimately work in this building and with what expectations, with the hope to get closer to the delicate balance between tailor-made and generic work environments.

In Part II, Chapter ④ went one step further in this regard from a spatial point of view, by focusing on the inter-dependencies between floor area and perceived comfort and satisfaction. Chapter ⑤ took a stab at the right compromise between a building envelope's performance and its embodied carbon footprint. Chapter ⑥, on the other hand, focused on optimizing energy management by looking into energy demand and renewable energy availability together with energy storage and grid.

In Part III, Chapter ⑦ examined the opportunity of integrating complex and multifaceted performance requirements into a process that could simultaneously promote architectural quality, environmental performance and actively involve all the actors in the process. Chapter ⑧ offers a new, software-based approach to support the exploration of design solutions by relying on lessons learned and on the cascading effects of decisions. Finally, Chapter ⑨ brings a synthetic perspective by presenting a limited set of ten operational recommendations that emerged from the research programme and are more directly applicable to a project with similar ambitions as those set for the *smart living lab*'s building.

In a project such as this one, the cross-fertilization potential offered by interdisciplinarity—and in this particular case, also by inter-institutionality—is tangible. By bringing different domains of expertise, competences and work culture together, and stimulating dialogue dynamics, the level of solvability of complex problems increases very rapidly. It is not, however, an easy exercise. Diversity in competences comes hand in hand with a diversity of languages and priorities, and to avoid ending up with the minimum common denominator, there is a need toremove all actors from their respective comfort zones, while asking them to remain anchored in their own specialization to ensure pertinence.

The next step is to move on with the actual design, then construction, of the *smart living lab* building. Towards this end, the results of the research effort presented in this book have been integrated into its design brief. From being a research object in itself, it now aims to become an embodiment of sustainable construction, an evolving research laboratory for its users and a lively demonstrator for its visitors. Towards this aim, an innovative parallel study mandate (MEP) will take place, which finds its foundations in the very outcomes of the research effort that was conducted in this programme. Beyond strictly programmatic and/or performative aspects, this publication is intended a source of reflection and motivation for the interdisciplinary teams selected for this unprecedented competition.

Beyond the scope of the future building hosting the *smart living lab*, we hope that this academic, but also human, adventure will serve as an inspiration to other quests for evermore sustainable places to live and work—towards 2050 and beyond.

List of acronyms

BED	building energy demand	
BFFSA	Blue Factory Fribourg Freiburg SA	
BI	building integrated	
BIPV	building integrated photovoltaic	
CAD	computer-aided design	
CEB	compressed earth bricks	
CED	cumulative energy demand	
CED_{nr}	non-renewable cumulative energy demand	
CF	characterization factor	
CO_{2-eq}	equivalent carbon dioxide	
CPU	Central Processing Unit	
CV^y	ratio of σ^y to e μ^y	
DHW	domestic hot water	
DP	domestic production	
DBPS	dynamic building performance simulation	
E	energy	
EI	environmental impact	
ELSA	Exploration tooL for Sustainable Architecture	
EPFL	École Polytechnique Fédérale de Lausanne	
ERA	energy reference area	
ES	energy storage	
EV	electric vehicle	
Exp	export	
f_{ap}	hourly factor for appliance use	
f_m	grid matching index	
f_{oc}	hourly occupation factor	
G	grid	
GDP	Gross Domestic Product	
GHG	greenhouse gas	
GUI	Graphical User Interface	
GWP	global warming potential	
h	efficiency	
HEIA-FR	School of Engineering and Architecture of Fribourg, member of University of Applied Science of Western Switzerland	
HI	heavy inertia	
HP	Heat pump	
HVAC	heating, ventilation, air conditioning	
i	interval of time	
LAST	Laboratory of Architecture and Sustainable Technologies	
LASUR	Urban Sociology Laboratory	
LCA	life cycle assessment	
LCER	life cycle efficiency ratio	
LCIA	life cycle impact assessment	
LI	light inertia	
LIPID	Laboratory of Integrated Performance in Design	
MEP	Architecture Competition with Open Dialogue	
m^y	mean annual value	
N	number of measurements	
NR	non-renewable	
NZEB	Net Zero Energy Building	
O	operative	

P_o	nominal energy density [W/m^2]	
P_a	nominal occupancy density [p/m^2]	
PCPs	parallel coordinate plots	
PEF	primary energy factor	
PV	photovoltaic	
R	ratio	
RES	renewable energy system	
RSSI	Received Signal Strength Indication	
s^y	standard deviation	
SA	sensitivity analysis	
SAM	Self-Assessment Manikin	
$SEER_{vc}$	seasonal energy efficiency ratio for ventilative cooling	
SH	space heating	
SLB	the *smart living lab*'s future building	
SUS	System Usability Scale	
TI	thermal inertia	
UNIFR	University of Fribourg	
UT	user testing	
UX	user experience	

Illustration credits

Pages 1–8   Jeremy Ayer, "Cardinal Brewery" (2011–2014).

Pages 21–24   Benoît Jeannet, from the projects "A Geological Index Of The Landscape" (2011–2015), "Synthetic Landscape Elements" (2017) and "Untitled" (2018).

Fig. 1.1–1.2   Poncety, Amélie, Arianna Brambilla, Endrit Hoxha, Didier Vuarnoz, Stefano Cozza, Vanda Costa Grisel, Cédric Liardet, and Thomas Jusselme. 2016. "Graphical Representation of the Smart Living Building Research Program." Gruyères, Switzerland.

Fig. 2.1   Poncety, Amélie, Arianna Brambilla, Endrit Hoxha, Didier Vuarnoz, Stefano Cozza, Vanda Costa Grisel, Cédric Liardet, and Thomas Jusselme. 2016. "Graphical Representation of the Smart Living Building Research Program." Gruyères, Switzerland.
Fig. 2.2   Jusselme, Thomas, Arianna Brambilla, Endrit Hoxha, Yingying Jiang, Didier Vuarnoz, and Stefano Cozza. 2015. "Building 2050 – State-of-the-Arts and Preliminary Guidelines." EPFL, Fribourg.
Fig. 2.3–2.4   Poncety, Amélie, Arianna Brambilla, Endrit Hoxha, Didier Vuarnoz, Stefano Cozza, Vanda Costa Grisel, Cédric Liardet, and Thomas Jusselme. 2016. "Graphical Representation of the Smart Living Building Research Program." Gruyères, Switzerland.
Fig. 2.5   Jusselme, Thomas, Arianna Brambilla, Endrit Hoxha, Yingying Jiang, Didier Vuarnoz, and Stefano Cozza. 2015. "Building 2050 – State-of-the-Arts and Preliminary Guidelines." EPFL, Fribourg.
Fig. 2.6   Thomas Jusselme and Vanda Costa, Building2050, EPFL.

Fig. 3.1   Thierry Maeder, UNI GE.
Fig. 3.2–3.3   Emmanuel Ravalet, LASUR, EPFL.

Pages 71–74   Benoît Jeannet, from the projects "A Geological Index Of The Landscape" (2011–2015) and "Untitled" (2018).

Fig. 4.1   Poncety, Amélie, Arianna Brambilla, Endrit Hoxha, Didier Vuarnoz, Stefano Cozza, Vanda Costa Grisel, Cédric Liardet, and Thomas Jusselme. 2016. "Graphical Representation of the Smart Living Building Research Program." Gruyères, Switzerland.
Fig. 4.2   Cédric Liardet, Building2050, EPFL.
Fig. 4.3   Corinne Cuendet, Lutz Architectes.
Fig. 4.4   Dominic Villeneuve, LASUR, EPFL.
Fig. 4.5   Cédric Liardet, Building2050, EPFL.
Fig. 4.6–4.8   Raphaël Dutoit, Atelier Oï
Fig. 4.9–4.12   Himanshu Verma, Human-IST, UNIFR.
Fig. 4.13   Hoxha, Endrit, Cédric Liardet, and Thomas Jusselme. 2018. "Measuring the Effect of Office Densification on the Energy and Carbon Lifecycle Performance."
Fig. 4.14   Endrit Hoxha, Building2050, EPFL.
Fig. 4.15–4.16   Derek Christie, LASUR, EPFL.
Fig. 4.17   Dominic Villeneuve, LASUR, EPFL.
Fig. 4.18–4.19   Hoxha, Endrit, Cédric Liardet, and Thomas Jusselme. 2018. "Measuring the Effect of Office Densification on the Energy and Carbon Lifecycle Performance."

Fig. 5.1   Jusselme, Thomas, Arianna Brambilla, Endrit Hoxha, Yingying Jiang, Didier Vuarnoz, and Stefano Cozza. 2015. "Building 2050 – State-of-the-Arts and Preliminary Guidelines." EPFL, Fribourg.
Fig. 5.2   SCBI, U. 2006. "Sustainable Building and Construction Initiative: Information Note." Paris, France *DTIE*.
Fig. 5.3   Barbara Haemmig de Preux / TERRABLOC.
Fig. 5.4   Arianna Brambilla, Building2050, EPFL.
Fig. 5.5   Amélie Poncéty, Building2050, EPFL.
Fig. 5.6–5.8 (left)   Arianna Brambilla, Building2050, EPFL.
Fig. 5.8 (right)   Brambilla, Arianna, and Thomas Jusselme. 2017. "Preventing Overheating in Offices through Thermal Inertial Properties of Compressed Earth Bricks: A Study on a Real Scale Prototype." *Energy and Buildings* 156 (December): 281–92. https://doi.org/10.1016/j.enbuild. 2017.09.070.
Fig. 5.9   Brambilla, Arianna, Jérôme Bonvin, Flourentzos Flourentzou, and Thomas Jusselme. 2018a. "Life Cycle Efficiency Ratio: A New Performance Indicator for a Life Cycle Driven Approach to Evaluate the Potential of Ventilative Cooling and Thermal Inertia." *Energy and Buildings* 163 (March): 22–33. https://doi.org/10.1016/j.enbuild.2017.12.010.
Fig. 5.10   Brambilla, Arianna, Jérôme Bonvin, Flourentzos Flourentzou, and Thomas Jusselme. 2018a. "Life Cycle Efficiency Ratio: A New Performance Indicator for a Life Cycle Driven Approach to Evaluate the Potential of Ventilative Cooling and Thermal Inertia." *Energy and Buildings* 163 (March): 22–33. https://doi.org/10.1016/j.enbuild.2017.12.010.
Fig. 5.11   Brambilla, Arianna, Jérôme Bonvin, Flourentzos Flourentzou, Thomas Jusselme. 2018b. "On the influence of thermal mass and natural ventilation on the overheating risk in offices." *Buildings* 8(4); 47.
Fig. 5.12–5.16   Brambilla, Arianna, and Thomas Jusselme. 2017. "Preventing Overheating in Offices through Thermal Inertial Properties of Compressed Earth Bricks: A Study on a Real Scale Prototype." *Energy and Buildings* 156 (December): 281–92. https://doi.org/10.1016/j.enbuild.2017.09.070.5.13.
Fig. 5.17–5.19   Brambilla, Arianna, Jérôme Bonvin, Flourentzos Flourentzou, and Thomas Jusselme. 2018a. "Life Cycle Efficiency Ratio: A New Performance Indicator for a Life Cycle Driven Approach to Evaluate the Potential of Ventilative Cooling and Thermal Inertia." *Energy and Buildings* 163 (March): 22–33. https://doi.org/10.1016/j.enbuild.2017.12.010.
Fig. 5.20   Arianna Brambilla, Building2050, EPFL.
Fig. 5.21–5.22   Brambilla, Arianna, Jérôme Bonvin, Flourentzos Flourentzou, and Thomas Jusselme. 2018a. "Life Cycle Efficiency Ratio: A New Performance Indicator for a Life Cycle Driven Approach to Evaluate the Potential of Ventilative Cooling and Thermal Inertia." *Energy and Buildings* 163 (March): 22–33. https://doi.org/10.1016/j.enbuild.2017.12.010.

Fig. 6.1–6.2   Didier Vuarnoz, Building2050, EPFL.
Fig. 6.3   Thibaut Schafer,

Institut Energy, HEIA-FR.
Fig. 6.4–6.7   Didier Vuarnoz, Building2050, EPFL.
Fig. 6.8   Agnès Lisowska-Masson, Human-IST, UNIFR
Fig. 6.9–6.10   Julien Nembrini, Human-IST, UNIFR.
Fig. 6.11–6.15   Didier Vuarnoz, Building2050, EPFL.
Fig. 6.16   Philippe Couty, Institut Energy, HEIA-FR.
Fig. 6.17–6.21   Didier Vuarnoz, Building2050, EPFL.

Pages 171–174   Benoît Jeannet, from the projects "A Geological Index Of The Landscape" (2011–2015) and "Untitled" (2018).

Fig. 7.1   Pieter Brueghel the Elder, bAGKOdJfvfAhYQ at Google Cultural Institute zoom level scaled down from second-highest, Public Domain, https://commons.wikimedia.org/w/index.php?curid=22178101.
Fig. 7.2–7.5   Florinel Radu, Institut Transform, HEIA-FR.
Fig. 7.6   Samuel Ludwig, www.samuelludwig.com.
Fig. 7.7   Mr. Nutt (Own work) [CC BY-SA 3.0 (https://creativecommons.org/licenses/by-sa/3.0)], via Wikimedia Commons.
Fig. 7.8   Florinel Radu, Institut Transform, HEIA-FR.
Fig. 7.9   Arch Photo, Inc., 112 Macdonough Street #4, Brooklyn, NY 11216.
Fig. 7.10   Florinel Radu, Institut Transform, HEIA-FR.

Fig. 8.1–8.2   Jusselme, Thomas, Emmanuel Rey, and Marilyne Andersen. 2018a. "Findings from a Survey on the Current Use of Life-Cycle Assessment in Building Design." *Proceedings of the PLEA 2018 conference: Smart and Healthy within the 2-degree Limit.*
Fig. 8.3   Kellenberger et al. 2012.
Fig. 8.4   Amélie Poncéty, Building2050, EPFL.
Fig. 8.5   Jusselme, Thomas, Emmanuel Rey, and Marilyne Andersen. 2018b. "An Integrative Approach for Embodied Energy: Towards an LCA-Based Data-Driven Design Method." *Renewable and Sustainable Energy Reviews* 88 (May): 123–32. https://doi.org/10.1016/j.rser.2018.02.036.
Fig. 8.6   Thomas Jusselme and Pedro Antunes, Building2050, EPFL.
Fig. 8.7   Raphaël Tuor, Human-IST, UNIFR.
Fig. 8.8   Andreas Koller, EPFL ECAL-LAB.
Fig. 8.9–8.12   Renato Zülli, EPFL ECAL-LAB.
Fig. 8.13   Amélie Poncéty, Building2050, EPFL.
Fig. 8.14   Thomas Jusselme, Building2050, EPFL.
Fig. 8.15   Stefano Cozza, Building2050, EPFL.
Fig. 8.16–8.17   Thomas Jusselme, Building2050, EPFL.

Fig. 9.1   Didier Vuarnoz, Building2050, EPFL.

Pages 253–256   Benoît Jeannet, from the project "A Geological Index Of The Landscape" (2011–2015).

Pages 273–280   Jeremy Ayer, "BlueFactory", (September 2018).

Authors

Marilyne Andersen holds an MSc in Physics and a PhD in Building Physics from the École polytechnique fédérale de Lausanne (EPFL), where she is a professor of sustainable construction technologies and Head of the Laboratory of Integrated Performance in Design (LIPID). Her research at LIPID focuses on the integration of building performance in design, with an emphasis on daylighting and themes such as health, perception, comfort and energy. She was Dean of the School of Architecture, Civil and Environmental Engineering (ENAC) at EPFL from 2013 to 2018 and is the Academic Director of the *smart living lab*. Before joining EPFL as faculty member, she was a Visiting Scholar at the Lawrence Berkeley National Laboratory, and Assistant then Associate Professor at MIT (USA), where she founded the MIT Daylighting Lab in 2004. She is the author of over 100 refereed scientific papers, several of which have earned distinctions, and was the first laureate of The Award for Daylight Research in 2016. She was also the leader of and faculty advisor to the Swiss Team, which won the 2017 US Solar Decathlon competition. She is co-founder of the start-up OCULIGHT dynamics, is a member of the Board of the LafargeHolcim Foundation for Sustainable Construction, an expert for Inno-Suisse and a Foundation Culture du Bâti (CUB) board member.

Emmanuel Rey earned a degree in architecture at École polytechnique fédérale de Lausanne (EPFL), followed by a European postgraduate diploma in architecture and sustainable development (1999) and a PhD from the Université catholique de Louvain (2006). His doctoral thesis was awarded the European Gustave Magnel Prize in 2009. Since 2000, he has worked at Bauart, an architectural and urban design firm based in Bern, Neuchâtel and Zurich, and has been a partner there since 2004. Through his work, he is involved in a wide variety of projects, competitions and achievements that have been published, exhibited and/or awarded on several occasions. He has also been professor of architecture and sustainable construction technologies at EPFL, where he founded the Laboratory of Architecture and Sustainable Technologies (LAST), since 2010. His contributions focus on the transcription of sustainability principles into architectural design, from the neighbourhood scale to construction components. He has been involved in the conceptual development of the *smart living lab* from its inception, and was Chair of the "Smart Living Building" Scientific Committee from 2014 to 2016. In 2015, he received an award from the Swiss Academies of Arts and Sciences and the swiss-academies award for transdisciplinary research (td-award).

Hamed Alavi is a senior researcher and lecturer at the Human-IST Institute (University of Fribourg) and a visiting research fellow in University College London. With a background in computer science, his research looks into Human-Computer Interaction as a design research field in the ever-evolving area of buildings and urban spaces, which is increasingly incorporating artificial intelligence. His current research on the notion of Human-Building Interaction questions the complexity of our interactive experiences with smart built environments.

Arianna Brambilla graduated from the Politecnico di Milano in 2011 with a degree in building engineering and architecture and a focus on sustainability and technological innovation. She got her PhD in 2014 (in collaboration with Aalborg University) for her work on the interconnections between energy efficiency and occupants' use of building equipment. In 2016, she completed a postdoc on thermal comfort and occupants' perception with the Building2050 research group at EPFL. She now works as lecturer in architectural technology at the University of Sydney, Australia.

Derek Christie is a public health biologist whose main research interest is the sustainable development of urban areas through a combination of health, transportation and environmental approaches. In 2018, he received his PhD from the Architecture and Sciences of the City doctoral programme at the EPFL with a project entitled "Frequent Walkers." He has been a board member of Geneva's Association for Transport and Environment for 20 years and has worked as a researcher and science writer at the University of Geneva and the World Health Organization, as well as in the private sector.

Anne-Claude Cosandey is the operational director of EPFL Fribourg and has been responsible for coordinating the *smart living lab* since 2014. She graduated with a degree in environmental engineering from EPFL in 1998 and earned a PhD from EPFL in 2002. She worked in a consulting engineering/biology company active in natural ecosystem protection for six years. In 2008, she became head of Ecoparc, a non-governmental organization that promotes sustainability in the built environment. In 2013, she coordinated the "demonstration projects for sustainable urban development" initiative from the Swiss federal office for spatial development. Throughout these experiences, she initiated and facilitated new projects involving a multitude of stakeholders including public, private and academic bodies.

Vanda Costa graduated in architecture from EPFL in 1998. She worked for several architecture firms in Lausanne before transitioning to a career in communications in 2003, honing her skills in graphic design, writing, event management and webmaster functions. A member of the association "Ville en Tête" since 2015, she leads children's activities to raise awareness about the built environment while helping to develop these programmes and their support material. She has been working as a scientific collaborator for EPFL at the *smart living lab* since 2016.

Philippe Couty began his PhD at EPFL in the field of turbine cavitation in 1997 after doing a Master's in physics and fluids mechanics. In 2004, he co-founded Karmic, Inc., which developed nanotechnology applications. In 2007, he decided to join the photovoltaic industry with Flexcell VHF-technologies, with a focus on increasing the cell efficiency of flexible solar panels. Since 2013, he has pursued a career in R&D and industrial development in the area of energy and industrial technologies. He has been the engineering leader for the Swiss Living Challenge for the past three years. In 2017, his team won the US DOE Solar Decathlon competition in Denver, Colorado. Today, he is self-employed as an energy and building consultant.

Stefano Cozza is a research engineer. He earned a B.Sc. MSc in Energy Engineering with a specialization in Renewable Resources from La Sapienza (University of Rome) in 2015. His Master's project, in collaboration with EPFL, concerned technical and architectural energy strategies for a sustainable building. After graduating, he continued to work as part of the Building2050 research group (EPFL), which looks at Building Performance Simulation and energy systems. Since June 2017, he has been pursuing his research as a doctoral candidate and teaching assistant at the Institute for Environmental Sciences of the University of Geneva. His research focuses on energy efficiency in the built environment and the energy performance gap in buildings more specifically.

Hugo Gasnier is an architect. He earned his degree at DSA Earthen Architectures (post-Master's training) and has been a researcher at CRAterre Laboratory, labex AE&CC and the ENSAG. He is in charge of the Dessin Chantier department, which works on the design and feasibility of architectural projects in France using earthen material. He is involved in research projects combining technique, training and architectural conception. His work brings together research and education, notably at DSA Earthen Architectures at the ENSAG. He is currently working on a thesis, which he began in 2015, on excavated earth as a resource for building environmentally-friendly towns.

Nicolas Henchoz is the Director of EPFL+ECAL Lab, EPFL's Design Research Center. With a background in Material Science and Journalism, he transitioned into art direction. His book, "Design for Innovative Technologies: from Disruption to Acceptance", defines a new vision of how technology can be turned into meaningful user experiences. His projects have been presented at various institutions including Harvard University, the Musée des Arts Décoratifs in Paris, the American Institute of Architecture in NYC and the Royal College of Art in London. His research work has also led to several articles and conferences such as ISMAR, Include and Siggraph. He is a visiting professor at the Politecnico di Milano and member of the board of the Global Alliance for Media Innovation.

Endrit Hoxha is currently a lecturer at EPOKA University, Albania. He earned a degree in Structural Profile Civil Engineering from the Polytechnic University of Tirana in 2010. An intern at École Spéciale des Travaux Publics du Bâtiment et de l'Industrie (ESTP) and EIFFAGE construction (Paris), he earned a Master's of Science from the École Nationale des Ponts et Chaussées (ENPC, Paris) in Mechanics of Materials and Structures in 2011 and a PhD in Environmental Science and Technology from the Université Paris-Est. In 2017, he completed a post-doc as part of the Building2050 research group at EPFL and later joined the Structural Xploration Lab at that same institution.

Thomas Jusselme is an eco-design engineer and researcher. He completed his education in 2003 with a Master's in Industrial Design at UTC Compiègne after earning a degree in environmental engineering in Lyon. He pursued his interests by studying sustainable architecture practices, travelling to 25 countries and subsequently co-founded exNdo (an architectural firm) and Milieu studio (an eco-design engineering office) in Lyon, where he was CTO for eight years. In 2015, he co-created COMBO Solutions, a start-up for energy and digital transition in buildings. He is currently a research associate with the Building2050 research group for EPFL at the *smart living lab* in Fribourg. He is also working on his PhD as part of the EPFL's LIPID and LAST laboratories.

Vincent Kaufmann is an associate professor of urban sociology and mobility at EPFL. He has also served as scientific director of the Mobile Lives Forum in Paris since 2011. After earning a Master's in sociology from the University of Geneva, he completed a PhD on the logics underlying transport modal choices at EPFL. He has been a guest lecturer at Lancaster University (2000–2001), École Des Ponts Paris (2001–2002), Université Laval (2008), Nimegen University (2010), the Université de Toulouse Le Mirail (2011) and Tongji University (2018). His areas of research include motility, mobility, urban lifestyles, the links between social and spatial mobility and land-use planning and transportation policies.

Denis Lalanne is a professor in the Department of Informatics at the University of Fribourg and heads the Human-IST Institute, an institute dedicated to research on and training in Human-Computer Interaction combining expertise in computer science, psychology and sociology. Human-IST aims to develop and evaluate new interface technologies that are useful, sustainable and attractive to a broad spectrum of people. At the *smart living lab*, his group is currently working on Human-Building Interaction to develop interactive technologies for understanding and improving building occupants' comfort and behaviour. He is a recognized expert in multimodal interaction and information visualization and has published over a hundred peer-reviewed scientific articles.

Jean-Marie Le Tiec graduated in architecture from the ENSAG and also holds a DPEA Architecture de Terre. He has worked for NAMA architecture, his own company, and with CRAterre as head of "dessin-chantier" section since 2005. CRAterre assists in the design and development of contemporary projects made of rammed earth and also is working to draft national regulations for earthen constructions in France. Through these two activities, he is involved in projects that focus on eco-responsible housing and constructive cultures.

Cédric Liardet earned a degree in Architecture from EPFL in 2008 and received the BG Consulting Engineers Award for Construction and Sustainable Development that same year. He then worked for the Dreier Frenzel architectural firm in Lausanne until becoming self-employed in 2011, led by his passion for economy of means ("doing more with less"). From 2016 to 2017, Liardet was also a scientific collaborator for EPFL's Building2050 group, where he worked on user environmental strategies.

Thierry Maeder is a geographer and a graduate of the University of Lausanne. He is currently working on a doctoral thesis in urban planning and development at the University of Geneva, where he also teaches the urban project. His research focuses on changes in planning policies by analysing patterns of production of art in the public space and the link between the arts, the city and critique. He previously worked as an urban planner for planning agencies and the city of Geneva's public art fund.

Marc Antoine Messer is an urban planner certified by the Federation suisse des urbanistes (FSU). He holds a PhD in urban science from EPFL, where he is now a post-doctoral scientific collaborator and lecturer. He is also the managing director of Mobil'homme, a spin-off of EPFL's Urban Sociology Laboratory. He is an expert in urban planning and metropolitan governance, and has developed an analytical method for understanding the interactions between stakeholders in urban regeneration processes. He was a member of the city council of the Greater Fribourg Area for 10 years, where he helped set up of the Greater Fribourg public authority.

Arnaud Misse is an architect and specializes in earthen building. He graduated from the ENSAG and earned a post-graduate degree in DPEA Architectures de Terre. He has been working in the field of earth architecture with CRAterre since 1998. He is currently responsible for the material department of CRAterre and also teaches a specialized course on earthen building systems at ENSAG. In 2006, he founded "NAMA architecture" with Jean-Marie Le Tiec to develop architectural projects that promote the use of local materials, know-how and building cultures to produce contemporary eco-responsible buildings.

Julien Nembrini has a background in mathematics and robotics, experience as a building physics engineer, and has worked on the use of digital tools for building and architectural processes ranging from design to post-occupancy evaluation. Committed to research with a potential for industrial applications, he currently focuses on the use of readily-available building data to study the interactions between buildings and their occupants. Combining data-centric techniques and visualization with user-centred qualitative approaches, the aim is to compare a fully-automated approach to mixed-mode automation that involves active users within the building context.

Cécile Nyffeler is pursuing a Master's in Environmental Sciences and Engineering with a focus in the monitoring and modelling of the environment at EPFL. She got her Bachelor's in autumn 2017. During the summer of 2016, she participated in the experimental phase of the *smart living lab*'s Envelope Design research project in Fribourg. Her main tasks were recording and processing data.

Luca Pattaroni holds a PhD in Sociology from the École des Hautes Études en Sciences Sociales (Paris). He is a senior researcher and lecturer at the Urban Sociology Laboratory at EPFL, where he heads the City, Habitat and Collective Action research group. He was visiting professor at the Federal University of Rio de Janeiro and the University of Columbia in New York. He is a member of the board of the "Swiss Journal of Sociology and Articulo-Journal of Urban Research". He also is Chairman of the Ressources Urbaines art cooperative and a member of the Cultural Council in Geneva. His research, which focuses on the expression of differences and the creation of the commons in contemporary cities, ranges from issues on housing and the public space to cultural and urban movements.

Florinel Radu is an architect and urban planner (UAUIM Bucharest, 1987). He earned his PhD from UAUIM Bucharest in 2000. He began teaching as a professor of architecture in the joint Master's of Architecture programme (HEIA-FR, HES-SO) in 2005. He has taught at several European schools including UAUIM Bucharest, EPFL and School of Architecture in Alghero, Sardinia, and has headed the TRANSFORM research institute since 2013. In addition, he has headed several applied research projects on user-centred sustainable architecture and urban planning.

Thibaut Schafer has a Bachelor's in mechanical engineering with a specialization in energy. With a background in the applied sciences, he earned a Master's at the University of Applied Sciences of Western Switzerland (HES-SO). His thesis looked at the energy efficiency of machine tools. He is currently working as an R&D engineer for the *smart living lab* at the HEIA-FR's Energy Institute.

Raphaël Tuor is currently working on a PhD at the Human-IST Institute in the department of Informatics at the University of Fribourg. In 2016, he earned a Master's in Computer Science with a focus in Advanced Information Processing. His Master's thesis focused on enhancing the visualization of mixed multidimensional data in parallel coordinates. He is now conducting research on the challenges of building data visualization and human-building interaction under the supervision of Professor Denis Lalanne.

Himanshu Verma is a postdoctoral researcher at the University of Fribourg, Switzerland. With a background in Human-Computer Interaction, his work focuses on users' sociotechnical interactions and experiences with artefacts and environments, as well as interactions mediated through artefacts. He has contributed methodologically to ways of acquiring knowledge about latent aspects of users' contexts and demonstrated ways of leveraging this knowledge in Context-Aware Applications. His current research as part of the *smart living lab* aims to create knowledge about occupants' living experiences and behaviours to help architects to make informed design decisions with a sustainable human-centric approach.

Dominic Villeneuve is a policy analyst and postdoctoral coordinator at the TUM's mobil. LAB Doctoral Research Group. He completed his PhD in Architecture and Sciences of the City under the supervision of Professor Vincent Kaufmann at the EPFL's Urban Sociology Laboratory in 2017. His thesis compared car dependence and social exclusion linked to mobility in the regions of Quebec City (Canada) and Strasbourg (France). He has a Master's in Public Administration from the University of Ottawa. He is also co-founder and chief technology officer of Urby-me, a startup project that is developing a smartphone app to measure the mobility, comfort and satisfaction of public transport users.

Didier Vuarnoz earned a degree in energy engineering from the University of Applied Sciences of Western Switzerland (HES-SO) in 1999 and a PhD from Kobe University in Japan (2013). His research looks at Phase Change Slurries (PCS), thermo-magnetism (magnetocalorics and hyperthermia) and energy strategies for carbon emission mitigation in buildings. His activities in both Switzerland (HES-SO and EPFL) and Japan (Kobe University) have been mainly academic. He was also a visiting scientist at Hokkaido University (Japan, 2002), Okayama University (Japan, 2003) and MIT (Cambridge, USA, 2008) for several months. He is currently working on the sustainable integration of renewables and energy storage in buildings at EPFL.

Renato Zülli is a UX/UI designer with a background in print-oriented editorial design. After doing Graphic Design studies at ECAL, he worked for various clients in culture and the sciences. In 2013, he started teaching and working as an Interaction Designer at the EPFL+ECAL Lab. His unique research in big data and data visualization synthesizes the history of interfaces and has enabled innovative experiments within massive information environments. For the COP21 in Paris, he developed a new way of understanding global issues in the context of interdependent controversies. In addition to working together with the EPFL's Social Media Lab and the *smart living lab*, he has also worked with Idiap and SciencesPo, as well as private partners like Faveeo.

Stakeholders

Project Team

Supervision
Prof. Marilyne Andersen, Academic Director of the *smart living lab*, Head of Laboratory of Integrated Performance in Design (LIPID) and of Building2050 Group

Principal investigator
Thomas Jusselme, Project Manager

Coordination
Vanda Costa Grisel, Scientific Collaborator

Members
Dr. Arianna Brambilla, Postdoctoral Researcher
Stefano Cozza, Scientific Assistant
Dr. Endrit Hoxha, Postdoctoral Researcher
Dr. Yinggying Jiang, Scientific Collaborator
Cédric Liardet, Scientific Collaborator
Amélie Poncéty, Scientific Collaborator
Dr. Didier Vuarnoz, Scientific Collaborator

Affiliates
Cecile Nyffeler, Master Student
Margaux Peltier, Master Student

Main collaborations

École polytechnique fédérale de Lausanne

EPFL+ECAL Lab
Nicolas Henchoz, Renato Zülli

Laboratory of Architecture and Sustainable Technologies (LAST)
Prof. Emmanuel Rey, Dr. Sophie Lufkin, Sergi Aguacil

Urban Sociology Laboratory (LASUR)
Prof. Vincent Kaufmann, Virginie Baranger, Dr. Derek Christie, Thierry Maeder, Dr. Marc-Antoine Messer, Dr. Sébastien Munafò, Dr. Luca Pattaroni, Dr. Emmanuel Ravalet, Dr. Dominic Villeneuve

School of Engineering and Architecture of Fribourg

ENERGY Institute
Prof. Jean-Philippe Bacher, Prof. Elena-Lavinia Niederhäuser, Dr. Philipe Couty, Gabriel Magnin, Thibaut Schafer

TRANSFORM Institute
Prof. Florinel Radu, Chantal Dräyer, François Esquivié

University of Fribourg

Human-IST Research Center
Prof. Denis Lalanne, Dr. Hamed Alavi, Thalia Georgardou, Dr. Agnes Lisowska Masson, Dr. Julien Nembrini, Dr. Himanshu Verma, Raphaël Tuor, Pierre Vanhulst

Private partners

Atelier Oï: Raphaël Dutoit, Patrick Reymond
CARPE: Elsa Cauderay
CRAterre: Jean-Marie Le Tiec, Hugo Gasnier
ESTIA: Dr. Flourentzos Flourentzou, Jérome Bonvin
Terrabloc: Rodrigo Fernandez

Committees

Joint Steering Committee

Canton of Fribourg
Olivier Curty, State Councillor, Co-Chair of the Joint Steering Committee
Jean-Pierre Siggen, State Councillor
Jean-Luc Mossier, Managing Director of the Canton of Fribourg Development Agency

École polytechnique fédérale de Lausanne
Etienne Marclay, Vice President for Human Resources & Operations EPFL, Co-Chair of the Joint Steering Committee
Andreas Mortensen, Vice President for Research EPFL
Marc Gruber, Vice President for Innovation EPFL
Marilyne Andersen, Dean of School of Architecture, Civil and Environmental Engineering EPFL

School of Engineering and Architecture of Fribourg
Jean-Nicolas Aebischer, Director of School of Engineering and Architecture of Fribourg

University of Fribourg
Astrid Epiney, Rector University of Fribourg

Operational Committee

Canton of Fribourg
Olivier Allaman, Director Company Foundation and Innovation at the Canton of Fribourg Development Agency

École polytechnique fédérale de Lausanne
Prof. Corentin Fivet, Head of Structural Xploration Lab (SXL)

School of Engineering and Architecture of Fribourg
Prof. Jean-Philippe Bacher, Co-Head of ENERGY Institute, *smart living lab* HEIA-FR Manager, Technology transfer manager

University of Fribourg (UNIFR)
Prof. Stephanie Teufel, Head of international institute of management in technology

smart living lab
Anne-Claude Cosandey, Director of Operations EPFL Fribourg and *smart living lab*

Former members (2014–2016)
Beat Vonlanthen, former State Councillor, Co-Chair of the Joint Steering Committee
Philippe Gillet, former Vice President for Academic Affairs EPFL, Co-Chair of the Joint Steering Committee
Adrienne Corboud, former Vice President for Innovation EPFL
André Schneider, former Vice President for Infrastructure EPFL

Commissions

Scientific Commission
smart living lab

Chair
Prof. Marilyne Andersen, Academic Director of the *smart living lab*, Head of Laboratory of Integrated Performance in Design (LIPID) and of Building2050 Group

Members
École polytechnique fédérale de Lausanne
Dr. Anne-Claude Cosandey, Director of Operations EPFL Fribourg and *smart living lab*
Prof. Corentin Fivet, Head of Structural Xploration Lab (SXL)
Thomas Jusselme, Building2050 Group, Project Manager
Prof. Dolaana Khovalyg, Head of Thermal Engineering for Built Environment Lab (TEBEL)
Prof. Dusan Licina, Head of Human-Oriented Built Environment Lab (HOBEL)
Prof. Paolo Tombesi, Head of Laboratory of Construction and Architecture (FAR)
School of Engineering and Architecture of Fribourg
Prof. Elena-Lavinia Niederhauser, Co-Head of ENERGY Institute
Prof. Jean-Philippe Bacher, Co-Head of ENERGY Institute / *smart living lab* HEIA-FR Manager
Prof. Florinel Radu, Head of TRANSFORM Institute
Prof. Daia Zwicky, Head of iTEC Institute
University of Fribourg
Prof. Martin Beyeler, Institute for Swiss and international construction law
Prof. Denis Lalanne, Head of Human-IST Research Center
Prof. Stephanie Teufel, Head of international institute of management in technology

Scientific Commission
"Smart Living Building" (2014–2016)

Chair
Prof. Emmanuel Rey, Head of Laboratory of Architecture and Sustainable Technologies (LAST)

Co-chair
Prof. Marilyne Andersen, Academic Director of the *smart living lab*, Head of Laboratory of Integrated Performance in Design (LIPID) and of Building2050 Group

Members
École polytechnique fédérale de Lausanne
Dr. Anne-Claude Cosandey, Director of Operations EPFL Fribourg and *smart living lab*
Prof. Corentin Fivet, Head of Structural Xploration Lab (SXL), Professor
Prof. Thomas Keller, Head of Composite Construction Laboratory (CCLAB)
Prof. Jean-Louis Scartezzini, Head of Solar Energy and Building Physics Laboratory (LESO-PB)
Prof. Paolo Tombesi, Head of Laboratory of Construction and Architecture (FAR)
School of Engineering and Architecture of Fribourg
Prof. Jean-Philippe Bacher, Co-Head of ENERGY Institute / *smart living lab* HEIA-FR Manager
Prof. Jacques Bersier, Head of Applied Research and Development
Prof. Elena-Lavinia Niederhauser, Co-Head of ENERGY Institute
Prof. Florinel Radu, Head of TRANSFORM Institute
Prof. Daia Zwicky, Head of iTEC Institute
University of Fribourg
Prof. Martin Beyeler, Institute for Swiss and international construction law
Prof. Denis Lalanne, Head of Human-IST Research Center
Dr. Arnold Rusch, Privatdozent
Prof. Stephanie Teufel, Head of international institute of management in technology
Prof. Jean-Baptiste Zufferey, Administrative Law Professor
Swiss Federal Laboratories for Materials Science and Technology (EMPA)
Peter Richner, Deputy Director
External consultant
Noël Schneider

Workshops

Design process workshop
Fribourg, March 7–8, 2017

Chair
Marilyne Andersen, Academic Director of the *smart living lab*, Head of Laboratory of Integrated Performance in Design (LIPID) and of Building2050 Group
Anne-Claude Cosandey, Director of Operations EPFL Fribourg and *smart living lab*
Organisation
Elvio Alloi, DII Constructions EPFL
Delphine Blauer, DII Constructions EPFL
Florinel Radu, TRANSFORM HEIA-FR
Paolo Tombesi, FAR EPFL
Coordination
Vanda Costa Grisel, Building2050 Group EPFL
Participants
Jean-Philippe Bacher, ENERGY HEIA-FR
Martin Beyeler, Institute for Swiss and International Construction Law UNIFR
Jonas Brulhart, DII Exploitation EPFL
Corentin Fivet, SXL EPFL
Thomas Jusselme, Building2050 Group EPFL
Denis Lalanne, HUMAN-IST UNIFR
Olivier Monney, HEIA-FR
Jean-Luc Mossier, Canton of Fribourg Development Agency
Emmanuel Rey, LAST EPFL
Kirstin Stadelmann, iimt UNIFR
Stephanie Teufel, iimt UNIFR
Barbara Tirone, ENAC-DO EPFL
Didier Vuarnoz, Building2050 Group EPFL

Scientific workshop
Gruyeres, October 5–6, 2016

Chair
Marilyne Andersen, Academic Director of the *smart living lab*, Head of Laboratory of Integrated Performance in Design (LIPID) and of Building2050 Group EPFL
Organisation
Thomas Jusselme, Project Manager Building2050 Group EPFL
Coordination
Vanda Costa Grisel, Scientific Collaborator Building2050 Group EPFL
Participants
Karen Allacker, KU Leuven
Sibylla Amstutz, Lucerne University of Applied Sciences and Arts
Annette Aumann, City of Zürich
Jean-Philippe Bacher, ENERGY HEIA-FR
Stéphanie Bender, 2b architectes
Arianna Brambilla, Building2050 Group EPFL
Hanspeter Bürgi, Bürgi & Shärer
Anne-Claude Cosandey, *smart living lab*
Enrico Costanza, UCL Interaction Center, University College London
Stefano Cozza, Building2050 Group EPFL
François Esquivié, TRANSFORM HEIA-FR
Stéphane Gerbex, Alpiq
John Haymaker, Perkins & Will
Per Heiselberg, Faculty of Engineering and Science Aalborg University
Endrit Hoxha, Building2050 Group EPFL
Niels Jungbluth, ESU-service
Denis Lalanne, Human-IST UNIFR
Benson Lau, University of Westminster School of Architecture
Cédric Liardet, Building2050 Group EPFL
Heinrich Manz, Lucerne University of Applied Sciences and Arts
Emanuele Naboni, The Royal Danish Academy of Fine Arts
Steffi Neubert, Emmer Pfenninger Partner
Wim Pullen, Center for People and Buildings Delft
Florinel Radu, TRANSFORM HEIA-FR
Emmanuel Rey, LAST EPFL
Josep Ricart, H arquitectes
Philip Ross, Unwork
Igor Sartori, SINTEF
Jean-Louis Scartezzini, LESO-PB EPFL
Philippe Stolz, Treeze
Didier Vuarnoz, Building2050 Group EPFL
Paul Wargocki, Department of Civil Engineering, Technical University of Denmark

Acknowledgements & Imprint

The editors would like to thank, first of all, the numerous researchers involved in the different steps of this ambitious interdisciplinary research programme and all the authors who have contributed to the different book chapters. We would also like to express our sincere gratitude to the many experts who participated in the interdisciplinary Scientific Workshop in Gruyères in October 2016 and the Design Process workshop in March 2017, which have become important milestones towards the achievement of the research programme.

Our thanks also go to the different members of the Joint Steering Committee, the Operational Committee, the Scientific Commission of the *smart living lab* and the Scientific Commission of the "Smart Living Building" for their support during the development of this project.

The editors are grateful to everyone who made this book and its distribution possible: the designers Marco Walser and Marina Brugger, the artists Jeremy Ayer and Benoît Jeannet, the infographist Barbara Hoffmann, the copy editor Jessica Strelec, the proofreader Emily Darrow, the printer Kösel and the publisher Park Books.

Last but not least, the editors' thanks also go to the Canton of Fribourg for its essential financial support and, more broadly, to the multiple stakeholders from the three Swiss universities—the School of Architecture, Civil and Environmental Engineering (ENAC) at the École polytechnique fédérale de Lausanne (EPFL), the School of Engineering and Architecture of Fribourg (HEIA-FR) and the University of Fribourg (UNIFR)—who have, directly or indirectly, contributed to this research and publication.

Design and typesetting
Elektrosmog, Zurich
Marco Walser and Marina Brugger

Editorial coordination
Vanda Costa Grisel, Lausanne / Fribourg

Graphic coordination
Sophie Lufkin, Lausanne

Photography
Photo reportage in Fribourg
Jeremy Ayer, Zurich / Fribourg
Artistic contribution
Benoît Jeannet, Neuchâtel

Cover image
Benoît Jeannet, Neuchâtel

Infography
Barbara Hoffmann, Leipzig / Zurich

Typeface
Alpha Grotesk
Simon Mager, Omnitype

Color separation
Color Library
www.colorlibrary.ch

Copy editing
Jessica Strelec, Valgorge

Proofreading
Emily Darrow, Brussels

Printing
Kösel GmbH & Co. KG, Altusried-Krugzell

Publisher
Park Books
Niederdorfstrasse 54
8001 Zurich
Switzerland

Park Books is being supported by the Federal Office of Culture with a general subsidy for the years 2016–2020.

All rights reserved; no part of this publication may be reproduced, stored in a retrieval system or transmitted in any form or by any means, electronic, mechanical, photocopying, recording, or otherwise, without the prior written consent of the editors and the publisher.

ISBN 978-3-03860-132-6